ENVER HOXHA'S LONG SHADOW

ENVER HOXHA'S LONG SHADOW

TRAVELS IN ALBANIA

JOHN WATKINS

Signal

Signal Books
Oxford

First published in 2023 by
Signal Books Limited
36 Minster Road
Oxford OX4 1LY
www.signalbooks.co.uk

A catalogue record for this book is available from the British Library.

ISBN 978-1-8384630-9-0 Paper

Typesetting, pre-press production and cover design: Tora Kelly
Cover Image: Bildagentur-online/Sunny Celeste/Alamy Stock Photo
Photographs: John Watkins
Printed in the UK by 4edge Limited

Contents

Foreword

Miranda Vickers

In this absorbing and engaging book, John Watkins gives us a refreshing new look at Albania, which is surely Europe's most enigmatic and perplexing country. The Albania that Watkins gives us is of two halves - the first following his footsteps through northern and central Albania during initial visits to the country in 1987 and 1988, the second retracing those steps in 2018 and 2019. In one sense this is a guidebook as Watkins travels from the town of Shköder in the north of Albania, through the central lowlands and down to the southern coastal region. Everywhere he describes in detail the people, topography and historic monuments he encounters, insights that are combined with an entertaining narrative on the turbulent and complex history of Albania.

This history is largely one of isolation, the country having been cut off from much of mainstream European life under the Ottoman occupation which lasted 500 years until independence was gained in 1912. There followed the turmoil of two world wars culminating in nearly half a century of the most secretive, isolationist, dictatorial regime, led by Enver Hoxha, mirrored only by North Korea today. With the death of Hoxha in 1985, the regime struggled on until 1991 when, in the wake of communist rule collapsing throughout Eastern Europe, Albanians took to civil unrest and the country's first multi-party elections saw the old one-party system swept away and a new democratic government installed.

Albania's transition from a rigid and often brutal dictatorship to a democracy has been traumatic. Initially, Albanians had expected quick returns from their investment in democracy, but disillusionment soon grew as they saw little improvement in their living standards. Violent social and political unrest followed, and the country was close to drifting into virtual civil war in 1997 and 1998. Since then, the democratic process has gradually progressed, albeit alongside pervasive corruption and a stagnant economy, which in turn has forced tens of thousands of young Albanians to emigrate in search of a better life. Through discussions with some of those who remain, people from all walks of life, Watkins has been able to glean an understanding of what life is like in contemporary Albania and how almost 30 years after his death in 1985, the long shadow cast by Enver Hoxha remains today.

The most striking feature of this work is how Watkins takes us deep into the momentous and tortuous events that followed the end of the one-party state in 1991, using a unique method to anchor his story - that of comparisons between the photographs he took in the 1980s with the same scenes and vistas in 2019. During his first visits Watkins took copious notes and numerous photographs alongside a 1970s official Albturist guidebook and map. For those of us fortunate enough to witness Albania at that time, the journey amounted to leaving the modern world behind us. Towns and villages were eerily quiet with no cars, pedestrians wandered in the centre of the streets and bicycles manoeuvred between horse and mule carts. The countryside was reminiscent of Thomas Hardy's 1880s England as peasants toiled the field in rows and ploughed with oxen.

By retracing his journey in 2019 and contrasting his early photographs with what we see nowadays, Watkins has managed to record the immense changes that have occurred throughout Albania during the past 30 years. The reactions of various Albanians when shown these before and after photographs are illuminating, as are ensuing discussions. They tell a story of a generational divide between those old enough to remember the communist regime and those born into democracy who know nothing of the horrors their parents' generation went through. The young are not taught in schools about the dark years of their recent history. They hear their parents' and grandparents' tales of old, but their concerns now lie with finding employment and a decent livelihood in a country rife with political and economic uncertainties.

As Watkins travels through Albania, he reflects on much of the beauty of the country, but also on the dramatic changes caused by hasty and tasteless development, which has frequently had a severely detrimental impact on the environment. In 2019 he returns to the coast around the town of Durres where in 1987 he had wandered through the dense pine forest that hemmed the beach. "In years past, pine forests along the shore stabilised the sand; now there was not a single pine tree to be seen. The overwhelming impression was of a building spree where every bit of spare land had been built on." The same sensation greets him in the once tiny remote settlement of Ksamil straggling a stunningly beautiful beach which had, by 2019, been destroyed by the rapid and uncontrolled development that has turned Ksamil into a ragged sprawl.

Continuing his journey through the southern coastal villages, Watkins describes the somewhat sensitive issue of Albania's ethnic-Greek minority population, which according to Greek sources was harshly treated by the communist regime. He finds that since 1991 a large majority of ethnic Greeks have left Albania to live in Greece, yet those who remain appear content with their current lives and can travel freely to and from Greece where healthcare and shopping are more affordable.

Outwardly, the Albania that Watkins discovered in the 1980s bears no resemblance to the modern-day country that has embraced modernity at a breakneck speed - in part to distance itself from the stigma and traumas of its dark past. The majority of older Albanians accept that their lives have vastly improved since the repression of the communist regime, while at the same time bemoaning the rampant corruption, bitter political infighting and ineffective governments that democracy has bestowed on them. The young meanwhile have no recollection of the past. They see themselves as modern Europeans in a Europe still largely reluctant to welcome them.

Albania and its Borders

Introduction

1972: Albania, a forbidden country

I saw Albania for the first time in May 1972. I was eighteen, just out of school. I'd hitched south through Italy to Corfu and had set up camp at Kassiopi on the island's north-eastern corner. One afternoon, I was having a beer at the harbour. The waiter pointed across the water and said "Alvania", and told me the name of the town we could see. He called it by its Greek name: Agioi Saranta. He waved a warning forefinger and switched to German, saying, "Alvania kommunist, Alvania verboten, Alvania nicht gut."   Like the mountains behind it, Agioi Saranta was sensitive to light. The early morning brightness drove it back into the mountain. If you didn't know it was there, you could mistake it for a natural rock formation. Later in the day, as the sun climbed, Agioi Saranta became less coy; by evening, its white apartment blocks stood along the edge of the bay like broken teeth.

What was going on there? What were people doing? There must be schools and hospitals, shops and cafés. Were Albanians strolling along the waterfront, as Greeks were here? Were they, like us, looking across the water and imagining what life was like on this side of the bay? And what was beyond those mountains? My knowledge of communist states was minimal, but I knew they were big on industry. Was inland Albania like Fritz Lang's *Metropolis*, a place where workers slaved in factories producing... what? The more I tried to conjure up an image, the more elusive it became.

1972-1975: a scarcity of information

The money ran out at the beginning of July, and I went home. In the autumn I began studying English at Birmingham University. Albania didn't go away. It was lodged at the back of my mind like an itch, but information was hard to find. A trawl through the university library produced a meagre return of two articles. One was a background piece written by André Blanc in the 1961 edition of Larousse's *Gazetteer of the World*. It described "wild mountains" in the north, "unhealthy plains" along the coast and a "hilly and populated fringe" between mountain and plain where most people lived. It also gave a short account of Albania's recent history: internationally recognised statehood in 1913, occupied by Italy and then Germany during the Second World War, now a People's Democracy.

The other article was "Albania: The Last Marxist Paradise", written by James Cameron and published in *The Atlantic Monthly* in 1963. It was the first eye-witness account I'd read of an actual visit to Albania. Cameron had managed to join a West German tour group visiting Tirana, Durrës and Krujë. As he walked in central Tirana, "the desolation of the streets was eerie. At each intersection stood a smart white-uniformed traffic policeman, rigidly poised to direct a press of vehicles that never came… In all Albania today there exists, as I was formally told, not one single private automobile."

Cameron enjoyed the "wonderfully rakish air" of Tirana's backstreets and was amused to see men "of most ferocious mien, darkly moustachioed, from whose scornful lips drooped a rose or a spray of honeysuckle". The mood changed when he sent a telegram to London describing Albania as a "small, proud, isolated Republic which has gallantly challenged both east and west". He was confronted by some "very tight-lipped functionaries, clearly in a markedly hostile frame of mind". Unsure about the cause of their indignation, it became clear that they had taken exception to the word "isolated" which, Cameron was told, had "fascist undertones and was an intolerable breach of my status as a visitor". The conversation, wrote Cameron, was "verging on the preposterous"; it made him feel "deep down in Alice in Wonderland country".

Second-hand bookshops produced more information, but it was random and never more than a trickle. I found two books about what was known as the Corfu Channel Incident: Leslie Gardiner's *The Eagle Spreads His Claws* (1966) and Eric Leggett's *The Corfu Incident* (1974). The books told the story of two British destroyers, HMS *Saumarez* and HMS *Volage*, steaming through the Corfu Channel in October 1946. Both ships hit mines that might or might not have been planted by Albania. Forty sailors were killed and forty-three injured. In retaliation, Britain refused to return almost 1,500 kilos of gold taken from Albania by Nazi Germany and subsequently held in the Bank of England.

The real value of these books lay in their reportage. *Albania - China's Beachhead in Europe* (1962) was written by a German journalist, Harry Hamm. Hamm was in Albania in August 1961, the month when relations between the Soviet Union and Albania became so bad that the Soviet Union withdrew its ambassador. Hamm was astonished to receive an invitation at such a sensitive time. Despite the rift, "Soviet-Albanian Friendship Week" went ahead as planned. Hamm describes streams of workers from textile and food processing plants, and "countless bureaucrats" converging on Scanderbeg Square at the centre of Tirana. Then he heard car engines as the Party leaders arrived and "practiced groups began to shout Communist slogans, which were taken up in a kind of chant by the thousands waiting for the programme to start". When the Albanian leader Enver Hoxha mounted the dais, "all the chants merged into one deafening roar that sounded like a battle cry, 'Enver Hoxha, Enver Hoxha!' Hoxha replied with a smile and a patronising wave of the hand."

Hamm saw signs of Soviet disengagement everywhere. In Tirana, the unfinished Palace of Culture was "a confusion of pillars, iron frames and wooden planking". On the coast at Durrës, he spoke to students who had been studying in the Soviet Union; they were "quite baffled by this sudden political about-face which seemed to have cut the ground from under their feet". As the Russians pulled out, the Chinese moved in. Hamm tried to talk to some Chinese engineers who were staying in Durrës, "but it was difficult, if not impossible, to get into conversation with them, not only for the few foreigners living in the hotel, but even for the Albanians."

Leslie Gardiner was in Albania in 1965. The final chapter in his book describes a whistle-stop tour around 1960s Albania, from Tirana to Durazzo, Korça, Scutari, Valona and Butrint (he uses the Italianised names for the cities). Because of the Soviet boycott, Durazzo was quiet, "but there is a beer tent, brightened with a larger-than-life Hoxha or Castro or Chou en-Lai in full colour on its sides". Valona to the south was "bright, flower-laden and touristy". Inland Korça had been "specially favoured" with the Hammer and Sickle knitting factory, a carpet-weaving combine, a sugar refinery and a tannery. Gardiner concludes:

> Even the dullest parts of Albania - the selected sites, the complexes and cooperatives, round which the visitor reluctantly tramps, have an especial fascination. Every town in the land, in spite of efforts to turn it into a carbon copy of the classic industrial Communist conurbation, has a grotesque, mixed-up exoticism all its own.

Who wouldn't want to visit Albania after reading that?

1975: Radio Tirana

One night I was in my room listening to the radio. I was doing what I often did, which was tune through medium and shortwave bands to see what foreign stations I could find. That was when I first heard Radio Tirana. I can't say I heard Radio Tirana loud and clear, because it wasn't. The signal fluctuated; sometimes I could hear it, sometimes it was lost in static. Broadcasts were preceded by a short call sign, a kind of trumpet fanfare that was both martial and melancholy. Then one of the announcers said, "This is Radio Tirana" and for the next half hour you could listen to a compelling mixture of news, music and ideology Albanian style.

The news wasn't like a normal news. It majored on speeches given at the People's Assembly or comments made by Politburo members. The bulletins were sonorous and weighty, but although the delivery was deadpan, the vocabulary was emotive. Reports were spiced with phrases like "revolutionary unity" and "peace-loving masses". There were attacks on "bourgeois democracy". Americans were "Yankee imperialists"; the Soviet Union was "revisionist" or "anti-Marxist". The mixture of emotive language and didactic delivery made Albania *sound* different.

As I became more familiar with the schedule, I began to see a pattern to the transmissions. Broadcasts at the beginning of the week were more ideological with programmes like "The Marxist-Leninist Movement Throughout the World is Growing in Scope and Strength" and "The Capitalist World, A World in Disintegration". On Wednesdays and Saturdays the mood lightened with programmes about music and culture. Sunday was a touch schizophrenic. "Introducing You To Albania", a catch-all magazine about the history and geography of the country, was followed by "Marxism-Leninism - An Ever Young and Scientific Doctrine".

Radio Tirana was as close as you could get to the authentic voice of the state. Listening to it was like eavesdropping on a forbidden world.

1985: death of a dictator

By the late 1970s, global politics were shifting. In May 1979, Margaret Thatcher became Prime Minister of Britain. In January 1981, Ronald Reagan became President of America. Political realignment provided Radio Tirana with a new cast of villains, but the underlying message was the same. Albania was stuck in a groove.

INTRODUCTION

Then, at the end of 1981, Albania hit the headlines. The Times reported that the Albanian Prime Minister, Mehmet Shehu, had committed suicide. This was significant because Shehu was second only to Enver Hoxha in the ruling clique and had generally been thought of as Hoxha's successor. But something was amiss because Shehu was not granted a state funeral. On 12 January 1982, *The Daily Telegraph* ran a story under the headline: "Albanian PM 'shot dead at dinner'". According to this report, an argument between Shehu and Hoxha over the dinner table had led to a fatal shooting: "It is not known whether Mr Shehu was killed by Mr Hoxha's shots, or by shots from aides or security men at the table." Hoxha was apparently injured in the incident. A report in *The Times* tried to make sense of the suicide/shooting and concluded lamely that "there are growing signs of a power struggle within the leadership". Then it all went quiet again, until 11 April 1985.

The death of Enver Hoxha, First Secretary of the Party of Labour of Albania since 1941, was an event of international significance. Even the British tabloids had obituaries. *The Sun* thought Hoxha had been "the world's grumpiest dictator" who had presided over "a grim, fear-ridden Stalinist society". The *Sunday Mirror* went further. Hoxha was not just "the world's most savage dictator"; he was also "a homosexual, psychopathic killer" who murdered his lovers after sex. This latter claim had been made by Hoxha's "personal interpreter", Ilir Sulka, who seems to have calculated that slandering his late boss would bolster his chances of being granted political asylum in Greece.

Obituaries in *The Times* and *The Guardian* were more measured. According to Jon Halliday in *The Guardian*, Hoxha "combined the attributes of a salon charmer and a Balkan brigand... He was highly cultured, well read in several languages – and even an admirer of Jerome K. Jerome." *The Times* emphasised Hoxha's "remarkable capacity for political manoeuvre, and a quality of ruthlessness, which led to a succession of party purges at home and to startling switches of allegiance abroad".

A few days after Hoxha's death, *The Guardian* reported that Albania's new leader, Ramiz Alia, had pledged to defend Hoxha's "Fortress Albania", which would remain "always strong, always red". But as the months passed, the regime began to make small but significant changes. In August 1986, an international freight railway line opened between Shkodër and the Montenegrin capital Titograd (known today as Podgorica). The following month, *The Guardian* reported that Swiss and French officials had recently visited Tirana "in search of trade and political openings".

The thaw continued. In August 1987, the Greek government announced that it was ending the "state of war" that had existed between the two countries since 1940. According to Radio Free Europe, Greece's decision was "an important step in Tirana's emergence from its long period of self-imposed isolation".

At about the same time as Albania was fixing its relations with Greece, I got a call from my father-in-law, Dag. Dag was a GP and peace campaigner. He was active in CND and a member of the International Physicians for the Prevention of Nuclear War. He and his wife Alison were frequent visitors to Eastern Europe, often as members of peace delegations. Dag's main focus was on Czechoslovakia - he collected its stamps - but he was also interested in the Balkans. He told me he'd seen an advert in *The Observer*. The paper was organising a four-day tour to northern and central Albania with departures in October and November. He wondered if I'd like to go with him.

1987-1990: The Albanian Society

The tour was so interesting that the following year we booked another one, this time to southern Albania which included Gjirokastër, Sarandë and Butrint. While we were there, I bought three books. *Our Enver* was a hagiographical account of Enver Hoxha's life written by Ramiz Alia. *Albania:*

General Information gave an overview of the country. As well as a historical survey, the book described how the state was organised and how its structure derived its authority from the working class, "the leading class of our society". It listed Albania's 26 administrative districts and gave a brief overview of each: its towns and villages, its geography and economy. I also bought a *Tourist Guidebook of Albania*. It was published by the state tourist agency, Albturist, and aimed to "help the foreign tourist and visitor to come to know Albania better".

Back in the UK, I joined the Albanian Society. Its Secretary, Bill Bland, was a bespectacled, portly figure with a passing resemblance to Arthur Lowe. For an annual £5 subscription, I received the society's magazine, *Albanian Life*, and invitations to events where typically a talk would be followed by a film. There was usually a bookstall, and I built up a collection of pocket-sized booklets with titles like *Proletarian Democracy is Genuine Democracy*, *Socialist Albania Will Always Remain Loyal to the Great Cause of Socialism* and *Stalin and his Work - A Banner of Struggle for All Revolutionaries*.

Another source of information was the Albanian Shop in Betterton Street, Covent Garden. It was an intimidating place with statuettes of Enver Hoxha in the window. On the owner's recommendation, I took out subscriptions to two magazines, *Albania Today* and *New Albania*. Because Britain had no diplomatic relations with Albania, I had to send a cheque to the Albanian Embassy in Paris.

If you took the magazines at face value, you'd think that life in Albania continued serenely. Factories and farms overfulfilled their targets. The government continued to invest in new factories and mines. The people looked well dressed and well fed. But Albania was not immune to the revolutions sweeping other Eastern European nations.

To head off growing resentment and disillusion, Ramiz Alia proposed economic reform. In April 1990, he unveiled what became known as the New Economic Mechanism. You knew it was important because *Albania Today*'s report on it ran to ten pages. Alia wanted to liberalise the "socialist economy" but at the same time "to carry forward the banner of Marxism-Leninism". The most contentious part of his package was to offer workers financial bonuses. It was suggested that in certain circumstances, workers could triple their wages through increased productivity. Conversely, falls in production could lead to a wage cut of up to 10 per cent. The Party wanted the mechanism to be implemented by the beginning of 1991.

But promises of economic reform were not enough. At the beginning of July 1990, Albanians began forcing their way into foreign embassies in Tirana. On Friday 6 July, *The Daily Mail* devoted the whole of its front page to what it called the "Scramble for Freedom". The article described hundreds of Albanians "courageously clawing their way to freedom from Europe's last bastion of Stalinist repression". By the middle of the month, around 5,000 people were occupying embassy compounds. The Embassies of France, West Germany and Italy were the most popular, but those of Greece, Poland, Czechoslovakia and Turkey were also targeted. Ramiz Alia called them "vagabonds, former prisoners and deceived adolescents". Then he let them all go.

As the crisis deepened, Albania began to jettison some of the bedrock policies of the Hoxha era. Through the summer and autumn, newspapers reported on efforts to restore diplomatic relations with the Soviet Union, the US and Britain. In another major policy reversal, on 14 November, *The Daily Telegraph*'s Michael Montgomery informed readers that "Church services have returned to Albania for the first time since the country's Stalinist rulers banned religion and declared 'the world's first atheist state'." Religion had been banned since 1967.

By now, the whole political system was being challenged. In December 1990, after sustained pressure from university students, Ramiz Alia announced that multi-party elections would be held on 10 February 1991. Despite his concessions, the country was rocked by anti-government protests. Workers fought pitched battles with the police and army. Buses were burnt and shops looted. In Tirana, barricades were erected around the headquarters of Albanian radio and TV.

For the Albanian Society, a loyal supporter of the regime, the Western media's view of an Albania in turmoil had to be refuted. When reports started circulating about unrest, the society issued a press statement chastising newspapers for "reporting completely fictional anti-Albanian propaganda as though it were fact". It was harder to dismiss the occupation of the embassies as fiction, but at the end of July 1990 Bland sent out a second press release. "The July Events in Tirana" came with a covering note explaining that the release was "a personal analysis and has not been approved by the Committee of the Society". In Bland's view, far from being a "spontaneous outburst of popular dissatisfaction with socialism", the embassy invasions had in fact been "a well-planned paramilitary operation organised by domestic and foreign forces hostile to socialism". Its aim, said Bland, was "'the elimination of socialism in Albania and the subordination of Albania to foreign powers".

Shortly afterwards, Bland resigned as Secretary of the Albanian Society, a post he had held for thirty years. A new committee was elected and at the next AGM, an "updated constitution" was ratified. The committee also agreed to a name change. From now on, the Albanian Society would be known as the Albania Society of Britain, but its magazine would still be called *Albanian Life*. By then, Bill Bland had moved on and set up the Stalin Society (UK). Both *New Albania* and *Albania Today* ceased publication at the end of 1990.

February 1991: a statue toppled

After being ignored for decades, Albania was now a major news story. I tried to clip the reports as they were published, but events were unfolding at such speed that it was hard to keep up. Unsorted newspapers began to accumulate in the corner of our living room. Eventually, the pile got so large I had to put them all in a plastic bag which played havoc with the chronology.

The year 1991 began as badly as 1990 had ended. Strikes, riots and violence forced Alia to postpone the election until 31 March. But this was no longer about reforming the existing system. Communism itself was at stake, and once again students were the catalyst.

On 18 February 1991, five hundred university students and staff began a hunger strike in support of a demand for better living conditions. The news spread quickly, and thousands of citizens gathered in the city centre in a show of solidarity. Two days later, huge crowds converged on Scanderbeg Square. They gathered round the statue of Enver Hoxha that had been erected in 1988 to mark the 80th anniversary of his birth. That evening, Albanian footage rebroadcast on UK television showed crowds on the plinth at the foot of the statue. Riot police fired tear gas to clear them. For a few moments, the police occupied the plinth, then suddenly another group rushed up the steps and retook it. The police responded with dogs. But the crowd had momentum and despite the clouds of tear gas drifting across the square, young Albanians began throwing bricks and stones at the police. The crowd started pushing at the statue. The statue began to rock. It tilted, teetered and then, almost in slow motion, fell sideways and crashed to the ground. Everyone was shouting and cheering. The police stepped back and watched as the statue was submerged beneath the crowd. Some people clambered onto it and waved Albanian flags.

August 1991: *Vlora*

The election, Albania's first multi-party contest for more than fifty years, went ahead on 31 March. Unsurprisingly, the communists won. Ramiz Alia lost his seat but remained Chairman of the Presidium of the Albanian People's Assembly. On 30 April he became President of Albania, the first since Ahmed Zogu, who had created (and held) the post in 1925 before he became King Zog.

INTRODUCTION

The election did nothing to halt the violence. In May, Albania's newly formed Union of Independent Trade Unions called a general strike. Appeals to call it off were ignored. At the end of the month, *The Guardian* reported that the strike "represents a grave challenge to the communist government that is barely a month old... All attempts to negotiate an end to the strike have failed." Five days later, the government blinked. After less than two months in office, the communist Prime Minister Fatos Nano stepped down. President Alia appointed the Minister of Food, Ylli Bufi, to head a government of "national salvation" that would, for the first time, include members of the opposition Democratic Party.

Food was now the issue. On 5 July, under a headline "Famine fear over unrest in Albania", *The Financial Times* reported that milk production had dropped by 50 per cent and flour production by 66 per cent "due to prolonged political unrest and half-hearted land reforms". At the beginning of August, Albanians once again took matters into their own hands. They headed for the ports - Durrës, Vlorë, Shëngjin and Sarandë - but most went to Durrës. Over the next few days, tens of thousands crossed to Italy in decrepit freighters and fishing boats. One ship came to epitomise the crisis. It was the *Vlora*, a freighter built in Ancona in 1960, 147 metres long and weighing just over 5,000 tons.

The *Vlora* had recently returned from Cuba with a cargo of sugar. On the voyage, its main engine had failed and it was now in Durrës awaiting repairs. On 7 August, the ship was boarded by thousands of Albanians. Photographs showed people in the water around the ship, trying to grab hold of rope ladders dangling from its sides. The freighter was already dangerously overloaded; one report put the number on board at more than 20,000. Some had clambered into the rigging. *The Daily Telegraph*'s Rome reporter, Bruce Johnson, graphically described them as "packed like starlings onto a battered monument".

Despite having no main engine and no radar, the captain decided his safest option was to attempt the crossing to Italy using the ship's auxiliary engine. The *Vlora* reached Brindisi at about four in the morning and was told to divert to Bari, 55 miles up the coast. It took the ship another seven hours to reach Bari. Police launches blockaded the port, but the *Vlora* was eventually given permission to dock.

Like the toppling of Hoxha's statue, the story of the *Vlora* and its cargo of desperate Albanians made for graphic television. Footage of the ship arriving in Bari showed Albanians crammed on the decks, on the superstructure, in the lifeboats, in the rigging. If ever there was an image that summed up the trauma of a nation, this was it.

1992-1996: travel guides

One of the consequences of Albania's revolution was a greater openness not just to journalists but to adventure-seeking travellers. Diplomatic relations with the UK had been re-established on 29 May 1991, and the Spring 1992 edition of *Albanian Life* contained advice from the Foreign and Commonwealth Office about visiting Albania. It wasn't recommended:

> Travellers should consider carefully the need to visit Albania as public order cannot be guaranteed in all parts of the country. There have been a number of attacks against British and other foreign aid consignments. There are also widespread and severe shortages of food, fuel and medical supplies.

But the mere fact that guidance had been issued had to be a step forward.

Tucked into the Spring/Summer 1993 edition of *Albanian Life* was a flier for an "EXCLUSIVE OFFER, brand new for 1993". The offer was for a guidebook, *Traveller's Guide to*

Albania, almost certainly the first to be published since the fall of the old regime. According to the flier, the book contained information "designed for both group and individual visitors". I sent a cheque off to the publishers, ACO, and the book arrived a few days later.

The book's authors, Agim Neza and Miranda Hanka, had both worked for the state travel agency, Albturist, and the itineraries they suggested were the same as the ones in the Albturist guidebook I'd bought in Albania. What made their book interesting were its insights into how Albania was adapting to the post-communist world. One of the major changes was on the roads, where the traffic "is not well organised". But the main issue for drivers was not other drivers but pedestrians who, after decades of almost traffic-free roads, "are not afraid of cars". It was the drivers who were terrified, "seeing hundreds of pedestrians walking carelessly on the street, so the blowing of the horns sometimes is really irritating". On country roads, you might be "confronted by animals" or get stuck behind ox-carts or horse-carts. The authors were optimistic. They thought that these more traditional forms of transport would be temporary, "as in the future, with the development of the economy and improvement of the roads, ox-carts and horse-carts will exist no more".

Established travel guides began to include information about Albania. The 1991 edition of *Let's Go: Europe* described it as "the Rip Van Winkle of Europe". It advised readers to "move quickly to glimpse the land and people as they have lived in their 40-year isolation". In 1993, Lonely Planet published the first edition of *Mediterranean Europe on a Shoestring* which included a short but remarkably upbeat section on Albania. Written by David Stanley (who also contributed to *Albanian Life*), it advised travellers to ignore the stories about violence and food shortages; they were all "a pack of lies". Most things were available to foreigners if you had hard currency. Dollars were best. It was safe to change money unofficially: "look for the men with a pocket calculator in hand" but "make sure you count their money twice before tendering yours".

In January the following year, *Blue Guide* published its guide to Albania. Written by James Pettifer, it was a typically erudite addition to the *Blue Guide* list with a lengthy historical introduction and detailed information about Albania's towns and cities. But its tone was more cautious than Lonely Planet's. Pettifer's view in 1994 was that "all first-time visitors, however experienced as travellers, should take an organised tour". Backpacking involved "very real security risks" and was not recommended. Money should be carefully hidden, "for example, in the sole of a shoe". If you were unfortunate enough to be confronted by armed thieves, they "should not be resisted". In an expanded second edition published two years later, generalised warnings had become more specific and were written in bold type. If you flicked through the book, they immediately stood out. There were warnings about changing money - all currency should be checked before acceptance - and about organised crime - if local security staff or bodyguards are employed for any purpose it is essential for their references and backgrounds to be checked by experts. And if you were thinking of travelling independently and using local buses, avoid overloaded vehicles.

April 1995: the Albanian Ambassador to Britain

The slow process of rebuilding UK-Albanian relations continued. On 28 February 1993, the BBC's Albanian Service reopened. It had been off air since January 1967. One of its programmes was "Letters Home", an Archers-style soap about the life of an Albanian student studying agriculture in England. The programme was full of tips for Albanian farmers about how to modernise farming practices.

In March the following year, the Albanian President Sali Berisha made his first visit to Britain. Just before he arrived, two Albanian journalists, Aleksander Frangaj and Martin Leka, had been arrested for "divulging military secrets".

The "secret" turned out to be a circular sent to all Albania's military bases advising personnel to hand in their weapons when they went off duty. *The Independent's* East Europe Editor, Tony Barber, wondered if "the post-Communist Albanian authorities were using security concerns as an excuse to silence their critics... The case shows that the legacy of Communist intolerance and intimidation is still strong in Albania." Under pressure from a number of international bodies including Human Rights Watch, Berisha was forced to pardon the two journalists.

In April 1995, Pavli Qesku, Albania's Ambassador to Britain, came to address the Albania Society of Britain. Qesku had been appointed in 1991, the first Ambassador to Britain since 1939. He was a slight figure with immaculate steel-grey hair. He wore a dark brown suit and matching tie. As he waited for the audience to settle, he flicked tiny flecks of dust from his cuffs.

The Ambassador began with an apology. He was not, he said, a public speaker. For most of his life, he had been an academic at the Institute of Linguistics and Literature and was currently working on an English-Albanian dictionary. Qesku spoke first about the economy and the old regime's obsession with "gigantism" - huge state farms and enormous manufacturing plants like the steel mill at Elbasan which employed 30,000 people. During what he called "the upheavals", Albania had suffered two years of lawlessness. Industry had come close to collapse and state farms had disintegrated. If you had driven from the north of Albania to the south, all you would have seen was brown, uncultivated soil. It had been, Qesku said, "a period of lethargy".

The plant at Elbasan was uneconomic. It had been built with Chinese aid and had cost 6 billion yen. Albania was still paying off the debt. The plant polluted the environment. Olive trees had been coated with industrial deposits. The river downstream of the plant was dead. But to close the mill would cause even greater hardship. So the government had been forced to keep these oversized and wasteful complexes open so as not to add to high levels of unemployment, which currently stood at 19 per cent.

In what was beginning to sound like a session of self-criticism, the Ambassador said that during communism, size alone had been seen as a mark of socialist virility. Albania now understood that this had been wrong, and these "errors of the past" were being corrected. In the Ambassador's view, Albania was turning an economic corner. Inflation had been running at 400 per cent and had been pegged back to 20 per cent. A new entrepreneurial class was emerging.

But there was a downside. Democratising the economy had deprived many sectors of state support. These included irrigation systems which the state had paid for and maintained. Pensions had also suffered, as had healthcare and schools which often had no heating. Pensioners were increasingly reliant on remittances sent by relatives working abroad. The country needed a modern legal framework. The Parliament was drafting a new constitution that would include a Declaration of Human Rights. But laws, even good ones, do not fill stomachs.

Then his time was up. He ended with an emotional "thank you" to all the friends of Albania who had stood by his country. Better, he said, a full small hall than a large empty one. We clapped him, touched by his sincerity and dignity in the face of such monumental challenges.

1997: the pyramid schemes

Albania's economy seemed to be making good progress. Sali Berisha's Democratic Party had implemented an aggressive privatisation programme and GDP was growing at something close to 11 per cent annually, then the highest rate among Eastern European nations. The Democrats were re-elected in 1996 with a huge majority. But at the tail end of the year, newspapers began picking up on a financial story which demonstrated how far Albania still had to go in its understanding of capitalism.

On 21 December 1996, Joanna Robertson filed a report for *The Guardian* under the headline, "Penny drops in Albania as savings scam collapses". She reported that hundreds of thousands of Albanians had invested in a pyramid savings scheme run by Sudja Kademi, described as "an Albanian gypsy and former shoe factory worker". Tempted by interest rates of 50 per cent or more, Albanians had invested their cash and had then sold houses and land so they could invest more money.

Sudja was one of seventeen savings schemes that had sprung up across Albania. So long as they continued to attract new funds, they were able to pay out. But when the investments began to slow, the payments were first delayed and then suspended. As the size of the scam became apparent, protests turned violent. Albania was once again in the spotlight.

On 7 February 1997, Robertson was in the southern city of Vlorë which had become the centre of the revolt. She watched as "protesters and more than 1,000 riot police took their battle to the rooftops of Vlorë's tatty concrete blocks… Demonstrators dragged wrecked cars and oil drums to the police station, erected barricades and set them alight. They captured several riot police, stripped them naked and burned their uniforms." In the hospital, "men with soiled and bloody bandages lay on makeshift beds covered with coats".

Andrew Gumbel in *The Independent* was also monitoring the crisis. Under a memorable headline, "Albania enters the twilight zone", Gumbel characterised Albania as being "in the grip of a rule of terror". The population, he wrote, was "in growing ferment against a crumbling, corrupt government". Sali Berisha and his confidants had "resorted to repression in a desperate attempt to restore order". Gumbel concluded with an ominous prophesy: "it will be almost impossible for any government to reassert control over a restive, angry population, now armed to the teeth".

It was as if Albania had been snared in a time warp where the clocks had been reset to 1990 and the battle to rid the country of dictatorship had to be run all over again. Except that this time, opposition forces were as well armed as the government's. It wasn't just guns. Rebels in Gjirokastër and Vlorë had looted heavy artillery and tanks from government armouries. In Sarandë, there were reports that rebels had seized a warship and opened fire on the town.

The headlines during March were apocalyptic. Albania was a "tinder box"'. It was "on the edge of anarchy". And then, "Albania prepares for war", "Rebels close in on Albanian capital", "Death and panic on Tirana's streets". Desperate to escape the violence, Albanians, as they had done in 1991, headed for the ports. Joanna Robertson, now in Durrës, watched as "more than 1,000 Albanians tried to storm their way into the heavily guarded docks". She reported that more than 4,200 refugees had already crossed to Brindisi and Bari.

The violence continued through April and May. Children's Aid Direct launched an appeal - "Albanian children face food crisis" - citing government figures that "food stocks are down to a tenth of normal levels". And then, as if a switch had been thrown, interest evaporated. By the autumn, my folders of news cuttings that had bulged during the first months of the year now shrank to a few random stories. Attention had shifted to Kosovo, where war had broken out between the Kosovo Liberation Army and Milošević's Serbia.

1990-2000: Enver Hoxha and the internet

Around this time, in the mid-1990s, electricians and engineers descended on Broadcasting House where I was working. They pulled up carpets and removed ceiling tiles. For weeks the building shook with the sound of drilling as new cables were installed. The BBC was readying itself for the next step in the information revolution. It was called the World Wide Web.

INTRODUCTION

From its earliest days, you could see what a powerful tool it was going to be, offering a way of disseminating information instantaneously without the inconvenience of national borders. A few sites even focused on Albania; some of them were listed in the Autumn 1996 edition of *Albanian Life*. They were mostly student forums and newsgroups run by American universities, but one site was based in the UK. It belonged to Eastern Books and claimed to have "probably the largest stock of rare and out-of-print-books on Albania in the world".

Having titles, publishing details and prices on a screen in front of you was game-changing. You still had to phone the bookshop to place your order and then pay with a card over the phone, but the serendipity of second-hand bookshops had been superseded. All you had to do now was peruse a list and decide what you wanted.

Another UK site with an online catalogue was John Buckle Books in Stockwell, south-west London. John Buckle Books was the headquarters of the Revolutionary Communist Party of Britain (Marxist-Leninist). As well as Marx, Engels, Lenin and Stalin, its catalogue also listed books by the North Korean leader Kim Jong-il and Georgi Dimitrov, the first communist leader of Bulgaria. But by far the largest number had been written by Enver Hoxha. More than twenty titles were listed, a mixture of speeches, reports and memoirs.

From the outside, John Buckle Books didn't look much like a bookshop. It stood at the end of a terraced row of shops on a bleak stretch of suburban road facing one of Lambeth's largest housing estates. In a room with plate-glass windows and red curtains, there were a couple of battered armchairs and bookshelves from floor to ceiling. It was like a cross between a library and a rather neglected sitting room. I walked around, looking at the names on the spines. It felt like I'd been transported back thirty years, to the days when communism had been a vital political and intellectual force.

Enver Hoxha's books occupied five shelves. It's true that many were duplicates - one whole shelf was filled with copies of *Two Friendly Peoples*. But what really struck me was Hoxha's enduring status in the communist world. He was up there at the top table, rubbing shoulders with his mentor Stalin.

I asked the man in charge why they had so many books by Enver Hoxha. He said that after 1978, when Albania had split from China, RCPB(ML) had switched its allegiance to Albania because Hoxha's version of Marxism-Leninism was the only one untainted by revisionism. Nowadays, he said, Hoxha's books were more of a historical resource. Every so often, young Albanians came to the shop to read or buy them because they could no longer get them in Albania or Kosovo. They wanted to arrive at their own decisions about Enver Hoxha. It was John Buckle's duty to keep his flame alive.

I left the shop with two carrier bags full of Hoxha's major works. They included *Laying the Foundations of the New Albania*, *Imperialism and the Revolution*, *The Anglo-American Threat to Albania* and *With Stalin*. I also bought a copy of *The History of the Party of Labour of Albania* published in 1982. I wrote John Buckle a cheque for £60.

In his homeland, Hoxha had been vilified, but outside Albania he was still an influential player. Left-wing political groups around the world were quick to harness the power of the internet to promote Hoxha's ideas. One of the first was revolutionarydemocracy.org, the website of an online journal called *Revolutionary Democracy* based in India. The Marxists Internet Archive was another early online publisher. Enver Hoxha was one of its Selected Marxist Writers and you could read entire books on its website.

There were plenty of others. An Italian website with a dramatic red and black front page described Hoxha as an "inspirer" who had become "a unique heroic fighter against modern revisionism". The Revolutionary Communist Party of Turkey praised Hoxha for his contribution "to the great cause of the international working class". A Swedish assessment was more nuanced. It praised Hoxha for revolutionising Albania's economy but added that "Hoxha's government resorted to very brutal tactics to reach its goals".

2004: an Albanian living room

In 2000, I joined the BBC Science Unit. Its offices were in Bush House, on the sixth floor of South-East Wing. The Albanian Service was next to us. The partition walls were so flimsy you could hear Albanian conversations from our office. The Macedonian Service and the Serbian Service were on the same corridor. Nearby were the Greek and Croatian Services. The Turkish Service was on the floor below. It was a Balkan hotspot. And because I was now based in Bush House, I could pitch programmes to the World Service.

At the end of 2004, I began researching a four-part series called "Controlling Science" with presenter Richard Hollingham. The idea was to look at how the attacks on the World Trade Centre in September 2001 had impacted on international science. We planned to use Albania as a case study: could Albania bring its scientific institutions into line with Western academia at a time when the 9/11 attacks had made America wary of foreign collaborations? With help from the Albanian Service, I put out feelers to the Academy of Sciences, the University of Tirana and Albania's Department of Education and Science. Email was unreliable, so I sent faxes. There was an almost palpable sense of connection when the fax machine bleeped and screeched as it typed out a response.

One morning I came into work and was handed a leaflet which read: EXPLORE, EXPERIENCE, SEE, TASTE, HEAR AND BE TOUCHED BY THE LIVES OF OUR AUDIENCES. It was Audience Week, and to give staff an insight into how audiences listened to their programmes, the World Service had devised eight "typical listening environments". These "provocative, three-dimensional, life-size exhibits" were on the landings in the South-East Wing stairwell. BBC Bengali had built a mock-up of a Bengali market. BBC Arabic had recreated a Syrian Living Room with "soft cushions, intricately woven rugs and elaborate chairs". BBC Spanish American had mocked up a Mexican car interior because "on busy Mexican streets the car rules".

BBC Albanian's contribution was on the second floor. Their Albanian Living Room consisted of three chairs and two tables, one with magazines on it, the other with a TV. Albanian objects were displayed in a cabinet: a shoulder bag, dolls in traditional dress, some books and a bottle of *raki*. We were invited to sit and listen to BBC Albania "on a locally produced transistor radio". A sign by the lift said "Tirana". It was all a bit surreal, a mundane collection of items marooned in an Art Deco stairwell. Soon enough I'd be seeing the real thing.

2005: back to Albania

On Monday 14 March 2005, Richard and I caught the Malev flight from Heathrow to Rinas via Budapest. As the plane made its final approach, it broke through thunderclouds and came in low over fields cultivated in neat strips and dotted with Alpine-style villas. A sign on the terminal building said: "Welcome to Mother Teresa Airport".

Stepping out of the terminal was like moving from one world into another. The internal order of the terminal had been displaced by the external disorder of a world still struggling to reconstruct itself after a decade of violence. On the other side of the road was a line of half-demolished buildings, a rubble of concrete shells and spars at crazy angles. It wasn't clear if this was destruction from 1997 - there had been fighting around the airport - or whether it was ongoing redevelopment. Either way, enterprising Albanians were making use of the wasteland. Under billboards for Nescafé and Peter Stuyvesant, they had set up stalls selling canned drinks, music cassettes, cigarettes and sunglasses. We drove into Tirana along a rutted highway where car showrooms, furniture stores and petrol stations filled the spaces between communist-era factories. When we were dropped outside the Tirana International Hotel on Scanderbeg Square, a doorman came out to meet us and helped with our baggage.

INTRODUCTION

For the next three days, Richard and I shuttled around Tirana's research centres. We went to the Academy of Sciences in a historic mansion in the grounds of what was left of Tirana's Byzantine castle. Then a taxi to the Institute of Applied Nuclear Physics at the end of a dirt track in a residential district called Fresku. Then back to the centre to meet Gudar Beqiraj, Director of the Institute of Informatics and Applied Mathematics. The Institute had had a key role compiling statistics about the socialist economy and had been one of the first to get Chinese-built computers. There was one in the hallway outside Gudar's office. It had a Chinese keyboard for inputting information and a metal cabinet with twin spools for data storage. The following morning we were at the Ministry of Education and Science on Rruga e Durrësit to meet the Minister, Luan Memushi.

Everyone agreed that science was chronically underfunded and that scientific institutions needed reform. Mentalities had to change. But there was pride too in what Albanian science had achieved during communism, especially after the break with China. The Chairman of the Academy, Professor Teki Tartari, told us how the Academy and its institutes had supported agriculture and animal husbandry, medicine, metallurgy, hydropower and electrification.

Inevitably, we saw a lot of Scanderbeg Square. At dawn, shoe-shiners set up their stalls on the steps of the National Historical Museum. Moneychangers gathered by Scanderbeg's statue with wads of dollars, euros and leks. Young Roma hawked biros and chewing gum. Around the plinth where Hoxha had stood, entrepreneurial citizens were hiring out mini 4x4 buggies to anyone with a bit of spare cash to indulge a child. Day and night, cars raced around the square, turning it into a giant traffic island. It was noisy and polluted, but the energy was intoxicating.

This was one face of the new order. At the same time, a more aspirational Tirana was taking root among the city's crumbling apartments. Developers had been quick to grasp the economic value of construction. But there was a darker side to the building boom. Unresolved issues about land ownership encouraged corrupt alliances between politicians and developers. One of the first to exploit the regulatory vacuum had been a Kosovar businessman, Hajdin Sejdia. In 1991, Sejdia had set up one of the pyramid savings schemes and had persuaded the authorities to let him use the profits to build a luxury "Sheraton" hotel behind the Palace of Culture. Work began on digging the foundations until Sheraton objected to their name being used without permission. Sejdia abandoned the project and decamped to Switzerland with a substantial amount of money, some say as much as several million dollars. The hole was still there. It had become an unofficial visitor attraction: a swampy, rubbish-filled reminder of the planning chaos of the early 1990s.

Our fixer Ardi had arranged a visit to the Metallurgical Combine "Steel of the Party" at Elbasan. The Combine was communist Albania's biggest industrial complex. To get to Elbasan, you had to cross Mali i Krrabit, a mountain that rose to almost a thousand metres. The road was narrow, just wide enough for two vehicles, and soon we became part of a slow-moving convoy crawling up the hillside behind a truck belching fumes that stung our eyes. Our driver, Eno, shrugged as if to say, what can you do?

We pulled off the road above the Combine. It was, as Pavli Qesku had said, gigantic. It filled the valley. It was overwhelming, mesmerising, a vast industrial conurbation the size of a small city. Although most of it was derelict, a few parts were operational. Smoke was billowing from a chimney near the power station. At a rough count there were at least fifteen chimneys representing fifteen different processes. Each would have been spewing out toxic fumes. Workers would have been exposed to a noxious cocktail of noise, dust and stench. There would have been trains shunting between the units. Trucks would have been delivering supplies. Now, the only thing moving was the smoke drifting down the valley.

INTRODUCTION

Kosma Biba met us outside what had been a nickel processing plant. Kosma was the steelwork's General Manager. He'd started working at Elbasan in 1975, at the time when relations with China were deteriorating. He was one of the young men detailed to complete the plant when the Chinese pulled out. He remembered working "with the strength of youth... there were days when we didn't go home, we just had to work to meet our targets". In those days, Kosma said, the state controlled everything. So when the system changed, it was very confusing. There had been different opinions about what to do with Combine: some wanted to keep it going; others highlighted the problems with pollution. Eventually, most of it closed and 10,000 people lost their jobs. Elbasan now had one of the highest unemployment rates in Albania.

But despite all that, Kosma remained optimistic. The site still had its own infrastructure, its own railway and roads, its own power station, its own water supply. Thirty new companies were now trading on the site employing around 2,000 people. Some of Kosma's friends had returned from Greece and had installed welding equipment in one of the units. Kosma was hopeful that more businesses would soon be opening. Like so many, Kosma believed that *privatizimi* was the answer: "as soon as the site is privatised, the problems will be solved. Privatisation will lead to the transformation of the whole area."

Kosma wanted to show us a refurbished steel mill. We set off through a landscape of wrecked and derelict buildings. Overhead, metal buckets that had once delivered coke to the smelters swung in the breeze. Despite the toxicity, trees had taken root and the roadside verges were grassy. As we walked we could hear goat bells tinkling. Then a shepherd appeared from a side road and exchanged greetings with Kosma. An open space criss-crossed by railway lines must have been a marshalling yard. Much of the track had been torn up or buried in mud and rubble. Whatever Kosma might like to think, this was not a viable infrastructure. In front of us were the towers and pipework of the new furnace. A pile of scrap - car parts, old railway trucks, metal sheeting and fencing, fridges and freezers - was waiting to be sorted. The scrap, said Kosma, came from all over Albania.

Inside the mill, it was hot and noisy. We watched molten metal running out of the base of the furnace and being shaped into still-glowing bars which were then picked up by a gantry crane and swung into a holding area. Kosma said that eventually the bars would be rolled into rods for construction. The air above them shimmered.

We were standing near a single, modern electric furnace. An extraction system removed heat and fumes. It was, relatively speaking, a clean process. If you try to imagine at least seven smelters all operating at the same time, as well as a brick works, a coking works and a power station, not to mention the trains and trucks rumbling through the site, you begin to get just the tiniest sense of what it must have been like here in the late 1980s, when "Çeliku i Partisë" was operating at full capacity.

The trip was over far too quickly. I spent the final morning walking around the city centre. I went to Tirana's main market at Pazari i Ri, located in a courtyard overlooked by communist-era apartments. Produce was piled high: trays of eggs, crates of tomatoes and citrus fruit, barrels of olives, apples and pears, spring greens, cabbages and leeks. For meat or fish, you had a choice of two market halls. One was Ottoman with its shops in a parade of arches. The other hall was larger and grander. Purpose-built in the 1930s, it had a tiled interior and air bricks to keep the space cool. An ice-cream freezer had been commandeered for frozen joints. The market was a congenial space, a synthesis of different eras and regimes. In a city where so much was changing, it felt like a haven where people whose lives had been disrupted could find a degree of normality.

There was just time for a late-morning coffee at Hotel Dajti. The hotel was one of Tirana's iconic buildings. Built by the Italians during the occupation, it had been famed for its luxury; for many years, it had been Tirana's main tourist hotel. James Cameron had stayed there in 1963, in a "large, dispiriting, but spotless room with a most elaborate bathroom, complete with bidet". The hotel had also played its part in the war. When partisans had liberated Tirana in November 1944, Hotel Dajti had become their headquarters for a few weeks. Its ballroom had been used by the Allied Operational Military Mission for a celebratory banquet on 1 January 1945. An international menu included *Dindon à la Jugoslave*, *Salade à la Russe*, *Rosbif à l'Anglaise*, *Oeufs en aspic à l'Americaine* and *Escalopes de veau à l'Albanaise*.

I ordered *kafe ekpres* and went to sit outside on the terrace. A few minutes later, a waitress in a blue suit brought me my coffee, a glass of water and a bill for 100 leks. Through the trees you could see the park on the other side of the road. If you could somehow block out the cars, you felt that not a lot had changed here since the end of communism.

After I'd drunk my coffee, I went inside. Despite its shabbiness, you could see what a grand place it must have been in its heyday. A spacious lobby with a marble floor opened onto a bar where men were relaxing in armchairs, smoking and chatting. Overhead were light fittings that might generously be called chandeliers, but only just. The reception desk was along the corridor. The receptionist was plucking her eyebrows and didn't look up as I walked past. Room keys were in pigeonholes behind her; there were plenty of empty rooms. Beyond the reception desk was a souvenir shop and an Albturist office. Both were closed, but the hotel still had souvenirs displayed in communist-era cabinets along the wall: wooden pipes, dolls in traditional costume and, acknowledgement of time passing, ashtrays shaped like bunkers.

When I got back to the Tirana International Hotel, Eno was waiting outside. He put my luggage in the boot and then presented me with a gold-painted statuette of Scanderbeg. He hoped that I had enjoyed my visit to Albania and that some day I would return.

I didn't go back again until 2012. By then I had retired and Albania filled a gap. I started going two or three times a year, seeing as much of the country as I could. I began learning Albanian.

Every time I went, Albania had changed. There were new apartment blocks and shopping centres, new hotels and restaurants. Roads were improved. In provincial towns like Tepelenë and Ersekë, central squares had been repaved. Coastal regions, especially around Durrës and further south at Sarandë and Ksamil, were being developed at breakneck speed. Even so, reminders of the old Albania were everywhere: in the derelict industrial sites, in the run-down housing estates, in the abandoned collective farms and their leaky irrigation systems.

During those first visits with Dag in 1987 and 1988, I had taken photographs. Some were prints, most were colour slides. The images began to seem like a resource, a record of a disappearing world. It wasn't exactly scientific, but an idea was taking shape. I began to wonder if I could use the photos as a barometer of change, a way of assessing the physical impact of transition on Albania. What changes would they reveal? And what would Albanians make of them? Would they be interested or offended by them?

Scanning and cleaning old slides is a laborious business, but the images brought the old world back into focus. I also had diaries and notes. And I still had the old Albturist map and the *Tourist Guidebook of Albania* to help find the routes.

In 1987, Dag and I had crossed into Albania from Yugoslavia. It made sense to start again in the same place.

1: Shkodër

The Adventure Begins

The First Glimpse
1987

The cold air hit us as the bus door opened. We collected our luggage and formed a queue at the Yugoslav border control where a guard checked our passports. When we had been processed, we began walking across the strip of no-man's land between Yugoslavia and Albania. It was very dark. Then someone on the Albanian side turned on a spotlight and when we were caught in its beam we were momentarily blinded. We shuffled to a halt by a metal barrier. Two guards were waiting for us. As names were called, we came forward one by one. Because of the way the guard pronounced our names, it was sometimes hard to know who was being called. I was worried about my beard. But when I was called forward, my passport was added to the pile without comment. When all our passports had been checked, we were directed to a customs house. We were now officially in Albania.

The customs house was being upgraded. Its windows were unglazed. There was no electronic equipment, no desk, no cubicles, only soldiers in green greatcoats carrying guns. In the corner, surrounded by potted plants, was a bust of Enver Hoxha. We were each given a customs declaration. Were we carrying a radio transmitter or receiver, drugs, printed material, camera, watches, explosives, different currencies? There were bursts of nervous laughter as we struggled to answer the questions. Suppose you had binoculars - they weren't on the list but should they be declared? Was a radio a "receiver"? I put my case on the table by the glassless door. A soldier looked at the form: "Camera?" I showed him my camera. "Please…" I unzipped the bag; he looked inside and felt round the edges. He found my newspaper. He leafed through it then put it back in my bag and with exaggerated politeness zipped it up.

An Albturist coach was parked by the customs house. When we were seated, the microphone clicked and our guide introduced himself. His name was Edi. He apologised for the delay and hoped that coming through customs hadn't been too painful. The drive from the border post at Hani i Hotit to Shkodër would take about forty minutes. Through the window we saw dim lights apparently suspended in mid-air. The trees along the road had luminous trunks that flared in the headlights. As we came into Shkodër, we passed blocks of flats with ground-floor shops and wooden counters. In one, vegetable crates were piled up on the floor; in another, rolls of material were stacked at one end of the counter. The intercom clicked: "Ladies and gentlemen, in a few minutes we will be arriving at Hotel Rozafa where we will spend the night. We are on time. You may collect your keys and you can go to your rooms. Dinner will be at, let us say, two o'clock. It is now one-forty."

I woke early and looked out of the window. The rising sun had turned distant mountain ranges to silver. A pale lemon gauze hung over the city. Below us, people were going to work, but no-one seemed in much of a hurry. It was mostly men, either walking singly or in small groups. A few were on bicycles. There were no cars. A horse-drawn cart clattered past. Then a bus came slowly along the road; it was painted cream and red, and the doors were broken. It left behind a plume of blue smoke hanging in the air. It was as if time had slowed and the air had become viscous. We seemed to be looking down on a slow motion world.

1: SHKODËR

After breakfast, Dag and I went outside. We stood for a moment on the steps, unsure if we were allowed to leave unsupervised, but no-one stopped us. Opposite Hotel Rozafa was a five-storey apartment block with washing on the balconies. Between the two buildings was a plinth and bust. Some men had stopped by it for a chat and a cigarette. When we got closer we realised it was Stalin. On the corner on the other side of the road, there was a huge banner with a profile of Enver Hoxha on a red flag.

A vast boulevard ran north from the hotel. On a roundabout was a statue of five huge figures. They must have been six or seven metres tall, all dressed for combat in heavy boots, military fatigues and greatcoats. They made me think of Ted Hughes' story, *The Iron Man*. You could imagine them clambering down from their pedestal and walking stiffly along the boulevard, their joints grating and feet scraping as they walked. Each step would have made the earth tremble. The men and women on their way to work seemed to shrink as they passed by.

Near the statue was a park with a sculpture at its centre celebrating children. Then we came to a noticeboard with a photograph of a smiling Enver Hoxha. We couldn't understand the text, but we could pick out words which gave a hint of its meaning: *organizator, transformimeve revolucionare, socializmit per idealet komuniste*. There were more pictures of Enver Hoxha: Hoxha in his study, Hoxha in military uniform, Hoxha surrounded by children, Hoxha taking a salute.

We turned into a smaller street lined with Italianate villas with wooden shutters over the windows. The villas were in a poor state of repair, but it was a pretty street with pavements and ornamental street lamps. There was even a quiet hum of conversation. The women were wearing white headscarves. The men preferred flat caps; a few wore the traditional white Albanian fez like the ones for sale in the hotel. Bicycles were leaning against the wall outside Pastiçeri Dibra. There were curtains over the windows and we didn't go in. Opposite the cake shop was a barber. There was a bookshop, a butcher's, a clothes shop and more snack bars. In the bookshop, the counter was piled high with books by Enver Hoxha and Albania's current leader Ramiz Alia. Hoxha had the larger pile. I bought an Albturist map of Albania. On the back were street plans of Albania's fourteen largest towns.

"Are you English?" "Yes." Two youths were standing by the post office at the end of the street; one of them had very blonde hair. "Where are you from?" "From Birmingham and from London." They nodded. The blonde one was holding a newspaper. Dag asked him about it and he said, "It's for youth." "What stories are in it?" He pointed to an article. "This is about young people in Russia, they take drugs, it is very bad." I asked: "Are there drugs in Albania?" "No - and in England?" "Yes, a lot of young people take drugs." I had a sudden intimation of the gap between our lives and theirs. How could they understand life in England? How could we understand what it meant to be young in Albania? "What else is in the newspaper?" "Weights." "Weights?" I didn't understand, so he demonstrated. "Ah, weights! Weightlifting! Is there a competition?" But we didn't get an answer because at that moment an older man appeared and leaned against the wall. "English?" "Yes." That was the end of the exchange. We said goodbye and walked back to the hotel.

How could we have we missed it? It was quite astonishing. The façade was smothered in Russian vine. It was growing unchecked, inching its way upwards like a malevolent triffid. The first four floors had already been colonised, and now tendrils had launched an assault on the fifth. It seemed odd to permit such a dramatic horticultural experiment on Shkodër's only tourist hotel, especially in a country that disapproved of beards.

2019

Stalin had gone. The five outsize figures had gone. A new mosque took up most of the children's park. But Hotel Rozafa had survived. It had lost its shaggy beard, but it was still a landmark, a point of stability in a rapidly changing city.

1: SHKODËR

The hotel had recently been modernised. As my partner, Kirstie, and I checked in, a screen by the reception desk was running a loop of images "before" and "after". Pictures of sub-standard toilets, cracked windows and grubby rooms with Albturist rugs on the floor contrasted with well-equipped bedrooms and king-size beds. If there was any doubt about the state of the old hotel, here was the proof.

Like other state assets, after regime change Hotel Rozafa had been privatised. In a curious, perhaps even unique, legal judgement, the National Privatization Agency had awarded ownership of the hotel to a consortium of forty ex-political prisoners, even though the hotel had never belonged to them. After a number of legal challenges, Albania's Constitutional Court overturned the ruling and found in favour of the owner of the land where the hotel had been built in 1971. Hotel Rozafa had then been bought by the Uldedaj Group in 2010.

I'd stayed at Hotel Rozafa in the summer of 2014. At that stage, the reception area and bar had been refurbished with marble floors, plush settees and chandeliers. It had become the place to go to eat ice-cream served by liveried staff. I was given a room on the third floor which cost 2,000 leks a night, about £11.50.

It was weird. Downstairs, the new Albania was sipping coffee and slurping ice-cream. Upstairs, nothing had changed. The room key had a wooden fob but the number was so faded I had to ask the woman patrolling the corridor (another reminder of the old order) for help. When she unlocked the door, the TV was on, always a nice touch, and the fan worked. The room still had its original 1970s G-Plan style furniture: bed, bedside table, wall lights. At the back of a wardrobe was a typed inventory of the room's contents which could well have been there for thirty years. Doilies were on every surface. Some were fabric and decorated with leaves; others were plastic and printed with images of acorns, hazelnuts and fir cones. Doilies had been a feature of our room in 1987. If you ventured beyond the third floor, you did so at your peril. The upper floors were derelict. The stairwell was blocked by a mass of fallen plaster and bird feathers.

By 2019, everything had been renewed. The stairwells had been recarpeted; there were pictures and settees on the landings. Our room had a flat-screen TV, minibar and aircon. It was all very comfortable and unexceptional.

When I'd woken that first morning in 1987, I'd taken photos from the hotel window. I did the same again now, trying as best I could to match the original images with their modern equivalents. One of the old photos was of Stalin on his plinth. Another was of the banner with an image of Enver Hoxha on a red flag. There were also some general street scenes, pictures of people on their way to work. Some of the men were wearing woollen jumpers; most were in dark jackets and bell-bottom trousers. A woman pushing a pram wore a brown, knee-length skirt and orange cardigan. In another photo, men were laying a rounded concrete plinth.

In one sense, what we were seeing was unremarkable, even banal. What made it so mesmerising was the location. The light was hazy which was due to autumnal mist or pollution from Shkodër's large *zona industriale*, most probably a mixture of both. Apart from the red flag and red letters on the banner, this was a monochrome world. For some of the images, I'd used a telephoto lens which exaggerated the softness of the light. The effect was to make what was already mysterious even more so. Trying to match the images now, it was as if the gauze had been removed and Shkodër had been flooded with colour.

Stalin had been replaced by Luigj Gurakuqi, a Shkodran who had been one of the leaders of the independence struggle and who had served as Minister of Education in Albania's first government. On the corner opposite where the banner had been there was now a statue of Mother Teresa. In 1987, the apartment block across the road from the hotel had been the tallest building. On a rise to the left, you could see the distinctive, curved roof of Shkodër's Franciscan

Church. Now, in 2019, the boulevard had been transformed by new offices and apartments. The apartment block was still there with the post office at its base, but it was dwarfed by the buildings around it. On the corner now occupied by Mother Teresa, there were more hotels and the headquarters of Shkodër's water utility, Ujësjellës Kanalizimi Shkodër. Hotel Colosseo partly blocked the view of the Franciscan Church's curved roof, but its rebuilt bell tower rose above all the new development.

I also had some photos looking north; they must have been taken from the hotel stairwell. Those five enormous figures on the grassy roundabout were Pesë Heronjtë e Vigut, the Five Heroes of Vig, who had put up heroic resistance to the Germans in 1944. The statue was erected in 1969, designed by one of communist Albania's leading sculptors, Shaban Hadëri. In the photo, the figures stood in front of a handsome neoclassical building with an arched façade. This was (still is) Teatri Migjeni, a post-war addition to the city built largely by voluntary labour. Parked outside were three buses, two jeeps, a minivan and a blue snub-nosed lorry. With one exception, those are the only vehicles in any of the old photos of Shkodër. To the left of the theatre was that enormous boulevard. It cut through the city, straight as a die. The people walking along it looked miniscule.

The boulevard and theatre were still there, but the ambience of the square had changed utterly. New developments on each corner towered over the theatre - although there were still minibuses parked outside it. These new buildings altered the sense of scale. The boulevard no longer seemed so huge, and trees planted along it made it a much less exposed space. The Five Heroes had been replaced by a fountain at the centre of what was now Sheshi Demokracia. There were benches around the fountain, but without pedestrian crossings, getting to them was risky.

When we came down to breakfast, I brought the photos with me. As well as street scenes, there were several of the hotel covered in Russian vine which I thought might be

1987: The Five Heroes of Vig by the theatre in Shkodër's central square...

2019: ....have been replaced by an ornamental fountain.

interesting to the staff. Astrit was on breakfast duty. He was a solicitous man approaching middle age. He kept himself busy checking the warming trays and juice machine. When we'd eaten, I got out the photos. Astrit smiled at the ivy: he didn't like it, it must have been full of dust and insects, the hotel was much better now, *shumë i përmirësuar*, much improved. All this, gesturing at the photos, was *shumë vite më parë*, many years ago.

On a wall outside the hotel, a trader had laid out a selection of second-hand books, postcards and bank notes. The postcards were 30 leks each, or 3 for 100 which seemed strange pricing. I picked out six which included a fine picture of Hotel Rozafa and the Five Heroes of Vig. I gave the man 200 leks and he threw in two more postcards for free, both reproductions of paintings: one by Vilson Kilica was called "Denoncimi i Traktatit të Varshavës", Denunciation of the Warsaw Pact; the other by Sadik Kaceli was titled "Brezaret"', Terraces, and showed a section of the Ionian coast banded with terraces. When I tried to interest the trader in my pictures of Shkodër, he brushed them aside. He was focused on trying to make money from his old images.

It wasn't hard to piece together the route that Dag and I had taken around the city centre in 1987. From Sheshi Pesë Heronjtë e Vigut we must have walked past Sahati i Inglizit, the English Clock Tower - I had a photo of it. The tower was built by an Englishman, Lord Paget, in the late nineteenth century. Paget wanted it to be an Anglican Church; Shkodrans were loyal to Catholicism. Up until 1990, the building had been Shkodër's Historical Museum.

From the Clock Tower, we would have joined the main road running north-east towards Shkodër's *zona industriale*. The street had been renamed; it was now Rruga Qemal Draçini. Qemal Draçini was a poet and writer from Shkodër who had been arrested in 1946 and died in prison the following year. A right turn would have taken us past the University and then another right into Rruga Kolë Idromeno. This was the street lined with Italianate villas - both Dag and I had taken photos of it. In the old photos, the street looked down-at-heel; now the villas had been restored. Cafés and restaurants ran the length of the street. One mansion had been turned into the Marubi Museum of Photography - the Marubi family had been pioneering photographers from Shkodër whose work chronicled Albania from the mid-nineteenth century until the 1950s.

At the western end of Rruga Kolë Idromeno, near the new mosque, was a restaurant called San Francisco. I had a photo of it from 1987; back then, it had been Pastiçeri Dibra. It was mid-morning and a group of young waiters were hanging around outside waiting for customers. I showed them the photos and they crowded round to look and went "Wow" and whistled in disbelief: *e mahnitshme! e pabesueshme!* Amazing! Incredible! Some of the places were easier to recognise than others: the banner defeated all of them. They asked if I had any more pictures, and called over an older waiter; he thought that, despite the visual evidence, the *berber* had been further down the street on the right. The photos became a good-humoured game of "guess the place", the older man giving his younger colleagues a gentle rap on the head when they got it wrong.

As Kirstie and I strolled up Rruga Kolë Idromeno, we bumped into Djon who worked at the Rose Garden Hotel near the cathedral. We'd stayed at the Rose Garden several times, and we'd booked again for a couple of nights. He'd been to the market and invited us to join him for a coffee. The cafés were busy. People looked well dressed. There was a gentle buzz of conversation, and it was very pleasant.

Djon was his early fifties and had three children: two were at university, the third was still at home. I asked him about life in Shkodër - it must be better now than it had been before 1990. Of course it was better, he said, people could come and go freely. The main problems nowadays were high prices and corruption. Djon said that many Albanians had set up businesses importing goods from China because Chinese imports were cheap, especially furniture and sanitary fittings. There was also a lot of trade with Turkey.

1987: A run-down Rruga Kole Idromeno has been ……

2019: …refurbished and is at the heart of Shkodër's vibrant café culture.

I asked Djon if he'd ever learned Chinese when China and Albania had been allies. He shook his head, but he did speak some Russian. Had there been marriages between Chinese and Albanians? He thought not, but some Albanians had married Russians. I asked him about the city - how many people lived here? He thought about 90,000, which made it Albania's fourth largest city after Tirana, Durrës and Elbasan. Shkodër, he continued, had a large student population. He pointed up Idromeno: the University and *konvikti*, the halls of residence, were at the top of the street. The University served the whole of northern Albania, for students from Kukës, Fushë-Arrez and Bajram Curri, as well as Shkodër. Djon thought it was good for the city to have so many young people studying in the town. Was the university free? No, you had to pay, but not very much because it was a state university. The trouble was corruption, people paying bribes to get their qualifications. It was, said Djon, the same people in charge now as it had been during communism. And then, when students do qualify, there's no work, so what to do they do? They all want to leave Albania.

I showed Djon the old photos. He commented on the width of the boulevard by Teatri Migjeni - which in fact must have been the same now as it was then, but without traffic and the trees it looked vast. He thought the villas along Rruga Kolë Idromeno looked better after restoration, and he liked the greenery on the front of Hotel Rozafa, adding that there wouldn't have been much of a view from the windows it covered.

Shkodër was one of the first cities to embrace communism. A cell had been set up in the city in 1934 and Shkodrans were instrumental in the founding of the Communist Party of Albania on 8 November 1941. Shkodër was the last Albanian city to be liberated from occupation on 29 November 1944.

In the years following the end of the war, Shkodër was treated harshly. Its Catholic clergy were abused and imprisoned. Punitive taxes were levied on its merchants.

Properties were seized. The repression was so extreme that citizens in Koplik and Postribë rebelled in 1945 and 1946. When the regime began to falter at the end of 1990, Shkodrans were among the first to challenge its authority. On 13 December 1990, they toppled a bust of Enver Hoxha which had stood in front of the 28 Nëntori High School. That was two months before Hoxha's statue in Tirana was pulled down.

Perhaps because of its historic opposition to communism, Shkodër has done more than most Albanian cities to memorialise the suffering inflicted on its citizens. The Diocesan Museum next to the cathedral tells the story of religious persecution. Churches were destroyed. Shkodër's cathedral was converted into a sports hall. Rather than saints on its façade, there were images of Politburo members. A display commemorates the 36 priests who died during communism, and who were beatified in November 2016.

Another museum, the Site of Witness and Memory, gives a searing account of what happened across the city as a whole: 2,890 imprisoned, 1,924 interned, 601 executed, 61 clerics persecuted, 136 tortured to death. When the National Liberation War ended, Shkodër had a population of around 30,000. At a rough reckoning, that means around 20 per cent of its citizens were either persecuted or killed, not to mention the devastating knock-on effect on families who now had "bad biographies". One of the most chilling displays is not the torture chambers or the accounts of torture, appalling as they are. It's a map of the city showing where the prisons were. There were more than twenty of them dotted around the town. Some were in appropriated religious buildings, others in what had been private homes. In a literal sense, the city had been turned into a prison.

In the violence that came with the collapse of the old regime, more Shkodrans died. On 2 April 1991, four students - Arben Broci, Bujar Bishanaku, Besnik Ceka and Nazmi Kryeziu - were killed by security forces in protests over a disputed election. Many more were injured. A monument in Sheshi Dy Prilli commemorates the four students. It was designed by a Shkodran sculptor Sadik Spahia, with arrays of marble columns topped with plain cornices. From a distance, the monument could almost be mistaken for the ruins of a classical temple.

In the same park, another memorial commemorates the bravery of Shkodër's "anti-communist people" who pulled down Hoxha's bust in December 1990. In May 2019, another memorial was unveiled. Bronze tableaux depict two despairing women in jail, three gaunt figures hugging themselves against the cold, and political prisoners stripped to the waist working in a mine. A plaque in English and Albanian states that the monument was in memory of "the persecution, sacrifices and resistance of the people of Shkodër during the communist dictatorship".

One of the strangest commentaries on the communist period is in the Franciscan Church. From 1967 to 1990, it had been used as a cinema. When it was returned to the Franciscans, they commissioned a series of frescoes that told the story of the church during communism. One of the frescoes dramatised an incident that had happened in January 1947. The state security organisation, Sigurimi, had been using the church to store weapons. When the authorities "discovered" the weapons, they accused the priests of using them to "fight the people's power". In a panel entitled *Shpifja e madhe*, the Great Slander, Franciscan priests with bare feet and manacled wrists stand in front of the altar holding the rifles. Facing them, enveloped in a cloud of sulphurous red smoke, communist partisans, with horned devils whispering in their ears, berate the priests. The congregation beg the partisans for mercy.

Memorialising Shkodër's opposition to communism is an essential part of the post-communist political dialogue. But for younger Shkodrans born after 1990, awareness of the communist era seemed sketchy.

1: SHKODËR

One afternoon, Kirstie and I went to a juice bar called Shega e Egër, the Wild Pomegranate. It was on Rruga Gjuhadol. Like other historic streets in Shkodër, Rruga Gjuhadol was crumbling at the end of communism. In 2013, the European Union gave Shkodër €1.2m for its restoration. The only trouble was that some of the owners of the properties couldn't be traced, so not all the façades were renovated. In some cases, even where owners agreed to the refurbishment, they then allowed their properties to decay. But the general sense was of a slow ripple, as more small businesses opened along the street. Already there were jewellers, a high-end clothes shop, cafés and bars, a balloon shop, a print shop and a web design company. Shega e Egër was one of those new businesses.

A young woman called Greta was serving, and after we'd had our drinks I asked if I could show her the photos. Greta was in her mid-twenties, born in Shkodër and spoke very good English. I laid the pictures out along the bar and her eyes widened. "Wow, amazing... was it really like this?" She was almost laughing in disbelief. "Look at the clothes! When were they taken?" Greta wanted to see all the photos, even the poor quality ones. She looked closely at the photo of men laying a concrete base. "Is that still there?" she asked. I said it was; it was on the corner by the new mosque. A sign on it said that on 16 July 1990 young Shkodrans had held the first anti-communist demonstration there to honour the "Martyr of Democracy", Pëllumb Pëllumbi. Pëllumbi had been shot by guards when he tried to cross the border. He was seventeen. Greta looked at the pictures of Hotel Rozafa with its shaggy vine. "Was that there then?" she asked.

Then she started asking me questions: Why did you come? Was Enver Hoxha still alive then? Where did you go?

Once she'd got over her amazement, she told us more about Shkodër. OK so she was born here and was biased, but Shkodër was her favourite Albanian city. At its heart were the old streets, Kolë Idromeno and her street, Gjuhadol. Gjuhadol still had lots of empty shops and properties;

Greta thought that some of the derelict ones were owned by people who now lived abroad or in other parts of Albania. More tourists were coming to Shkodër and she hoped that more shops would open along Gjuhadol. But the Bashkia (municipal authorities) weren't investing in the city; they were only doing some restoration now because local elections were coming up. Greta was particularly exercised about the way the city treated its Roma community: "If you come into the city from the north it's not so bad, but if you come from the south, when you get to Xhabiaj, you see the Roma camp." The Bashkia should be doing more for those people.

The next afternoon, Edris was behind the bar. He was twenty-four and had highlights in his hair, designer stubble and ear piercings. I laid the pictures out on the counter and, like Greta, he looked at them in amazement. The photos were definitely Shkodër but Edris was having difficulty connecting them to the city he knew. "Where did you get these photos?" I said I'd been to Albania with Albturist in 1987. "Wasn't it dangerous? ... O my God, is that Stalin? In Piazza Park?" There was now a pizza restaurant on the corner; Edris wondered if Stalin would have liked pizza. He looked at the banner with its red flag and image of Enver Hoxha. Then he started reading the words on the noticeboard: *Nderimi më i madh për veprën e shokut Enver, mirenjohja më i madhe për gjithshka ai ka bërë për Partinë e popullin tone...* The greatest honour to Comrade Enver, the greatest gratitude for everything he has done for our People's Party... "What a brainwash!"

Born in 1995 and too young to remember the chaos of 1997, Edris had spent time in Serbia. He was fluent in Serbian and loved Belgrade. It was, he said, "a city without rules", which clearly endeared it to him. He advised us to go there. Edris had a modern sensibility and saw nothing wrong with an Albanian making his home in Belgrade. But he still had to live with the fall-out from the old regime. Jobs, he said, weren't a problem for young people; they could open a business and that was usually enough to support a family. It was much harder for older people to find work because, as he put it, "they weren't educated", by which I think he meant they weren't educated in the ways of capitalism.

Like others, Edris identified corruption as a major problem. He told us about a Vetting Commission that was supposed to check that Albania's judges and prosecutors had no connections with organised crime. The Commission was part of a judicial reform that would make Albania's legal system more acceptable to the European Union. In the first instance, legal experts from Europe and America would vet the applicants who wanted to serve on the Commission. Edris was unimpressed: "Let's suppose a judge has two houses. A member of the Vetting Commission says: how can you afford two houses, you must be corrupt!" Edris thought the Vetting Commission would change nothing. In his view, everything came down to power and money: "Only the strongest win."

Edris also told us what had happened to Pesë Heronjtë e Vigut, the Five Heroes of Vig. In the 2007 local elections, the Democrats had held onto Shkodër and they wanted to rid the city of its communist monuments, known throughout Albania as *lapidars*. In January 2009, a bulldozer had pulled up next to the statue. It smashed the stone plinth and then a crane lifted the five figures and swung them onto the back of a truck. At first it seemed they wanted to break the statue up and sell it for scrap. Then they changed their minds and moved it to the Martyrs' Cemetery on the outskirts of town. Moving the statue really annoyed people and it became a national issue. Eventually the Bashkia put it on a roundabout at Dobraç on the north side of the city. Edris thought it should have stayed where it was, in the centre of Shkodër. The politics didn't bother him. The statue was a part of history.

As I showed the photos to more people, a pattern began to emerge. Broadly speaking, younger people were more willing to engage. Older people - in other words those with some personal experience of the communist regime - were polite, but non-committal, limiting their comments to generalities. It would be dangerous to draw conclusions from such a small sample, but I began to wonder if people like Astrit and Djon who've lived through such difficult times have learned that if you're going to survive it's safer not to express strong opinions.

That evening, we ate at Arti'Zanave, a slow food restaurant in a side street off Rruga Gjuhadol. The restaurant was run by women to support female victims of domestic violence. After we'd eaten, I showed the pictures to the woman in charge. She told us that she had been fifteen in 1987, but she made it clear she didn't want to talk about communism. She was far more interested in telling us about all the different nationalities who'd eaten at her restaurant: Dutch, German, Ukrainian, even Chinese.

Aldis was the owner of the Rose Garden. He was doing well and was about to open a second hotel in one of the old mansions on Gjuhadol, close to Shega e Egër. Aldis was older than Greta and Idris. Born in 1986, he had experienced four years of communist rule; he was eleven when the pyramid schemes collapsed.

When I showed him the pictures, he expressed the same sense of surprise as Greta and Idris, but, like the older people, was cautious about the comments he made. "The streets are so wide and so clean," he said. He commented on the clothes, the lack of cars and the crazy greenery on Hotel Rozafa - which in retrospect seemed to symbolise the stagnation of the old regime; why didn't anyone cut it back?

Then I asked him about education, because it seemed to us that people born after 1990 had very little knowledge about the old regime: were children taught about it at school? No, said Aldis, they weren't. He was at school in the 1990s and hadn't been taught about Enver Hoxha. I asked why he thought that was. Aldis thought that the authorities wanted that period "cancelled from history". He went on: "Anything the younger generation learns about the old regime comes from their parents and grandparents.

They talk about how green it was back then, how safe, how everyone had work." There was, he thought, *nostalgji* for some aspects of life before 1990, but there was no desire for a return to the old days.

The question of how to teach about the decades of communist rule has not been resolved. Some years ago, the Ministry of Education and Science produced a glossy booklet laying out the command structure of education: from Parliament, through the Council of Ministers and then to the Education Department and local authorities. It talked about "developing the intellectual, creative, practical and physical abilities of the students" so that they would have "the basic elements of general culture and civic education". History of the Albanian Nation and Knowledge about Society were compulsory subjects in secondary schools, but there were no details about how these subjects should be taught.

In 2016, the Organization for Security and Co-operation in Europe (OSCE) published a research paper, "Citizens understanding and perceptions of the Communist past in Albania and expectations for the future". OSCE researchers quizzed 995 people of all ages, backgrounds and experiences. Among younger citizens, the report said: "It is interesting to note how low the importance of school seems to be in terms of informing people about the Communist era… Overall the education system seems to have little impact in informing people about the Communist era."

In their conclusion they wrote: "Television has a very important role in teaching people about the past, while school seems to have an extremely limited role. As schools are responsible for teaching youth about history, there seems to be ample opportunity to strengthen the role of schools in teaching about the Communist era."

When asked specifically about Enver Hoxha, 42 per cent of respondents thought his impact on Albania had been "positive".

Rozafa Castle: a bird's eye view
1987

We clambered onto the bus and a group of ragamuffin children sitting on the pavement waved as we departed. Edi wished us a good morning and introduced his co-guide, Ilir, who took over the commentary. Ilir said that our first stop today would be the Castle of Rozafa. It wasn't far but before we got there, he would like to tell us a bit about the history of Albania. So as we drove through the southern suburbs, past rows of tower blocks, he gave us a potted résumé that began brightly with the Illyrians and then descended into centuries of occupation - Greek, Roman, Byzantine, Barbarian, Bulgarian, Venetian, Ottoman - illuminated only by the bravery of national hero Scanderbeg who, for a few years, held the Ottomans at bay. Then on into the nineteenth century and the struggle for independence, nationhood in 1912, occupation during the First World War, then a feudal monarchy under Zog, then more occupation, this time by Italians and then Germans, before final liberation by Albanian partisans at the end of 1944. As he was talking, we passed a statue standing by housing estates on the southern fringe of the city. That, said Ilir, was Isa Boletini, one of the heroes who had fought for Albanian independence. He'd been killed in Montenegro in 1916.

We parked at the bottom of the hill and climbed the zigzag path to the fortress. Concrete bunkers, almost buried under vegetation, protected its flanks. On a flood plain to the east, a mosque stood among cultivated fields. It was the Lead Mosque, said Edi, the oldest mosque in Shkodër and was currently being restored. Two boys kicking tiny unripe pomegranates came down the path and smiled cheerily.

We entered the castle through an enormous triple doorway. Edi told us that it had been named after Rozafa, a young bride who'd been buried alive in the walls to ensure that the castle didn't fall down. A group of modern-day workmen were having an early lunch. They were putting a new floor in a building at the southern end of the fortress. Someone asked if it was going to be a bar or café. "No," said Edi, "it is not for tourists. We are a poor nation but such monuments are important to us, they are a part of the history of our country, we believe it is important to preserve them."

The castle occupied a commanding position with a 360-degree view. Shkodër was to the north; haze still hung over the city, but the wedge of apartments in the foreground glittered in the sunshine. To the north-west was Lake Shkodër, a huge expanse of pale blue water bordered by marshland. A flock of sheep was grazing by the water. A broad river flowed out of the lake, crossed by a wooden bridge. On the far bank, an ox-cart moved at a snail's pace along a track and then stopped outside a low building facing the river.

To the south-east, a flood plain stretched into the distance until it reached the mountains. A river had cut sweeping curves through the soil. As it slowed, the river had broken into innumerable channels creating a watery lattice that ran through gravel and shale beds. The plain was intensively cultivated; fields laid out with mathematical precision divided the plain into a series of huge rectangles. Some fields were green with winter wheat; others were rusty-golden with maize that would soon be harvested; others were fallow.

The scene had a hallucinatory intensity. After fifteen years of imagining, here it was laid out in front of me, my first proper view of an Albanian landscape.

2019

Kirstie and I took the narrow road that winds up the hill to the castle. We passed the Liria nine-year school with a fine *lapidar* in the playground celebrating the creation of the Shkodran branch of the Albanian League in 1878. The footpath had been repaved; souvenir stalls along it sold woven bags, fridge magnets and a large variety of hats. In 1987, I'd taken a photo of the castle ramparts; bunkers had been embedded in the rock below the walls. The bunkers were now hidden under trees. By the castle entrance was a whitewashed grave belonging to Muja Baba, a Sufi holy man who had died in 1583. That hadn't been there in 1987.

We went in through the triple doorway and followed the path past the ruins of what had been Kisha e Shën Stefanit with a stump of a minaret at its eastern end, and then walked across the grass to a row of arches overlooking the River Drin. This was where I had taken the original photo of the flood plain and river. I lined it up as best I could, with the arches in the foreground. Much of the old brickwork had disappeared, but the river was still beautiful. It flowed in lazy meanders out of the mountains and across the plain. The shale beds that had been such a prominent feature in 1987 were green with trees. Villages along the eastern edge of the plain - Renc, Kotaj, Guri i Zi, Jaban - had all expanded, as had Kuç on the plain. Those huge cooperative fields had been broken down into strips. To the south, new building around Bahçallëk had brought the village to the river's edge.

There were other post-communist changes. A new bridge crossed the Buna; the old one was now pedestrian-only. On the far bank, a mosque had been built next to buildings that had once been a meat processing plant. The lake's marshy shoreline which had been used for grazing had been abandoned and had become a forest of willows.

The castle museum was in the courtyard in the south-eastern corner. This was where the workmen had been installing a new floor in 1987, the year the museum had opened. Spread over two floors, it told the story of the castle from its Illyrian beginnings up until 19 March 1914, the day Shkodër was incorporated into the Albanian state. As well as historical objects and modern busts of Illyrian royalty - Agroni, Teuta, Genti - the museum highlighted the story of Rozafa with a statue showing her immured but still able to breastfeed her baby. Upstairs were maps and displays. There was information about the Bushatlliu family who had governed the city in the eighteenth century and had tried unsuccessfully to create an independent Albanian principality. Another display featured two of Shkodër's most famous medieval scholars, Marin Beçikemi and Marin Barleti, the latter known for his history of the Ottoman siege of Shkodër in 1478. There was an impressively large wooden chair carved with floral motifs and double-headed eagles. As the story moved into the early years of the twentieth century, photos showed crowds gathered in the castle to witness the Albanian flag being raised for the first time. Another photograph showed the flag being raised over the Bashkia on 28 November 1913 to mark the first anniversary of the Albanian state.

We bought some postcards and I said to the curator that I'd been here in 1987 and that I had some photos of the castle. He told us that he had worked at the museum since 2002; he had a tiny budget and it was a struggle maintaining the site. The photo that caught his attention was the one of the Drin meandering across the plain. But it wasn't the river that interested him. It was the brickwork in the foreground. Those ruined walls were all that was left of an Ottoman *kazerma*, a barracks. A fig tree had already weakened the walls and then during the troubles in 1997, the building had been vandalised by "the people". It seemed an odd target.

On our way back down the hill, I showed the photos to the man in the ticket office. I had to wait while he watered the grass around Mujo Baba's grave. When he'd finished watering, he leafed through the photos and I asked him about the *kazerma*. He said that during communism there'd been anti-aircraft guns sited there. He mimed firing - *bam, bam, bam*. There'd been more guns on the hill to the left. That's why the people had attacked the building, because of its connection with the state. They had also attacked the communist-era barracks by the museum.

One of the old photos showed Shkodër from the castle; it had been a compact settlement bisected by two roads. To the east, the town pushed up against the hills, but to the north and west was agricultural land. There was a green cordon between city and castle. During communism, the region had been an important agricultural zone growing wheat, tobacco, olives and vines. Now the city sprawled across the plain. Agricultural land had been built on. A new bypass was being constructed. The green cordon had disappeared beneath apartment blocks. All this new building, said the man approvingly, was *biznes*. The only part of the landscape that hadn't altered was the castle.

2: South to Laç

Fields, Ditches and an Airport

1987

We crossed the Drin and headed south along a single-lane road. Edi took up the commentary in his precise English: "For most of this journey you will see mountains to your left and the plain to your right. Albania is a mountainous country, but for us, in so short a visit, we will stay mainly on the plain. As you can see, much of the plain is under cultivation…"

Through the window, the fields slid silently by, large fields of rich, black earth. Hypnotic rows of irrigation channels ran across the fields. People were at work; headscarved women were digging ditches with adzes, hoeing the soil or resting by the roadside. Caterpillar tractors were turning the soil. Bullock carts lumbered along muddy trucks. As we drove, Edi told us about socialist agriculture and the increases in productivity it had brought. There were, he said, two types of farm: cooperative and state. On cooperative farms, peasants earned money by selling their produce to the state; on state farms, workers received a wage of between 500 and 1000 leks a month. Ratios set by law controlled highest and lowest wages in all branches of the economy, so that at most, no worker could earn more than twice another worker. As a conversion, 500 leks was about £45. It wasn't a huge amount, but Edi said that food and accommodation were provided by the farm, and that Albanians didn't pay tax. We saw children coming out of school and going into the fields. Edi told us that education for children aged between six and fourteen was compulsory (and free), and that working in the fields was seen as part of their education.

The irrigation channels continued to flicker in the sunshine and Edi continued to drip-feed us statistics over the intercom. He told us that in the current Five Year Plan, the number of cows would increase by 90,000 and the number of sheep and goats would increase by 1.4 million. Fertilizer production would increase by 55 per cent; pesticide production by 44 per cent. As he talked, I got a feeling that the world outside the window wasn't in step with its description inside the coach. There seemed to be two classes of reality: one was rational and "scientific" in a Marxist-Leninist way, all facts and figures; the other was earthy, backbreaking and relied heavily on bullock carts. Which version to believe? Eyes or ears? It was confusing, and the more Edi spoke, the wider the gap became.

The plain began to narrow; we were approaching Lezhë. Above the town was a castle with *PARTI ENVER* written on its walls. Edi drew our attention to a large concrete structure by the river. It looked like a Brutalist Parthenon, a rectangle of pillars supporting a concrete roof. Edi told us that it had had been erected a few years earlier, in November 1981, to protect the ruins of the cathedral of Shën Nikolla where Albania's national hero Scanderbeg had been buried in 1468. We drove past blocks of prefabricated apartments, their flat roofs bristling with TV aerials. The blocks were new, built after a devastating earthquake in 1979; the ground around them was puddled and muddy. Firewood had been stacked on the balconies, and huge revolutionary banners hung down their sides. One was a portrait of Ramiz Alia. Another celebrated the Party of Labour of Albania: workers with raised fists marching under a red flag.

2019

It was a sunny Sunday morning and everyone who could was off to the beach at Velipojë. By the bridge over the Drin, street traders sold fresh fish laid out on newspaper and sacks of charcoal. As we crossed the river, we got a good view of the old bridge going nowhere.

The first settlement south of the river was Bahçallëk, once famed in the words of the little Albturist *Guidebook of Albania* for "the numerous gardens that surrounded it". Not anymore. Modern Bahçallëk had become a commercial suburb serving Shkodër, with a main street lined with garages, builders' merchants and showrooms. Along with other northern settlements including Lezhë and Shkodër, Bahçallëk had been flattened by that earthquake which struck on 15 April 1979. It measured 7.1 on the Richter scale and remains the most powerful earthquake in modern Albanian history.

In a neglected park near the main road, a *lapidar* commemorates Bahçallëk's rebuilding. One face of the monument shows a homeless family standing amidst falling masonry. A clock has stopped at 7.20 a.m., the time the earthquake struck. Another face shows the reconstruction: a work party marching into action behind an Albanian flag; tents for their accommodation; men and women laying bricks, pushing wheelbarrows; trucks and buses parked nearby. A date, 1 July 1979, suggests that the rebuilding was completed in less than three months.

But the *lapidar* wasn't just a celebration of Bahçallëk's reconstruction. Its real message focused on the 20,000 *aksionistë* who came from all over the country to help. Their effort was taken as evidence of unity between northern and southern Albanians. A rhyming inscription on the *lapidar* read:

> *Sup me sup jug e veri*
> *U ngri Bahçallëku i ri*
> *Ky bashkim Popull - Parti,*
> *Monument në Shqipëri.*

ENVER HOXHA'S LONG SHADOW

Shoulder to shoulder south and north
Have raised a new Bahçallëk
This union of the People and the Party
A monument to Albania.

The old road had continued south from Bahçallëk to Bushat. For a few kilometres, the new road followed the same route. Then, just before Bushat, a smaller road branched off to the right. This was where old and new diverged. We took the smaller road and it was as if a brake had been applied. Everything slowed. It was hard to believe that until 1981 when the railway reached Shkodër, this had been one of the most important routes in Albania, the only link between the northern regions and Tirana.

The road had been improved several times since the end of communism, but it was still narrow, and we went slowly. For the most part traffic was agricultural, a mixture of tractors and horse-drawn carts. Cows grazed on the verges. Although the fields had been broken down into strips, you began to get just an inkling of what had made these spaces so memorable in 1987.

Bushat - the home of the Bushatlli family mentioned in the castle museum - was a long, straggling village with red-roofed houses clustered on the hillside. According to the Albturist guide, "on the hills that line up along the road there are new plantations of mulberry trees, the leaves of which serve to feed silkworms." Albania had had a long tradition of indigenous silk production, especially around Bushat, and its friendship with China gave the sector a boost. In the late 1950s, Albanian engineers had been despatched to the East is Red Silk Factory in Hangzhou to improve their skills. Large-leaved varieties of Chinese mulberry trees had been imported from China. The cocoons were processed and spun in a factory in Shkodër. After 1990, the industry collapsed. Bushat had also been known for its milk production, with yields of more than 4,000 litres per cow. That tradition continues; modern Bushat has a thriving dairy. It seemed a prosperous village, but you didn't have to look hard for remnants of the old order.

South of Bushat, the Albturist map showed the main road veering south-west and passing behind a low mountain range called Mali Barbullush. This was not the route described in the Albturist guidebook, which stated that "the road runs along the banks of the Drin and through the villages of Berdicë, Bushat, Barbullush, Kakarriq, Balldren, all situated in a plain." So why the discrepancy? It turned out that the map was right, in the sense that it had marked the tourist route correctly. But the road marked on the map wasn't the main road. And so what didn't the authorities want visitors to see?

Barbullush, was nothing out of the ordinary. A *lapidar* in a small roadside cemetery commemorated seventeen villagers "massacred by Nazi Germans". The monument showed five men, traditionally dressed in baggy trousers and waistcoats. The concrete was so pitted and blackened that the figures had been almost eaten away, giving them an unearthly, almost spectral quality. The date of the massacre wasn't recorded on the *lapidar*, but all the graves, each with a five-pointed communist star, had the same date of death: 22 November 1944.

During communism, this region was intensively farmed. Since the 1990s, farming patterns had changed, but it was still rich agricultural land. Roadside stalls sold squashes and pumpkins. Horses pulled trailers loaded high with hay. The fertility of the land was one of the reasons why, when the changes came, so many people chose to stay. The lushness has also allowed diversification into tourism.

The next village was Kukël. It was tiny, and we wouldn't have stopped if we hadn't seen signs to a museum. The signs led to a Catholic church on high ground overlooking the plain. It was an unexpectedly grand building for such a small settlement, a fine neoclassical church painted in shades of pink with a pale blue double staircase up to the entrance. A plaque on the gatepost read, *Qendra Muze Ndre*

Mjeda. We parked, walked up to the church and asked if the museum was open. A rather grumpy man said it was and then disappeared into an office. We waited for a few moments and then another man appeared with a large key and took us to the church.

The Church of St Stephen the First Martyr had been consecrated in 1913 and was a gift from Austria-Hungary. Closed during communism and used as a *vatër kulturore*, a hearth of culture, it had been severely damaged during the atheist campaigns in 1967. Restoration began in 1993 and the church reopened for worship in 2005. By 2011, it had undergone a more thorough restoration. Our guide drew our attention to two stained glass windows in the nave, a gift, he said, from a family in Tirana. The glass was modern, a stylised resurrected Christ, but incorporated into the design were two very lifelike heads. One was bald, the other hirsute; both had large moustaches. The bald one, said our guide, was Ndre Mjeda; the other was his brother Lazër.

The reasons for Ndre Mjeda's importance became clear in the museum. Mjeda was many things: a scholar, a theologist, a politician, a linguist, a poet, a musician. Born in Shkodër in 1866 and educated by Jesuits, he had been sent abroad to study theology in Italy, France, Dalmatia and Poland. When he returned to Albania in 1899, he settled in Kukël. He built a rectory from which he could serve the local community and supervise the construction of the church.

Although a priest, Mjeda's commitment to improving the lives of ordinary people was praised by Enver Hoxha who described him as one of the "outstanding figures of our national cause and culture". During the years of communism, his house had been a *shtëpi muze*, a Museum House. But because Mjeda was also a Catholic priest, Hoxha felt obliged to caution readers not to "exalt" those parts of Mjeda's work where he speaks of Christian theology: "As Marxists and in the interest of the people and socialism, we must combat these negative aspects. In ideology we cannot make concessions to the beauty of verse or the language."

The museum was reopened in October 2014 by Albania's Minister of Culture, Mirela Kumbaro Furxhi, and it would have been interesting to know which parts of the current exhibition had been on display in the 1980s. The domestic items on the ground floor would have been uncontroversial: a coffee grinder and coffee pot, an inkwell, Mjeda's walking stick hanging on a hook between fireplace and window. The black and white family portraits would probably have been there, and the photographs of Mjeda as an international figure attending conferences across Europe. His death notice signed 1 August 1937 by Shkodër's Archiepiscopal Metropolitan, Gasper Thaçi, described Mjeda as "a notable writer" and a "veteran patriot". The communists couldn't have argued with that.

What definitely wasn't there was Mjeda's writing desk. It was removed from his house in 1966 and put in storage in Shkodër's Historical Museum. It was returned to the museum in time for the reopening and is one of its prize exhibits. What also would not have been on display were the fragments recovered from the desecrated church: the original rose window, wooden beams, a bas relief of a sailing ship. By far the most moving of these fragments were the letters of the original inscription that had been hacked off the church's façade. They were laid out in a glass-topped cabinet, a jumble of letters and parts of letters that could have been its own work of art. Meaningless in a literal sense, the letters have become invested with symbolic meaning, testimony to the violence that was inflicted on the church.

On the terrace in front of the church is a statue of Ndre Mjeda designed by Shkodran sculptor Sadik Spahiu. Mjeda stands in a billowing cassock with a broad-brimmed *cappello romano* on his head. His hands are clasped behind his back as he looks out across the plain.

From Kukël, the road hugs the mountainside. It crosses a canalised river on a Zog-era bridge and then skirts another small village called Gjadër. Then suddenly, completely

31

without warning, you find yourself crossing a thirty-metre-wide concrete strip. It takes a few moments for it to sink in. One moment you're admiring pomegranates in bloom, the next you're on a runway that was once one of communist Albania's most closely guarded military secrets. Now there's not even a fence.

So this was why we'd been diverted along the western side of Mali Barbullush.

It was mind-blowing. The runway was about two kilometres long, its northern end submerged in a shimmering haze. Grasses were pushing through the cracks, greening the concrete. But nature wasn't the only force eating away at the runway. Since 1990, Gjadër village had expanded and new villas had been built on both sides of the strip. Gardens backed onto the runway; cows and sheep grazed on the grass. Other roads through the village also joined the runway, turning it into a gigantic boulevard cutting through the fields. At its southern end, rusty gates said: *Ndal, Zone Ushtarake*, No Entry, Military Zone.

This was only the landing strip. The main runway was a kilometre to the east.

Construction had begun in 1969, at a moment in Albanian history when the country was even more consumed than usual by security fears. Albania had split from the Soviet bloc in 1961 but it continued to be a member of the Warsaw Pact. That changed in September 1968. In protest at the Pact's "fascist-type aggression" towards Czechoslovakia, Albania formally withdrew from the Pact, a move that, in the words of an official history, led to "a new outburst of revolutionary enthusiasm in carrying out the tasks in the various fields of socialist construction and the defence of the country". This was the moment dramatized by Vilson Kilica on the postcard I'd been given in Shkodër, and it wasn't by chance that in the same year, 1968, two specialist army units were created: Batalioni i Xhenios, an Engineering Battalion, and Kompania e Ndërtimit, a Construction Company. These two units took the lead in building the new airport.

It was a huge undertaking. The engineering corps provided about 2,000 troops and officers who worked twelve-hour shifts. Thousands more civilian engineers and workers were recruited from across the country. Many were housed at nearby Lezhë.

Agustin Gjinaj, a former air force officer who was interviewed about Gjadër in 2012, recalled that the base was built to a high specification "according to the scrupulous demands of our engineers and the Chinese specialists". Behind bomb-proof doors made of iron and concrete, a U-shaped bunker had been cut into the mountain with space for more than forty fighter jets plus fuel and weaponry. There were underground workshops, laboratories, conference rooms and a canteen. The bunker had its own fire and ventilation system and a dedicated electricity supply. The concrete vaults were covered in plastic to control moisture.

The base was handed over to the Minister of Defence, Beqir Balluku, in March 1974. The first flights started in July the same year, watched, says Gjinaj, by military personnel, foreign workers and specialists, and also by local residents. Its official purpose was to deter Yugoslav incursions into Albanian air space. At first a single squadron of Chinese-built Shenyang fighter aircraft was stationed at Gjadër. Later, two more squadrons were added, one from Rinas, the other from Kuçovë.

Gjadër continued to operate as a military airport until 1992. Then, keen to demonstrate its post-communist commitment to NATO, Albania allowed the CIA to use the base for unmanned spy missions over Yugoslavia. In March 1997, as violence gripped the country following the collapse of the pyramid investment schemes, the airport was ransacked and several planes damaged. At which point, Gjadër was abandoned as a military installation.

But its runways were still attractive. Bikers and owners of fast cars used them as a racetrack. And there were persistent rumours of the airport being used for drug running. An investigation in 2014 commissioned by the

Socialist government quickly became politicised when it found evidence that the airport had been used for narcotics during Sali Berisha's time in office, accusations vehemently denied by the Democratic Party. In October 2016, Berisha himself published a picture on his Facebook page of a light plane over Gjadër and wondered (mischievously) whether it was a *mushkonja e hashashit*, a hashish mosquito, looking for somewhere to land.

In April 2019, the airbase was in the news once again when the Socialist government announced plans to sell off the dozens of planes that had been quietly rotting in the underground hangars. Collectors are licking their lips at a rare opportunity to buy up a little bit of aviation history.

The Albturist guidebook said it was 41 kilometres from Shkodër to Lezhë. It seemed further. Then as now, Lezhë's importance lay in its connections with Scanderbeg. In 1444, the town hosted Lidhja e Lezhës, the League of Lezhë, where, under Scanderbeg's leadership Albania's feuding princelings agreed a common front against the Ottomans. It was also the place where Scanderbeg died on 17 January 1468. Lezhë, said Enver Hoxha, was "dear to our people".

The Brutalist memorial was still there, surrounded by parkland. So were the blocks of flats, but without the revolutionary banners. The apartments had been repainted and had new windows. On some of them, the corner balconies had been bricked in, which changed their profile, but they were still easily recognisable.

At the northern end of the park was Lezhë's industrial estate. During communism, the town had been an important food processing centre; it had also had plants producing tiles and paper. Now, only two factories were running. The tile factory had been privatised in 1994 and bought by a company called Milis. The meat processing plant had been bought in 2004 by Inca Casing and produced sausage skins. The other factory units were derelict and had been taken over by Roma. It was a desperate place, one of the most shocking examples of poverty we'd seen in Albania. Dark-skinned people thronged the streets; young girls balanced babies on their hips; children played in the dirt. Bags of recycled plastic and paper were everywhere, collected by litter pickers from the city's wastebins and sold on to a recycling centre for a few leks. All this only a few hundred metres from one of Albania's most important historical shrines.

Hoteli i Gjuetisë: a fascist retreat
1987

A couple of kilometres south of Lezhë, we turned off the main road onto a tree-lined track that led to a restaurant. Parked outside was a Volvo saloon, a minibus and a jeep, more vehicles than we had seen all morning. The minibus had been made in Poland. An arched entrance led to a complex of stone buildings and terraces that looked out over a landscaped garden with lawns and trees and a small lake. Someone in our group who had done their homework said that this had been a hunting lodge used by Mussolini's son-in-law, Count Ciano, during the Italian occupation of Albania in the Second World War.

A table had been laid and we sat down to soup, cold meat and grey mullet followed by an over-sweet gateau and red apples served in a bucket of iced water. Dag said quietly: "I wonder what they're having for lunch in those tower blocks." I could see what he was getting at.

2019

Hoteli i Gjuetisë had been one of Albturist's jewels where tourist groups were taken for lunch. The guidebook described it rather prosaically as "a modern characteristic hotel". A feature article in *New Albania* was more fulsome. Set amid what it called "the Albanian 'Amazon' in miniature", in its view, the hotel was "a very original architectural complex built in stone and timber... to eat a lunch of fish and game in the exotic surroundings of the restaurant is a pleasant experience." True, it was.

Since 1987, I'd been back to Hoteli i Gjuetisë several times. In 2017, the lodge still looked much as it had done in 1987. By the entrance where you turned into a still-grand tree-lined avenue, there was a yellow sign. It was partly obscured by foliage but you could clearly read: Hoteli i Gjuetise Lezhe, and across the top in Gothic script, "Filiali Albturist", Albturist Affiliated.

Apart from the trees that were noticeably larger, the space appeared to be unchanged. From the courtyard, a paved path ran through the garden to the restaurant. After the bright sunshine, it was almost dark inside and we had to wait a few moments for eyes to adjust. I can't call it a jolt of recognition because it wasn't, but as the room came into focus, at some deeper, subconscious level there was a memory that it mapped onto, and it must have been a near-perfect match, because for a few seconds it was as if I'd been caught in a weird time warp, as if the space I was standing in had blurred into the space as it had been thirty years ago.

In 1987, our Albturist group had sat around a large wooden table to eat. Now in 2017, the room was set out with smaller tables for a wedding party but the wooden walls and ceiling and the strip of red carpet on the parquet floor seemed to be exactly as they had been. Even the light, a flat light that seeped into the room through net curtains, was as I remembered. Apart from the visual clutter of the bar, the room was authentic, even down to the old radiators and the decorative ironwork around the fireplace.

We had a drink on the terrace and then walked through a stone arch into what had been the hotel. A shady arcade led to a derelict, overgrown courtyard, with uncut grass and untended trees. Wooden shutters dangled from windows that were clotted with cobwebs. It was lush, overgrown, a place of dappled sunshine, humidity and whining mosquitoes. Lezhë was only a couple of kilometres away, but this little wooded enclave felt like a different world.

Although the article in *New Albania* had chosen not to draw attention to it, the hotel had a notorious history. It had been built for Count Galeazzo Ciano, Mussolini's son-in-law and driving force behind Italy's invasion of Albania in 1939. In the years leading up to the invasion, Ciano had been a regular visitor to Albania. He had befriended King Zog and had been an official witness at the king's wedding in April 1938. Ciano wanted a base in Albania, somewhere to entertain friends and influence people, so he commandeered a private hunting reserve on Ishull Lezhë and commissioned an Italian company to build him a hunting lodge. According to the original plans which are held in Albania's National Building Archive, the contract was awarded to Legnami Pasotti, a company from Brescia who were specialists in wooden structures.

Legnami Pasotti's design was an Italian take on what a Balkan lodge should be. Its fireplaces and wood-panelled walls and ceilings were intended to evoke a highland *kulla*. But it also had to be comfortable. So there was a large dining room, guest rooms and a private suite for Ciano, plus a kitchen, servants' quarters, bathrooms and toilets. The lodge was completed only a few months before the Italian invasion and Ciano's wartime Diaries make no mention of him ever staying there. But Italian archive images show the lodge being used by hunters in March 1942. There are photographs of men with guns, hunting dogs and dozens of dead ducks laid out along a wall. In another image, two men inspect a small bear in a paddock.

After liberation, the hunting lodge became state property and was administered initially from Tirana by Hotel Dajti. In a seamless transition, the new communist government continued to use the lodge as Ciano had intended, as a place to entertain and impress foreign delegations. In the early days, the visitors were mostly Yugoslavs and Russians. When Albturist was founded in 1956, some rooms were converted into a hotel, but it wasn't until the 1980s, when more tourist groups began to come, that the authorities woke up to the wider potential of the hunting lodge and surrounding wetland. In 1985, a second dining room was added, part of a plan to redevelop the whole area as a tourist complex. There was a plan to dig a new canal that would link the lodge directly with the lagoon so that "the visitor will be able to enjoy the beauty of the forest while rowing or fishing". But when the old regime collapsed, its development plans were shelved and the canal was never built. The hunting lodge was ransacked and partly burnt during the disturbances in 1997. It reopened in 2003, but when we'd been there in 2017 you got the sense that it had never properly recovered.

By 2019, everything had changed, even the tree-lined drive. The Albturist sign had gone and the gates replaced by two hefty stone urns. The courtyard had been reshaped with a fountain at its centre. There were tables on the lawn, an outdoor bar, children's play equipment, ersatz statues and a horse-drawn wedding cart. I sat at a table, struggling to process the changes. It was too open, too bright. Hoteli i Gjuetisë had been shorn of its mystery.

One of the waiters offered to give me a tour of the grounds. He showed me the swimming pool and an annexe next to it that was, he said, "specially for weddings", and he insisted on taking a photo of me by the pool. He showed me an outdoor space which looked a little like an aviary, and I asked facetiously if it was for birds - no, he said, it was for dancing at a wedding. And even as he was explaining, a film crew with camera, sound boom and lights were making a video of a couple dressed in their wedding finery.

After I'd eaten, I went inside to look at the dining hall. Two years ago, the décor had hardly changed since communism. Now the room was lighter and brighter with doors opening onto the terrace and a new entrance by the bar. The fireplace was still there, but the rustic snug with cushions around the hearth had gone, and a grand piano had been installed opposite the fireplace.

I got out the photos of the lodge as it had been in 1987, and the waiters gathered round to look. One of them, Giri, spoke good English. He said he was an architecture student in Tirana and was working at the lodge to make some money. Giri had a good eye for architectural detail. He said that the photos showed two reception rooms, not one. The one with the fireplace was where we were standing. The other one had rounded window frames; it had been burned in 1997 and only recently restored. I asked if I could see it and off we went, around the outside of the building and along the colonnade past the hotel rooms. Giri said that four rooms had already been refurbished, another ten were being restored.

The room Giri took me to was a mirror image of the main dining room with dark wood-panelled walls, a wooden ceiling and a large fireplace. The fireplace was not as ornate as the one in the main dining hall and the windows no longer had rounded frames, as they did in the photo - they too had fallen victim to the rebuilding. But what had survived was the ambience. It was darker than its counterpart, pleasantly gloomy, with the light filtered by net curtains. Giri said that nowadays this room was reserved for receptions, weddings and birthdays. And bang on cue, in came the wedding party and the film crew began to set up their shots while the happy couple slumped exhausted in chairs on each side of the fireplace.

Giri was enjoying the break from waitering and was keen to continue the tour. We came out into the colonnade and he pointed to the room opposite. It had a heavy wooden door and a small window protected by net curtains. That room, he said, was the only one that hadn't been altered; it was still as it had been from Count Ciano's time. Unfortunately, the owner had the key and he was in Istanbul to watch Albania play Turkey in a Euro qualifier. I said I would have to come back and see the room another day.

Lezhë: irrigation and forced labour
1987

We drained our tumblers of wine, drank our small cups of Turkish coffee and returned to the coach. We continued south through a string of villages along the eastern fringe of the plain. We were very close to the mountains, and the road wound through orchards, over bridges, and past single-storey villas with red-tiled roofs, each with a small plot for vegetables and chickens. To our right, the plain stretched to the horizon, its flatness broken by occasional cooperative warehouses and farm buildings. A single-line railway ran close to the road. For a time, a train kept us company; most of its windows were missing. Edi told us that much of the plain was reclaimed marshland and was now used for wheat, rice and vegetables. I wanted to see it all and make notes so I wouldn't forget, but the combination of wine, sun on the window and the swaying coach was making it hard to stay awake.

Edi took pity on us: "After your late night you will probably want to rest… I will mention just a couple of things. You will have noticed how quiet the roads are; this is because in Albania we have no private cars. You will have seen some motorbikes and heavy vehicles; these belong to the factories or the state farms. The bikes are for experts to travel to different parts of the farm. Some people have also been asking about housing: many of the houses in the countryside are privately owned and people are free to sell them, but there must be no speculation. Most Albanians live in state-owned flats where the rents are very low, between 25 and 35 leks a month. The flats are built by the state or by volunteers. Some people build their own houses; Albanians can borrow money from the state and pay it back over twenty years…"

As Edi continued, ox-carts lumbered across the fields laden with maize stems. In a village, children were playing football and swinging from irrigation pipes. A man with an axe chipped away at a tree stump for kindling. Ragged plastic hung like dirty clothes from tobacco frames. Sunshine bounced off the roofs of a thousand greenhouses. A women's brigade, adzes and hoes on their shoulders, were making their way home along the railway track. Then our coach got stuck behind a tractor that took no notice of the driver's hooting. As the sun started to dip, those hallucinatory ditches filled with gold, as if the peasants had become alchemists.

2019

Just past Stadiumi Besëlidhja on Lezhë's southern outskirts, a canalised stream runs alongside Rruga Franz Josef Strauss. The stream is called Përroi i Manatisë. It was canalised in the early 1960s and was supposed to take flood water from the hills east of Lezhë to the River Drin. It's a typical urban watercourse that's showing its age. Its banks have collapsed and its sluggish water is clogged with rubbish. Përroi i Manatisë was one tiny element in a much larger scheme to drain and irrigate Bregu i Matit, the plain south of Lezhë. By the time the work had been completed in 1967, around 700 kilometres of canals and waterways crisscrossed the plain. This must have been another of those places where we'd been mesmerised by flickering irrigation channels.

In its description of this section of the route, the Albturist guidebook asks the visitor to take note of "the transformations that have taken place in the villages of this region and the irrigation schemes that have been set up and placed at the service of the collective farms". Irrigation made it possible to grow vines and fruit trees on the hillsides. On the plain, which ran west all the way to the sea, irrigation allowed collectivised farms to grow wheat, vegetables, rice and sunflowers.

Collectivisation and land reclamation went hand in hand. One of the first acts of the communist government was to drain marshland around Maliq, near Korcë. Other marshlands at Tërbuf, Hoxharë and Kakariq were also drained. Drainage not only increased the acreage of land available for growing food; flat fields and effective irrigation made "intensified agriculture'" possible. The old regime took pride in land reclamation. It has been estimated that during the communist era, 25,000 kilometres of irrigation canals were dug, of which 2,000 were main canals, 6,200 were secondary canals and 16,800 were tertiary canals like Përroi i Manatisë. That's an awful lot of canals.

On Bregu i Matit, two main canals ran in parallel across the plain to the coast more than nine kilometres away. One ran from Spiten to Hidrovor; the other from Zejmen to Tale. Secondary canals distributed water to the fields. The guidebook failed to mention that irrigation schemes were dependent on forced labour. Until 1990, there was a work camp at Zejmen to provide labour for *kanalizimi*.

In July 1991, Albania adopted Land Law 7501. This was a crucial piece of legislation that authorised land redistribution. Collectivised farms were broken up, and by the end of the decade it was estimated that as many as 470,000 family farms had replaced 550 state and cooperative farms. All those family farms needed to tap into the irrigation system. It was a logistical challenge that the state was unable to deal with. A precarious situation was pushed further into crisis in 1997 when pumping stations and irrigation channels were vandalised.

Recognising the importance of irrigation to Albanian agriculture - without it, there would be none - in 1994, the World Bank funded an Irrigation and Drainage Rehabilitation Program to repair existing networks and to ensure sustainability through farmer participation. In July 2000, the Albanian government transferred responsibility for irrigation to the municipalities and community groups. Since then, election-time promises to curb flooding and improve irrigation have become part of Albania's political discourse.

Which brings us back to Përroi i Manatisë. The stream would probably have gone unnoticed if it hadn't run through Lezhë's suburbs. In 2009, the Bashkia acknowledged that its concrete conduit had fractured and that the stream had become "unattractive". They promised improvements.

Nothing happened. Then in November 2016, there was widespread flooding in Lezhë's southern suburbs and Përroi i Manatisë was identified as a root cause. The Bashkia drew up a rehabilitation plan for a number of small waterways around Lezhë, including Përroi i Manatisë. Again, nothing was done. In September 2019, Lezhë flooded again, and again in January 2021, May 2022, November 2022 and January 2023.

As you leave Lezhë on the old road, a bridge crosses Përroi i Manatisë. From the bridge you can see the remains of a small reservoir, now overgrown with trees and bushes, that would have been another part of the original flood control system. We must have crossed this bridge in 1987.

The road takes you through a string of farming villages along the eastern edge of the plain - Manati, Tresh, Spiten, Markatomaj, Zejmen and Pllanë. It winds through the villages and crosses watercourses on communist-era bridges. It was a pretty road and although the asphalt had cracked and there were lots of potholes, there was not much traffic and we could go slowly.

Remnants of the old order were everywhere: in the warehouses and collectivised housing, in the industrial estates, in the irrigation canals, in the railway. For about five kilometres, from Spiten to Pllanë, road and rail ran side by side. It must have been along this stretch of road that we'd been accompanied by that windowless train in 1987.

As well as the old, there was plenty of the new: new shops, new houses, new businesses and most strikingly, new churches. By the time the ban on religious observance had been lifted in December 1990, churches and mosques had been closed for more than twenty years. Many were in ruins and it was easier and cheaper to build new ones. Bregu i Matit is still northern Albania, an overwhelmingly Catholic region, and it seemed that every village had a new Catholic church. In Spiten, Kisha 'Shpirti i Shenjtë' had been built right next to communist-era warehouses - old and new side by side.

At Zejmen, I took a smaller road that went west alongside the Zejmen-Tale canal. The road crossed another canal running north to south, then it crossed the abandoned railway into farmland. Since the collapse of collectivised farming, the plain has been transformed. Rather than a succession of vast fields, it has become a patchwork of small farms. Some were run as businesses, growing fruit and vegetables for local markets; others were subsistence farms, providing produce just for the family. Many of the plots had new houses on them. The SH1 highway, Albania's main north–south artery, runs through the centre of Bregu i Matit and has encouraged ribbon development: petrol stations, cafés, restaurants, hotels. It's only when you get west of the motorway that you start to have any sense of open space. Fields stretch away to the horizon. Tracks branch off from the asphalt at regular intervals, as if a mathematical grid had been imposed on the landscape. It all starts to look the same. If you didn't know your way around, it would be easy to get lost.

The same rigour has been applied to the canals and watercourses. The Zejmen-Tale canal cuts an undeviating line across the plain. At its eastern end near the village, its banks were overgrown and the watercourse weedy and full of rubbish. Closer to the sea, the canal widens until it's broad enough for small boats. At Tale, it abandons its rigour and meanders through a mini-wetland before emptying into the sea at Tale beach. This whole stretch of coast, from Tale up to Ishull Lezhë, is now part of a managed *Rezervati Natyror*.

Despite its size, the canal flooded in November 2016, in the same downpour that overwhelmed Përroi i Manatisë in Lezhë. In March 2019, the central government stumped up 5.5 million leks (about £40,000) for the canal to be dredged. The Minister for Agriculture and Rural Development, Bledi Çuçi, came to inspect the work. Mr Çuçi hoped that the removal of more than 5,000 cubic metres of silt would make floods a thing of the past.

Laç: "a majestic factory"
1987

Road and rail together crossed a wide river at Milot. Then, after more fields and irrigation channels, we came to Laç. On its outskirts was a huge factory; its chimneys must have been visible for miles. Edi told us that Laç was one of Albania's new industrial cities, built in the 1960s. This was why there were so many new housing blocks here, for the workers. On the site we were passing, there was a phosphate fertiliser plant and a copper smelter. "Albania is only a small country," said Edi, "but it places great importance on industry, and it has large mineral deposits: chrome, copper, aluminium, nickel." The current Five Year Plan emphasised the need to increase the efficiency of metal processing and to discover new reserves.

Edi was very good at his job. The way he put it, it sounded as if we were passing a state-of-the-art factory, a fine-tuned industrial complex. Through the window we saw disintegrating brickwork, and rusty cylinders and conduits. Asbestos cladding was peeling from the pipes. I'm not an engineer and we had only a brief glimpse, but the factory was definitely in a poor state of repair.

When Edi looked out of the window, he must have seen what we were seeing, but he spoke so rationally, so persuasively that he either believed what he was saying, or he was a consummate actor. It must have been the latter - or maybe Edi's description simply reflected the fact that in Albania, this was what heavy industry was.

2019

If irrigation was important, industry was even more so, the heavier the better. Albania, said Enver Hoxha, followed the Leninist maxim that "heavy industry is the basis of socialist industrialisation". South of Milot, you become aware of four chimneys. At first, the distance makes them hazy, but as you get closer, they come more sharply into focus and by the time you reach them they are the dominant presence in the landscape. The chimneys belonged to one of communist Albania's showcase industrial projects, Uzina e Superfosfatit.

The guidebook describes it like this: "In the place where not many years ago nestled a tiny village, on the right side of the road, today rises majestically, with its tall chimneys, the chemical superphosphate plant of Laç, an entirely modern plant. The road here is at all hours crowded with traffic; in the vicinity of Laç there is a huge automobile park for trucks, further on an industrial woodworking combine, and still further away, at the foot of a hill, the new town itself. Many storey buildings, schools, shops and various other institutions, all brand new, give this small town an attractive aspect."

Building began in 1963, at a time when Albania was trying to rebalance its economy from "agricultural-industrial" to "industrial-agricultural". And because the factory was a prestige project, film crews recorded its progress. A *Zhurnal* film crew recorded the moment when, amid much applause, Politburo member Spiro Koleka laid the first stone. Two years later, a newsreel, *Kinoditar*, gave viewers a progress report. The film showed a vast building site with scaffolding, cranes and half-completed chimneys. In the same year, the state-run film enterprise, Kinostudio, made a short documentary about the factory. This was a much more accomplished piece of filmmaking. In one sequence, a stream of men climb a wooden staircase up the inside of one of the chimneys. At the top, two workers are roped to a wooden beam and they step casually over the edge, dangling on the end of the rope, so they can inspect the exterior of the new chimney. It's dizzying even to watch.

The plant came on stream in 1966. China provided the technology. Over the next decade, the factory expanded. In 1979, a second phosphate plant and a copper smelter were added - a by-product of the smelter was sulphur dioxide, an ingredient in phosphate fertiliser. In 1987, a third phosphate plant using Polish technology was built. A bullish article in

New Albania at the beginning of 1989 stated that a fourth phosphate plant would be built at Laç with a capacity of 150,000 tons per annum. It would form part of a putative Ninth Five Year Plan that never happened.

When we came past in 1987, I had no impression of noise or traffic or even smoke from the chimneys. I took three photos from the coach window. The first caught two chimneys and a cluster of metal tanks and pipework. The metalwork by the chimneys was new and glittered in the afternoon sun - it could have been a part of the recently installed Polish phosphate plant. Next to the chimneys were two rectangular storage tanks mounted over six giant fans, three fans per tank. In the foreground was a jumble of discarded rusty pipes. The other two photos showed the pipework in more detail. Some of them seemed to be lagged with asbestos which was broken and peeling. In the background you can see a metal ladder giving access to an inspection deck.

I stood on the bank outside the factory trying to match the images. Time and depredation had taken their toll. The shiny pipework had disappeared, almost certainly taken for scrap. And the six fans under the storage tanks had also gone; there were jagged holes where they had been. Trees and shrubs had taken root on the waste ground where there'd been those discarded pipes; they too had probably been scavenged for scrap.

This wasn't the first time I'd been back to Laç. I'd been in Albania with our son Joe in 2012 and we couldn't resist stopping at the factory. An Albanian flag hung limply by the gates which had communist stars at their centre. The factory was deserted and we could walk along rubble-strewn paths that took us deep into the site. Sometimes the path was wet with an unnaturally bright orange effluent. In other parts, the puddles were yellow or bright green. Frogs burped in the ditches. Then we heard sheep bells and a few moments later saw a shepherd leading his flock through the ruins. We smiled and waved, and the sheep left hoofprints in the yellow mud.

On we went past ruptured pipes, smashed windows and

1987: The mighty phosphate fertiliser plant at Laç has been...

2019: ...abandoned and stripped of its metal. But the chimneys are still standing.

piles of bricks where walls had collapsed. We came to a large building that we thought might have been a bagging area; steel girders were still in place that could have supported machinery or a conveyor belt. Inside, a chaotic mass of masonry and rubble was illuminated by shafts of sunlight falling through a non-existent roof. In another building, a mass of rusty pipes ran between four metal tanks, and we wondered if this had been where phosphate dust had been mixed with sulphuric acid to produce superphosphate. Etched against a cloudless blue sky, the site looked like a piece of post-apocalyptic art. It was as if we had been transported into a dystopian video game with assassins hiding among the ruins.

Amid all this degradation, the four chimneys still stood erect. They looked in good condition, tribute to the skills of those aerial workers caught on film. In the early days of the communist regime, Hoxha had spoken about "the enemies of the people" who could not bear to see "the smoke from the chimneys of our thriving factories". When you stand next to them, you can understand why they were so fetishised. After the demolition of bell towers and minarets in 1967, chimneys came to symbolise the triumph of the atheistic socialist order. Although it wasn't wise, we went inside one, the one that had been in the film. Thanks to its portholes we could see all the way to the top. The concrete inner shell was large enough for a metal flue and ladder, and although much of the latter had rusted way, some sections were still in place, zigzagging skywards.

It was a mesmerising place, as much for what it had been as for what it now was. The size was humbling, even numbing when you think of the physical effort consumed by its construction - and this was only one of hundreds of similar sites across Albania. One of Ismail Kadare's darkest novels, *The Pyramid*, describes the construction of a giant pyramid at Giza, the building of which would force the Pharoah's subjects "to renounce their previous way of life". When construction began, workers suffered "exhaustion, the terror of execution and the fear of being sent to the quarries". For the Pharoah, read Hoxha; for Giza, read Laç.

Somehow, Uzina e Superfosfatit survived the transition. In 1993, USAID commissioned an evaluation to assess the factory's viability "under the current market economy system". The inspectors concluded that continued operation was "not feasible". Although it was not its intention, if you read the evaluation today it provides a detailed insight into working conditions inside the plant where more than 2,000 people had been employed. The inspectors noted that much of the equipment was "unreliable or worn out". Handrails, stairs and platforms were "corroded and/or damaged". Control room instrumentation needed "replacement and upgrading". There was "almost a total absence of guards on the mechanical drives thus exposing the workers to serious hazards". The electrical switching equipment was substandard. General maintenance had been "greatly hampered" by a lack of spare parts: "Almost all parts could not be imported and consequently had to be made in Albania or made or assembled from local castings at the Laç plant."

The inspectors also expressed concern about the factory's environmental impact. In the phosphate rock grinding area, dust levels were sometimes more than ten times above allowed limits. Outside, the inspectors reported that releasing "off-gases from copper smelting" through chimneys created "intolerable environmental conditions for plant personnel and the surrounding countryside and communities".

Despite all that, the factory continued operating until 1999. It reopened in 2002 and closed again the next year. In May 2010, the Department of Economy, Trade and Energy issued a liquidation notice. In 2011, Prime Minister Sali Berisha published a list of 300 businesses offered for privatisation. The superphosphate plant was on the list. So far, there have been no takers. But the factory continues to make headlines. Ground pollution remains a problem with high levels of copper and arsenic leaching into groundwater. In July 2018, one man was killed and two injured when a wall collapsed as they tried to remove metal girders for scrap.

Laç town: rivers of mud
2019

In 1987, we had only a brief glimpse of Laç. Touted as a "new city" built from scratch for the workers at the superphosphate plant, you get some sense of the pre-1990 town from a documentary called *Laçi, qyteti ynë*, Laç, Our City, made in 1976. The storyline is about a composer who is writing a song in praise of Laç. As he walks through the town seeking inspiration, the film presents us, the audience, with a series of images of town and factory. We are shown new apartment blocks and parks planted with flowers and trees; students studying; a crocodile of nursery children wrapped up against the cold; a health clinic; children and pensioners working together to dig a drainage channel through the town. At the end of the film, we join the audience in Laç's Pallati i Kulturës where the song is performed. In the words of the song, Laç represents *pranvera e socializmit, pranvera e Partisë*, the spring of Socialism, the spring of the Party.

When the fertiliser plant closed, it took the town's economy with it. Since then, Laç has become a hub for cheap and used clothes; most of its market is given over to them. The main square has been repaved and the Bashkia repainted, but structurally speaking, modern Laç is little different from the Laç in the 1976 film.

Although Laç was an industrial settlement, the plain south of the Mat river was one of Albania's most important agricultural zones where state and cooperative farms produced wheat, milk and vegetables. The plain is known as Fusha e Thumanës and, like Bregu i Matit, had originally been marshland. It was drained in the late 1950s and early 1960s, and in common with other irrigation schemes, it relied on forced labour. Internment camps were set up at Milot,

Bushnesh, Gjorm, Ishëm and Patok. We know a lot about the camps on Fusha e Thumanës from testimony recorded later by political prisoners.

Irrigation on Fusha e Thumanës began in June 1958 when the authorities ordered the relocation of prisoners from a camp at Bubullimë, about 120 kilometres to the south, to a new camp at Bushnesh near Thumanë. At two o'clock in the morning of 3 June 1958, 540 prisoners set off in a convoy of sixty Škoda and ZIS trucks. The convoy was escorted by 13 army officers, 26 police officers, 92 soldiers and three dogs. The escorts were armed with 11 machine guns, 20 rifles and 111 pistols. When they arrived at Bushnesh, the authorities decided that forests near the camp were a security risk and could be used by prisoners to escape. So in September, the men were relocated to Gjorm on the outskirts of Laç.

Mark Alija was one of the unfortunates interned there. Before his arrest, Alija had worked at Thumanë as an assistant to Hungarian engineers who were advising on irrigation. The Hungarians were critical of the Hoxha regime and spoke glowingly about life in the West. Alija tried to escape to Yugoslavia but was caught and sentenced to six years' imprisonment. He was sent to the internment camp at Gjorm to work on the canals. When he was sentenced, Alija was seventeen years old.

Conditions at the camp were harsh. In his testimony, Alija describes men sleeping on two-storey bunks made of planks. There was no washing water and no showers; if anyone tried to wash clothes in the canal they were locked in a cell for three days. There were no toilets; you just did your business in a field. It was a wonder, Alija says, that there was never an outbreak of cholera.

For the prisoners, living conditions were only one part of their trauma. The work was exhausting. All the digging had to be done by hand with wheelbarrows, spades and shovels. In his testimony, Alija describes a typical day. Prisoners were woken at six in the morning, given a bowl of soup and then driven five kilometres to the canal. They worked until three in the afternoon and were then driven back to the camp for a meal. In the evenings, prisoners read or sewed. Lights out at eight. The next morning when they returned to the canal, they found that the embankments had sunk by up to a metre, because the ground was so sodden.

Some tried to escape. In February 1959, eleven prisoners were given permission to leave the compound to collect wood. Three made a run for it; one was shot and killed, the other two were recaptured. In August the following year, an enterprising prisoner tried to leave the camp dressed as an ordinary worker. He was shot and wounded by a guard.

As work intensified, the numbers living at Gjorm increased. In 1959, the population had risen to 742. In 1960, it dropped to 624. The camp was closed in 1963. In June that year, Enver Hoxha told the Tenth Plenum of the PLA's Central Committee that thanks to large state investments, Fusha e Thumanës had been turned into one of Albania's most fertile zones.

The canal where Alija and the other prisoners at Gjorm worked was called Kanali i Drojes. It began at Shullaz, a small village near Laç, and ran south to Mamurras where it joined the river that gave the canal its name, Lumi i Drojës. The river was also canalised and ran west across the plain to the sea.

You can see the canal at Shullaz where it is crossed by a bridge. The water was black and sluggish. A man who ran a small garage watched as I took photos. He confirmed that the canal went to Laç and then joined the Drojë river. He said that other waterways from the hills also drained into the canal but the conduits (he called them *mure*, walls) had collapsed and they no longer controlled the water, so the canal ran low in the summer and flooded in the winter. I asked if his workshop ever got flooded. No, he said, because it was on higher ground, the water ran onto the plain. No-one, he said, was looking after the canal. Tree roots were damaging the banks and it was full of rubbish. The man ate seeds as he spoke, chewing, talking, spitting.

I picked the canal up again at Sanxhak, south of Laç, where it ran alongside the road. Sheep were grazing on banks piled high with rubbish and plastic bottles. It was the same at Mamurras. The canal here was in a dip behind collectivised apartment blocks by the railway. It looked like a sewer. Its banks were a toxic mixture of mud and rubbish. Someone had tried to shore up the banks with car tyres.

Further south at Thumanë, the road crossed Lumi i Drojes. The bridge had been swept away by flash floods in April 2018. It had been rebuilt, but the canalised riverbed had been damaged. Further west, out on the plain near Dukagjin i Ri, canal and river converge. I tried to find the junction but got lost in the myriad of tracks running through the fields.

It rained heavily overnight, and the next morning when I went to look again at the canal it was a scary sight. The level had risen by at least a couple of metres and the water had changed colour. It was now brown with earth and sludge. It hadn't breached the bridge at Shullaz, but the current had pushed tree branches, plastic bottles and polystyrene trays - anything that floated - up against the bridge. Even worse, Laç had flooded. The town centre was under several inches of sticky brown mud. Water was still pouring down the drainage channels that ran through the town, but at least the water was now contained. All along the banks there were piles of refuse that must have been blocking the channels when the rain started.

Homes and shops were flooded. The market was inundated. Stallholders were trying to rescue their stock. Some stalls had been swept away. Men and women with brooms and wheelbarrows had started to clear up the mess. Bashkia employees in orange jackets were scraping mud from the pavements. A fire engine followed them, spraying the pavements with clean water.

The terrible thing was that this was the second time Laç had been flooded in a month. In September, a retaining wall along Kanali i Drojës at Sanxhak had cracked, flooding houses close to the canal. A minister sent from Tirana assured residents that the government "would be moving very quickly" to fix both the canal and the drainage channels that ran through Laç. But not quickly enough.

Without industry, Laç is having to reinvent itself. The clothes market is part of that reinvention, but the town also has plans to resume its role as a place of pilgrimage. In the hills above Laç is a Franciscan church, Kisha e Shna Ndout, the Church of St Anthony. The church was built in 1557, and up until the mid-1960s continued to attract pilgrims in large numbers. On Easter Sunday 1964, Dymphna Cusack was in Laç and wrote a vivid account of the day in her book, *Illyria Reborn*. Although the communists had been in power for twenty years, Cusack thought that traditional village life had hardly changed. She was introduced to the village headman - she refers to him as "the Patriarch" - whose name was Ndue. Ndue sat by the hearth smoking a "long, richly-chased silver pipe with a bulbous amber mouthpiece" and was served coffee by his youngest daughter-in-law who wore "the Catholic folk costume of the region at its richest". When the bells rang out that Easter morning, Cusack joined the villagers as they made their way up the hill. The church was filled to bursting, men on one side, women on the other. Most of the women wore a white surcoat of homespun wool on which was embroidered a cross. All of them were veiled. It was, Cusack wrote, "a scene out of another age".

After the service, Cusack joined the Patriarch and his family for an Easter banquet of stewed pork, stewed beef and macaroni followed by "an enormous sweetish tart with much butter in it". But they knew change was coming. The Patriarch's son told Cusack that work had already begun on a new factory and soon they would have to join the agricultural cooperative. Three years later, during the atheist campaigns, Kisha e Shna Ndout was attacked and damaged, but the villagers continued to use it for worship. A story has it that in 1981, soldiers were sent to complete the demolition. But as they laid charges, thirty-two of them became paralysed from the waist down. Some were sent to Austria for treatment, others to the military hospital in Tirana. After six months of intensive treatment, they were not fully cured. The authorities blamed food poisoning. Villagers took it as a sign of divine intervention.

On 13 June 1990, St Anthony's saint's day, 60,000 people defied the authorities and gathered at the ruins of the church. That evening, Radio Tirana reported that people had come from all over Albania to take part in a "mass picnic". In 1991 the church was rebuilt, and two years later it was connected to the town by a good quality asphalt road. On a cool afternoon in October, there weren't many people around, just a few families lighting candles, kissing icons or praying to one of the saints.

From the church, there is a stunning view across the plain, all the way to the coast ten kilometres away. To the north is Laç's football stadium. Then the four chimneys of Uzina e Superfosfatit. The landscape has changed, but the chimneys still dominate, reminders of a social order that ground to a halt at the end of 1990.

3: Krujë

Battles among the Pines

1987

It was getting late and the setting sun had become hazy behind bands of cloud. At Fushë-Krujë, we turned off the main road and began to climb through pine forests. LAVDI NË 1908, GLORY to 1908, the year of Enver Hoxha's birth, was picked out in white stones on the hillside. The intercom clicked. It was Edi telling us that we were about to visit the Hero City of Krujë where, for 25 years, Scanderbeg had defied the Turks.

Just as he was launching into a longer exposition, we heard a klaxon. A local bus was trying to overtake. The road was narrow and twisting, but that didn't deter the other bus which drew level, smoke pouring from its exhaust. For just a few moments, the two vehicles were side by side. The Albanian bus was packed to its rusty seams with villagers returning home from the plain. Safe in our respective vehicles, each group could stare at the other without restraint. We saw dark, weathered faces; they saw pink, bourgeois faces, faces of the class enemy. Then our coach started to lose ground and by the next corner we had been overtaken. We ground to a halt on the bend and after a short discussion with the driver, Edi announced that there was a problem with the gearbox. The driver let the coach roll back to a straighter section of road, and after much roaring and juddering managed to engage first gear. We crawled into Krujë, a less than triumphant entry into the Hero City.

2018

The road up the mountain to Krujë had been improved since 1987. It still twisted back and forth though pine forests, but the surface was good and the carriageway wide enough for coaches to pass without danger. What I hadn't noticed on that first visit was the sheer number of *lapidars* along the road. They started on the plain and continued all the way to Krujë.

A *lapidar* by the track to Zgërdhesh commemorates the battles fought by Scanderbeg. The original monument that we would have passed in 1987 was a concrete monolith with a fine bas relief of Scanderbeg at full gallop, cape flying out behind him. It had been designed by Thoma Thomai to mark the 500th anniversary of Scanderbeg's death in 1968. For some reason, it had been replaced in 2012. The new *lapidar* still celebrated Scanderbeg, but instead of the bas relief there were fifteen metal shields, each stamped with the outline of Scanderbeg's goat helmet.

There was another one in the Martyrs' Cemetery. The best of the bunch was in a garage on the outskirts of the town. It commemorated 21 members of the Twenty-Third Brigade who had been killed during the war. A frieze showed five partisans in action - firing weapons, waving a flag, looking resolute. In the left-hand corner was an outline of Krujë's medieval castle.

You might wonder why there are so many *lapidars* along this stretch of road. There had been heavy fighting around Krujë, but what made the town unique was its connection with Scanderbeg. Memorialising the campaign to liberate Krujë strengthened the communists' links with Albania's national hero.

But the *lapidars* also carried a political message. Despite the rhetoric, not everyone in Krujë had been sympathetic to the communists. One of the non-communist leaders Enver Hoxha had had to deal with was Abaz Kupi. Kupi was born in Krujë in 1892. During King Zog's reign, Kupi had been in charge of Krujë's gendarmerie. After the Italian invasion, he went to Turkey but returned to Albania in April 1941 and set up a pro-Zogist resistance group, Legaliteti. In the early stages of the fight against fascism, Kupi had cooperated with the communists and been a member of the Anti-Fascist National Liberation Council, an umbrella organisation which brought together both communists and nationalists.

On 22 September 1943, a combined force of communist partisans and members of Legaliteti took control of Krujë in what became known as its "first liberation". Abaz Kupi claimed the credit for the liberation, which incensed the communists. In December, Kupi was summoned to Tirana to meet with Enver Hoxha. Hoxha later described the meeting in his memoir, *The Anglo-American Threat to Albania.* He accused Kupi of lying about the liberation of Krujë: "The people saw with their own eyes who did the fighting there. It was the partisan *çetas* led by Haxhi Lleshi that shed their blood. You arrived at the end just to appear as a 'liberator'." At the end of the meeting, Kupi was expelled from the National Liberation Council. "Thus we ended the meeting with Abaz Kupi and took our departure. Since that time I never again set eyes on him."

Animosity towards Kupi and Legaliteti continued long after the end of the war. Legaliteti was routinely referred to as "traitorous", "treacherous" or "reactionary". Kupi was a "traitor and bandit" who had "collaborated openly with the Germans". His claim to have liberated Krujë had to be refuted. The *lapidars* along the road, a public record for all to see, declared that it was the communists not Legaliteti who had done the liberating.

Krujë: "Whoever speaks of Scanderbeg speaks of Krujë"
1987

We parked by a statue of Scanderbeg with sword drawn astride a rearing horse, and we walked through the little town towards the castle. On the hillside above us were modern apartment blocks; there were more apartment blocks on the slope below the road. The air was chill, the light fading. There weren't many people around, just a few men strolling and chatting quietly. Edi said that on a clear day you could see all the way to the sea, but not this evening. Smoke from the cement works at Fushë-Krujë mixed with the evening mist and condensed into smog. A dense patch began to spread horizontally and then it pushed upwards, smothering the hillside. The smog drifted across the valley, and as the sun set, it took on a pinkish hue that made the landscape even more opaque and dreamlike.

A cobbled path led into the old bazaar. It wasn't a bazaar in the full-blown Turkish sense, just a narrow street of small wooden shops. All but two were closed. In one, a cobbler was working under a blue-white strip light. Another was selling painted plates, carved wood and postcards.

We emerged into a large open space overlooked by a medieval tower on a rocky outcrop. The site was dominated by a new building. This, said Edi, was the Scanderbeg Museum which had opened in 1982. Its pale stone had not yet weathered and although it had been designed to blend with the original architecture, it seemed more a fantasy than a genuine historical reconstruction, something imagined by Escher or de Chirico.

In the hallway was a larger-than-life, three-dimensional marble tableau of Scanderbeg and his warriors. Scanderbeg was standing with one hand resting on his sword hilt. It was surprisingly powerful. In front of a dramatic fresco of Scanderbeg battling with the Turks, a copy of his famous helmet and sword were displayed on a table covered with red velvet. The originals, we were told, were in Vienna.

We wandered round, admiring the furniture, the paintings, the sculptures, the maps and the books. Upstairs, there was a reconstruction of Scanderbeg's study with an outsize wooden chair and table. Some of our group who had been on this tour last year were surprised that our attention hadn't been drawn to a selection of Enver Hoxha's books on a shelf; they wondered if there was political significance in the omission. Then we all trooped across the courtyard to a restaurant where we sat around low tables drinking coffee. A concert of light music was on the television. The sound quality was fine but the line hold was faulty and the picture slowly revolved. Then Edi stood up to make an announcement: "Thanks to the attentions of our mechanics, our coach has now been fixed and we can continue our journey to Durrës where we will be stopping for the night." I had a sudden vision of an elite squad of mechanics, Albanian supermen, rushing up the mountain to fix our coach. As we went out into the darkness, some older members of the group grumbled about the uneven stones underfoot.

2018

Our visit to Krujë in 1987 had come at the end of a long day. I'd been back briefly in 2005 and again in 2014. This time I planned to stay for a couple of days.

I had some photos from that first visit. Two were of the bazaar; one was mine, one was Dag's. My photo had been taken from the castle gate. It showed a section of the bazaar and its shops. On the hillside behind the bazaar were two buildings. One was derelict and smothered in ivy. The other seemed to be inhabited. Along the skyline were communist-era apartment blocks.

There was a problem. When I stood in the same spot as I had done in 1987, the view was blocked by new houses. So I had to move and that messed up the angles. Perspective aside, there'd been big changes. In 1987, there had been a gap between the shop units along one side of the bazaar. The gap had been filled in. The derelict building covered in ivy was, once again, Xhamia e Pazarit, the bazaar mosque with a new minaret. The mansion next to the mosque had literally been sliced in half to make space for Hotel Panorama. The communist-era apartment blocks above the bazaar were blocked from view by an enormous new development called Castle Sight, a trio of tower blocks each ten storeys high.

Dag had taken his photo inside the bazaar. It showed the shop frontages in more detail. All had overhanging roofs and full-length wooden shutters. A whitewashed wall ran in front of them, with steps up to each unit. Using the steps as a guide, I tried to find the spot where Dag had taken his photo. I stopped outside a shop selling jewellery and tourist trinkets. The stallholder came out to see what I was doing. He shouted across to the stallholder opposite and almost at once a gaggle of people gathered to look at the photos. I laid them out on the step. One woman pointed to a house and said that was still her family home where she'd grown up with her three brothers. Another woman was particularly taken with Dag's photo because in 1994 she had taken a photo of her daughters in exactly the same spot. She asked if she could have a copy, and out came mobile phones to take photos of photos. Then someone produced a photo from 1926 which showed the original bazaar stretching on both sides of the street all the way along Rr Pazari i Vjetër. The caption under the photo read, "A bazaar as long as the town itself".

From the bazaar, you emerge into a small square in front of Hotel Panorama. A parapet wall made of semi-circular concrete hoops runs alongside the road. It had survived. I had a picture of it from 1987.

I hadn't taken the photo because of the wall. What had been memorable was the view - or rather, the lack of it because of the smog. At the time, the smog had seemed like a physical manifestation of the mystery that cloaked so much of Albania. The Albturist guidebook saw it differently. It fondly described "dense clouds of smoke belching from the chimneys of the numerous furnaces of the new cement factory which turns out cement of the highest quality". The plant at Fushë-Krujë played a crucial role in the socialist economy, producing more than 10 per cent of Albania's cement. It also produced a lot of smoke.

1987: Smoke from the concrete works in the valley below Krujë....

2018: ...has been cleaned up, but trees and new buildings block the view.

The curvature of the wall made it relatively easy to find where I had stood in 1987. To the left, in the gap between buildings, there had been a view of the smog-filled valley. Now the gap was filled by new shops and houses. Although they blocked the view, they were true to the original layout of the bazaar. In that 1926 photo, you can see a *tekke* at the far end, in what is now Sheshi Abaz Kupi. The *tekke* had been damaged during the atheist campaign in 1967. It has now been rebuilt.

This was also where I'd taken a photo of the castle. The museum's pale stone contrasted with the weather-beaten Kulla e Sahatit on its rocky wedge. In the old photo, a few small cottages clung to the hillside below the castle. Apart from the Clock Tower and museum, the most prominent structure was a rectangular brick tower to support telephone wires. When I tried to line up a matching photo, trees obstructed the view. So I walked down the hill a bit. An electricity cable looped across the frame, but at least I could see the castle. Since 1987 the bazaar had been extended up the hill, almost to the castle entrance. Picture windows looking out over the valley belonged to a restaurant called Kroi. The brick tower was still standing.

As I walked back through the bazaar, the young man with the jewellery store was standing by the door. His name was Donald and he invited me in to look around. As well as the usual range of souvenirs, Donald also sold jewellery. He opened a cabinet to show me a pair of silver filigree earrings with a circular design based on Illyrian jewellery found at Zgërdhesh. Other earrings used animals or flowers, especially *luledele*, daisies. These pieces, said Donald, were new, made by craftsmen in Tirana, Shkodër and Krujë. Donald also had some older pieces from communist times; the silver was duller but the quality was good. He got out a magnifying glass so I could see the craftmanship in more detail.

Donald spoke extremely good English; he said he'd taught himself from songs and films. He was also very knowledgeable, and with his help we pieced together a fuller history of the bazaar. There'd been a bazaar in Krujë for centuries, maybe even back to the time of Scanderbeg. These buildings, though, were Ottoman, probably eighteenth- or nineteenth-century. In March 1944, during the National Liberation War, more than half the bazaar had been burned. When the communists took over, the shops still standing were nationalised. Most were closed; a few became outlets for state produce. In the 1960s, the communists decided to rebuild part of the bazaar to celebrate the 500th anniversary of Scanderbeg's death in 1468. If you look carefully at the foundations, Donald said, you can see which shops are original and which have been rebuilt: the wood in the new ones is lighter in colour. As well as celebrating Scanderbeg, the authorities wanted to use the bazaar to promote Albanian handicrafts and earn foreign currency from tourists, and they brought skilled craftsmen to the bazaar to make carpets, metalware and jewellery.

After 1990, the shopkeepers reclaimed their shops and began trading again as private individuals. The bazaar got another make-over in 2015. It was paid for by the Albanian-American Development Foundation, AADF, who'd designated the bazaar a Tourism Development District, a TID. There was a "TID Kruja" plaque by Donald's shop. They'd started with the roofs, replacing broken tiles, and worked downwards. In my old photo, the wall and steps up the shops had been whitewashed. Donald said that when they stripped the whitewash away, they found that some of the steps and frontages were brick, so they were all replaced with stone.

I had one more photo to match - the truncated minaret in the castle compound. For once, the communists couldn't be blamed for its destruction; it fell down in a storm in 1917. There was at least another hour before dusk, so I set off towards the old settlement in the south-west corner. A man was standing outside the Ethnographic Museum. He spoke good English and asked if I had been to Krujë before. I said yes. Had I been with my wife? Yes. Did she have long hair? No. And when that line of enquiry foundered, he asked where I came from and finally, which was where all this was leading, would I like him to show me around.

My guide's name was Deni. He was fair-haired, in his mid-forties and lived in the old quarter with nine relatives, including his elderly mother. Life was hard. Deni's brother had recently died of cancer. His mother needed medicine, and her pension was nowhere near enough to buy what she needed. The family had been unable to pay their electricity bill. The power had been cut off and now Deni had to find 8,000 leks, more than €60, to have it turned back on. Deni used to work at the shoe factory, but when it moved to Shkodër he lost his job. So now he mows the grass around the castle and generally keeps the site tidy. The Bashkia don't pay him and to make matters worse, two days ago someone stole his mower.

By now we were deep in the old town, walking along a lane lined with high stone walls shielding Ottoman mansions. Some were inhabited, but many were derelict with buckled roofs and broken windows. We stopped at a crossroads where a wooden sign pointed to the sights: Dollma Tekke, Scanderbeg's Tree, the Old Hammam, the Secret Tunnel. Deni had made the sign. It was screwed to the wall but at night he took it down in case anyone stole it. Kids, teenagers, you know what it's like…

We went first to the Old Hammam. It was locked, but its roof had been retiled and its walls repointed. Then we went to the Secret Tunnel. It led to a led to a postern gate which opened onto a narrow ledge outside the walls with a fine view over the valley and plain. Below us was an old factory with a brick chimney. It had made ceramics, said Deni. It had closed. To the left was a quarry where a sizable chunk had been scooped out of the mountain. That too had closed. In the past, Deni said, the valley would have been filled with smoke from lime kilns, but the government had put a stop to it, and now there really was no work in Krujë.

When Deni mentioned the smoke, it seemed like a cue to show him the photos. He looked through them, but he didn't really connect, not even to the smoke billowing around the truncated minaret. The one thing that did catch his attention in the photo of the castle was not the castle itself but the road leading to it. In the old photo, the road ran straight up the hillside to the Ottoman fountain at the castle entrance. There was nothing along it, no shops, no apartments, no restaurants; its whole length was visible. He ran his finger up and down the road. There seemed to be something about the clarity of the line that took him back somewhere, triggered memories. Deni was struggling with the new order. It was marginalising him. Maybe he was thinking back to a time when life was simpler, before capitalism began to complicate his relationship with his town.

As we started to walk back, Deni finally came to the point. It was, he said, almost thirty years since the end of communism, but his life hadn't improved. "You have your memories", he said, the implication being that I was fortunate to have the time and money to indulge in memories. The pictures seemed to have fed a resentment. What use are memories if you can't feed your family?

I was quite happy to give Deni some money. After what he'd told me about his various hardships, I gave him 500 leks, which was about €4. He fingered the note, folded it and then said, "What can I buy with this?" "Do you want it or not?" I took it back and gave him 2,000 leks, about €15, which he accepted, and I was thinking, that's quite a lot of money for a walk around the old town. I think if I'd given him 8,000 leks to pay off his electricity bill he still wouldn't have been happy. It can't be easy having to spend your life cajoling money out of foreigners.

By eight o'clock the light was fading. I positioned myself on the steps in front of the museum, with the stump of the minaret on the right. The sky began to take on a pinky-purple hue and there was some smoke drifting across the valley. As well as the old communist-era cement works, now refurbished to EU standards, another plant had been built at Borizanë. It was operated by Titan and had opened in 2010. But the pollution was nothing to what it had been. In the original photo, buildings in the foreground had been lost in the gloom. As it got darker, a spotlight illuminated the minaret and lights began to twinkle in the valley. Soon the plain was sprinkled with a delicate network of lights that stretched all the way to the sea, where a bright cluster marked Durrës.

After I'd eaten I went back to the bazaar. Almost every unit had closed, shutters down, doors padlocked. Without visitors, you could appreciate how pretty the street was. It was in a much better condition now than it had been in 1987, but the stillness was closer to the atmosphere back then, and it wasn't a huge stretch to imagine you'd been transported back thirty years. At that moment, I saw Deni coming up the street, and with him, a reminder that reverie was luxury. He'd been to get some shopping. He'd bought bread, yoghurt and a set of lights he could run off a battery. He said he had a framed picture in his home. It was a painting of fruit, the only thing of value he had. Would I like to come and see it? Maybe I'd like to buy it. I shook my head. I said that even if I liked it, I only had a small case and it would be too big to carry. He nodded and walked on through the bazaar and out into the darkness.

The lights were still on in Donald's shop. He asked if I liked the bazaar at night; the streetlamps had been another part of the TID refurbishment. As he packed his stock away, he told me more about his life. He'd left school at thirteen. He wasn't naughty, he just didn't try very hard. He had the grades to go on to higher education, but he decided to work and get some business experience. When he was eighteen, he'd gone to Germany. Albanians could only stay legally for ninety days, and when his permit expired he did casual work and stayed in a dormitory with other migrants. Sometimes he had to sleep in the corridor. He'd stayed for four years, but wasn't happy. Donald thought Germans were cold; they'd say "good morning" but weren't really interested in you. Along the way, he met an ethnic-Albanian social worker who'd settled in Germany. Like Donald, the man was a northerner. Donald thought he would be able to help him, but when they arranged a meeting, he never turned up. Eventually, the authorities caught up with him. He was put on a train to the airport and flown back to Tirana. That's when he'd started working in the shop, which belonged to his uncle.

Donald was doing OK, but he knew there was a problem in Krujë with people who, for whatever reason, hadn't benefited from the changes: "There are a lot of poor people in Krujë, and now highlanders are coming. Some of them are rough types and it's hard to assimilate them." Donald reckoned that 88 per cent of Krujë's population were "proletarian", 12 per cent were "super-rich". There was no middle class.

The hotel where I was staying was in a restored Ottoman mansion near Kulla e Sahatit. The establishment next to it, Restaurant Kalaja, must have been where we had drunk our twilight coffee in 1987. Before independence, the mansion had housed the town's Ottoman garrison. When the Ottomans withdrew, the mansion was abandoned. In 1960, part of it had been converted into Krujë's first Scanderbeg museum, dedicated, said the Albturist guidebook, to "the struggle of the Albanian people against the invaders in general and to Skanderbeg in particular". On display in the museum were copies of documents and portraits of Scanderbeg: "The exhibits of the museum close with the National Liberation War as a crowning event of all the struggles for freedom and independence of the Albanian people."

It was only a short walk from the hotel to the new, purpose-built museum. A few minutes before nine, I had formed an orderly queue of one on the steps. There were metal double-headed eagles on the door. Over the arch, a decorative stone ribbon combined Scanderbeg's goat helmet and more double-headed eagles.

"Whoever speaks of Scanderbeg speaks of Krujë," said Enver Hoxha, but it took the state until 1982 to inaugurate what Hoxha called a "specialised museum" dedicated to Scanderbeg. Given his importance to the national narrative, you might wonder why it took so long. Part of the problem was what to put in the museum. Hoxha acknowledged that "material documents" were scarce. He suggested that paintings and reconstructions should strive for historical accuracy by drawing on contemporary sources, the most famous of which was Marin Barleti's account of Scanderbeg's life published in 1510.

There were also political reasons for the delay. At the end of the National Liberation War, Albania's overriding priority was to establish communism. To do that it needed Stalin's support. In those early years, there was reluctance to do anything that might detract from the pre-eminence of Stalin. Until 1968, it was Stalin not Scanderbeg whose statue stood in Scanderbeg Square.

Stalin died in March 1953 and Albania continued to be loyal to his interpretation of Marxism-Leninism. When relations with the Soviet Union began to cool, the Albanian leadership warmed to the idea of erecting a statue of Scanderbeg in Krujë. The statue was designed by Janaq Paço and unveiled in 1957. It stands in the town centre near the old Albturist-affiliated Hotel Skënderbeu.

In 1968, Albania celebrated the 500th anniversary of Scanderbeg's death. As well as commissioning the statue for Scanderbeg Square, the Presidium of the People's Assembly declared Krujë a "Hero City", for its "very important role in the legendary struggle of the Albanian people, under the leadership of Gjergj Castrati-Skanderbeg, against the Ottoman invaders".

Over the next decade, attention focused on the idea of creating a museum that would do justice to Scanderbeg's legacy. It would have to be "historical" in the sense of giving a meaningful account of Scanderbeg's life. And it would have to be "political", locking Scanderbeg into the communist narrative. A final concept was agreed in 1977 and a commission of architects, historians and politicians was assembled to manage the project. Enver Hoxha's daughter Pranvera, newly qualified as an architect, her husband Klement Kolaneci and Piro Vaso were responsible for the museum's design. Two eminent historians, Aleks Buda and Kristo Frashëri, oversaw the historical element. The architect in charge of construction was Robert Kote. Overall responsibility for the project was shared by the Ministry of Education and Ministry of Finance. Enver Hoxha took a close interest.

Just before the museum opened, a new road was laid to improve access. Enver Hoxha was too ill to attend the opening on 1 November 1982, but his wife Nexhmije was there with other members of the Politburo including Adil Çarçani, Manush Myftiu and Ramiz Alia. The museum they had come to inaugurate was primarily a symbolic structure. It paid lip service to medieval design, but the number of original objects on display which might justify it being called a museum were minimal. A church bell dated 1462 and a medieval cannon were about it. As we'd been told in 1987, Scanderbeg's goat helmet and sword were in the Kunsthistorisches Museum in Vienna.

The lack of physical evidence made it easier for the regime to mould a narrative around Scanderbeg that dovetailed with its own ideology. That's not to say that Aleks Buda's and Kristo Frashëri's historical insights weren't important. They were, and their knowledge of medieval manners and warfare was evident in the extraordinary detail of the murals. But in essence the museum's purpose was ideological. Scanderbeg's struggle to preserve Albania's freedom in the face of external threat was the same struggle as the one being waged by the Party of Labour of Albania. The museum was a symbol of communist Albania. It was the PLA's "Red Fortress".

Today groups are shepherded round exhibits that have changed little since the museum was inaugurated. There was the same ghostly tableau of a larger-than-life "Skënderbeu dhe Populli", Scanderbeg and the People, in the entrance hall, and the same dramatic mural in Salla Bashkim-Përballimi, the Unity-Resistance Hall, of Scanderbeg's forces routing an Ottoman army. This was the room where copies of Scanderbeg's weapons were displayed on a velvet-covered table that resembled an altar.

In the corridors there were the same shields, the same weapons, the same coats of arms. Scanderbeg's study was as it had been, with its desk and high-backed chair. Several exhibits had tried to articulate Scanderbeg's and the communists' shared ambition. A stained-glass panel on the first floor showed a musician sitting cross-legged, playing a single-stringed *lahutë*. Gathered around him were Albanians who represented the communist social order: a solder with a star on his cap; two young militia members with rifles, one still a boy; a Young Pioneer holding a book, *Historia e Shqipërisë*; an old man with a hand resting on his walking stick, listening to the music. Behind them were images of the "new Albania": a weird mix of flowers, pylons and belching chimneys. At the rear of the panel, Scanderbeg with sword raised and cape flying gallops by.

Even more interesting was a display of ceramics that brought together medieval and communist imagery. On one side, a partisan with a rifle on his shoulder and bullets around his waist; on the other, the partisan's medieval equivalent in *fustanella* and *opinga*, armed with daggers and an arquebus. Both, the display was saying, shared the same aim: the protection of Albania. Between the figures, other ceramics merged the two eras: a National Liberation War flag that featured Scanderbeg's goat helmet; a communist star with Scanderbeg at its centre; Scanderbeg's coat of arms next to a communist coat of arms, both with double-headed eagles.

The communist vision of Scanderbeg, as represented in the museum, still held good. No-one had tried to unpick the narrative and disentangle Scanderbeg from the communists. In uncertain times, while Albania is still struggling to find its place in the capitalist world, Scanderbeg's appeal as a point of stability is as strong as ever.

A local historian had set up a bookstall in the castle arches with his books laid out on the wall. I bought one about the history of Krujë and he signed it for me, *me respekt*. His name was Baki. He was a flamboyant, elderly gentleman with a straw hat and walking stick; his friends addressed him as "Profesor". I showed him the old photos. He wasn't very interested in them, but they did prompt him to reminisce about his life in Krujë. He'd been born in 1937 into an intellectual family - his father, he said, had studied jurisprudence at Oxford. Baki had taught in local schools for more than forty years, and because of his historical and linguistic expertise, he'd been made an associate member of the Institute of Linguistics and Literature which was part of the Academy of Sciences. His daughter was also a linguist and had translated some of his books into English. Now, he said, he was trying to make a little money to supplement his pension. As he was talking, he kept an eye on the castle gate and the moment any tourists came into view, commerce triumphed over reminiscence and he was off again, going through the languages - English, German, French, Italian - until he got a response.

There was a shop in the bazaar I particularly liked because it had piles of communist-era books and magazines to rummage through. It was called Antika and was run by two brothers; Altin was minding the shop today. I showed him the pictures, but all I got was "that was communism, this is capitalism". Like Baki, he wanted to sell books, even though his line of business owed its existence to the old regime. Everything has a value.

I put the photos away and went off to browse at the back of the shop. I found a book in English called *The Youth of New Albania*. There was no publication date, but judging from the text it had been published in the mid-1950s. A previous owner had doodled on the blank pages at the front and back of the book. The first photo was of a youngish Enver Hoxha surrounded by schoolchildren. Then there were pictures of young people studying, relaxing, debating, exercising, skiing, swimming, building factories and railways, attending youth conferences "in the spirit of proletarian internationalism". The text contained a welter of statistics, the most extreme (and precise) of which was a claim that compared with the "pre-war years", Albania now had 328.7 per cent more elementary schools and 302.7 per cent more secondary schools.

While I'd been browsing, Altin had selected more books he thought I might find interesting. These included a biography of Stalin, a history of Marxism-Leninism and a lavishly illustrated biography of Enver Hoxha published in 1986, the year after his death. I bought the biography. I asked Altin who his customers were, presumably not Albanians. Altin said that Norwegians and Dutch favoured books; Germans preferred medals and banknotes. Albanians weren't interested, Altin continued; they'd been abused by the communists and now they were suffering at the hands of corrupt politicians. Who could blame them if they were disenchanted with politics.

Next to Antika was a shop that specialised in communist-era medals and awards. As well as boxes of military red stars - poorer quality for conscripts, better quality (and costlier) for officers - it also had some civilian awards. There were medals for excellence in different branches of the economy. A medal for distinguished service in mining showed a miner's head next to an oil derrick. Another medal celebrated achievement in agriculture with a pastoral scene of wheat and grazing sheep. Mothers who had produced large families were called *Nënë Heroine*, Heroine Mother, and were awarded a badge with a gold star. A good quality enamelled badge had the English word "Tourist" on it. It showed a mountain scene with a tent, forests, compass and map. It must have been minted for visitors from other Eastern European countries who had come to Albania for a holiday.

Other badges were not so grand and were stamped on flimsier metal. One featured a book by Enver Hoxha and had been awarded to citizens who had been "flagbearers" in implementing Comrade Enver's teachings. Another was a lapel badge with "Albturist" written across an outline of Albania. I bought them both.

When I went to pay, I said to the man that I had been here in 1987 and he launched into an attack on modern Albanians. In the old days, he said, the party and the people had always been close; these badges were a symbol of that connection. How can a country function if its people take no interest in politics?

Beyond Hotel Panorama, next to the equestrian statue is Hotel Skënderbeu. Built in the 1970s when Krujë was starting to develop as a tourist destination, for many years it had been the only hotel in town. An Albturist brochure described it as a "4-storey, 33-room hotel with all the necessary facilities, situated in the heart of the 'Hero City', Krujë". From the hotel there was a view of "almost the entire city and of the historical castle".

With the collapse of the one-party state, Hotel Skënderbeu had faced competition from new hotels built to higher specifications and with more spectacular views. When the hotel was privatised in 1994, the rooms were mothballed but the bar and restaurant remained open. Its terrace was pleasantly shady although the view over the valley was blocked by trees and the extension to the bazaar. I asked the waiter if he thought the rooms would ever reopen. He told me that a three-stage plan had been put in place. Stage one had been the reopening of the bar. Stage two was the refurbishment of the reception rooms so the hotel could host weddings. Stage three was reopening the hotel. Did he think stage three would happen soon? He said that most of Krujë's visitors didn't stop overnight. They came to see the castle, do some shopping in the bazaar and then moved on. Krujë already had two big hotels, Hotel Panorama and Hotel Grand. He wasn't sure if it needed a third.

Across the square behind the Bashkia was another remnant of communist Krujë: a sports arena. A bas relief by the entrance showed children playing basketball, boys on one side, girls on the other. Along the street was a market where locals came to do their shopping. The stalls were laid out on the road, in the dust and dirt. There are markets like this all over Albania, places where people will try to sell anything to make a few leks. But it seemed worse to see one in Krujë which has a thriving tourist industry. You can see how little of that new wealth has trickled down.

I walked back up the hill and into the bazaar, the public face of Krujë. I liked it. And I liked the castle compound with its eccentric museum. Deni was by the truncated minaret talking with some visitors, almost certainly telling them his story, trying to hustle some money. When he saw me he came over. He told me he'd been to the bank to try to get a loan so his electricity could be reconnected. But the bank had refused him because he didn't have a job. He asked me again about the picture - why wouldn't I come and look at it? Then he had another idea. If I gave him the money, I could also give him my address so he could repay it when he got work. That wasn't a good idea. I gave him some more money, but he can't hold me personally responsible for the world's inequalities.

4: Durrës

A City Reinvented

Hotel Adriatiku: Stalinist style
1987

We spent the night at Hotel Adriatiku at Durrës. We went to sleep to the sound of the sea; and when we awoke, the grubby lace curtains were flapping in the breeze. It was a gloriously sunny morning. A broad golden beach ran in a crescent around the bay, all the way to the town about three kilometres to the north. To the south, the beach stretched as far as you could see. A cyclist rode along the water's edge with a bag of shopping swinging from his handlebars. Below us, some Albanians were breakfasting on bread and wine; they were using the top of a bunker as a table.

While Dag shaved, I sat on the balcony with our little radio, tuning through different stations. I couldn't distinguish between Albanian and Serbo-Croat, but Greek and Italian were both there, and if we could pick them up so could Albanians. If you can't block foreign transmissions, you can always take the fight to the enemy. Parla Tirana was an Italian-language service from Radio Tirana, and this morning its lead story was about an increase in the production of eggs, meat and milk. It was followed by a report on an anti-NATO demonstration in Spain. The bulletin concluded with a long list of people who were visiting Albania, some of them accompanied by voice clips. A French librarian working for a week at the National Library in Tirana said how much she was enjoying her visit; a German-speaking Swiss visitor expressed her delight at Tirana and Korçë. All of which, if true, goes to show that Albania isn't quite as isolated as Western newspapers would have us believe.

We ate our breakfast - omelette, bread, jam - in the dining room, and then took our coffee into the lounge. Unlike other parts of the hotel which were very run down - worn carpets in the corridors, even some broken windows - this space was well maintained. It had a marble floor, a ceiling supported on Corinthian columns and plate-glass windows looking out over the beach. A decorative cornice and glass chandeliers added to the sense of faded opulence. We sat in armchairs covered with a white stretch fabric, enjoying the luxury.

We had some free time before our tour of Durrës town, so Dag and I went for a walk. Steps led down to a well-kept lawn and palm trees. In the garden, Albanians were playing backgammon. Three black Volvos with CD plates were parked by the steps. A diplomatic party had come to play tennis on the hotel's dilapidated courts. The chauffeurs busied themselves polishing their cars while they waited. We walked past the tennis courts and along the palm-lined drive to the main road. At the hotel entrance was an Albturist sign and an exhortation: *RROFTË PROLETARIATI NDËRKOMBËTAR!* LONG LIVE THE INTERNATIONAL PROLETARIAT! I still wasn't used to seeing roads without cars.

We followed a track which took us through pine trees and back to the beach. Bunkers were everywhere. Some were leaning at crazy angles where they had sunk into the soft sand. Others had been broken apart by the sea. Among the pines you could see the maze of trenches that had linked the emplacements. From the water's edge there was a fine view of the hotel. It was a handsome building, symmetrical, solidly constructed with pine trees behind it. On the terrace, staff were putting out tables and orange plastic chairs. More Westerners had arrived and were unloading windsurfers. Even in its shabby state, the hotel was still an island of exclusivity in a deprived world.

2017

Looking back to 1987, it's easy to picture Hotel Adriatiku in isolation, commanding that wonderful crescent of beach. But when you look more closely at the photos, you can see that there were other hotels around it, and it would be more accurate to think of Hotel Adriatiku as the flagship in a cluster of hotels. Flanking it were Hotel Durrës and Hotel Apolonia. Both were four-storey buildings, each with more than a hundred rooms as well as restaurants and bars. Two others, Hotel Butrinti and Hotel Kruja, were on the same site. On the beach, only a few metres from Hotel Adriatiku, was a pre-communist restaurant with large windows, a veranda and a tower at the corner.

There was another factor. Our visit had been at the beginning of November, very definitely the low season. If we had come in summer, we would have got a very different impression. The official estimate was that around 60,000 "working people and their families" spent their holidays on Durrës beach. As well as the hotels, there were rest homes and Young Pioneer camps. Tens of thousands more came as day-trippers from Tirana. Most took the train; there were nine a day between Durrës and the capital. An article in *New Albania* described a "belt of multi-coloured umbrellas stretching for more than ten kilometres from the outskirts of the city of Durrës to the pine trees on the opposite side of the bay". Ever optimistic, the article outlined plans to build ten-storey apartment blocks, which would have made them some of the tallest in Albania. The beach was to be extended and new gardens planted. But not even the most visionary planner could have foreseen what would actually happen to Durrës beach when the old system collapsed.

Kirstie and I had booked into Hotel Adriatiku for a few days. We'd taken the overnight ferry from Bari and had arrived in a mist. Even so, you could see that the coast was lined with hotels. We docked near a wharf with cranes and hoppers for unloading cargo. Containers were stacked on the quay. Across the entrance to the Arrivals Hall was a message: "Welcome to Albania". From the Arrivals Hall a pedestrian bridge crossed the main road into the coach station where men with gruff voices bawled out destinations. We only wanted to go a few kilometres up the coast. We tried to find a local bus, then gave up and got a taxi.

In a previous incarnation, the coast road must have been a grand boulevard. In years past, pine forests along the shore stabilised the sand; now there was not a single pine tree to be seen. The road ran through unending ranks of apartment blocks and hotels. Some of this must have been here before 1990, and every so often among the high-rises you could see older single- or two-storey blocks that had so far avoided demolition. But the overwhelming impression was of a building spree where every bit of spare land had been built on.

Hotel Adriatiku had been one of Albturist's jewels. The guidebook described it as "first rate". As well as restaurant and bar, the hotel had sports grounds, table tennis halls and chess "for the amusement of the tourists". It was still a grand hotel, not the sort of place we usually stay, but nostalgia is a powerful driver. We were given a room on the third floor. It was comfortable and well-equipped - no balcony, but a full-length window overlooking the beach.

The history of the hotel mirrored the history of Albania. It was budgeted for in Albania's First Five Year Plan (1951-5), drawn up while Stalin was still alive. The hotel had been designed by a Soviet-trained Albanian architect, Gani Strazimiri. Strazimiri's design - a tiered, symmetrical, four-storey building with a pillared façade - was a homage to Stalinist neoclassicism. But its construction was dogged by worries over finance. By the time it opened in 1957, Stalin was dead and the rift between Albania and the Soviet Union was widening. The Soviet Union formally stopped its credits to Albania in 1961, and the financial squeeze impacted on every aspect of the Albanian economy, including its efforts to establish a tourist industry.

When the British journalist James Cameron stayed at Hotel Adriatiku in 1963, he noted that several hotels around it were in "various stages of half-completion". In Cameron's view, the hotel's interior did not live up to the promise of its exterior: "instead of fine timbers and rich marbles there was plasterboard and gritty cement; in the spacious hall the evergreen plants grew out of oil drums painted green". By 1987, marble floors had been laid, chandeliers hung from the ceiling and the plants had proper pots.

Soon after the collapse of the old regime, Hotel Butrint and Hotel Kruja closed, but Hotel Adriatiku continued. It was damaged in 1990 and again during the violence in 1997. In 2000 it was privatised and bought by the Dudaj family. The hotel was rebuilt and reopened in 2003.

I had several old photographs of Hotel Adriatiku. It was still recognisably the same building, but restoration had softened its Soviet rigour. At the front of the hotel, a straight flight of steps had been replaced by a curving staircase that led up to a new lobby with the hotel's logo on the pediment. Two new lift shafts with pointed roofs had been added to each side. Where there had been gardens and tennis courts, there was now an ornamental fountain and swimming pool. On the seaward side, the changes were more obvious. A fourth floor had been added and the side wings had been raised to accommodate the extra floor. Balconies had been enclosed. The ground-floor terrace had been extended. The pointed roofs of the new lift shafts rose above the roofline. The same and not the same.

Inside, I had a photo of the lounge with marble floor, chandeliers and plant pots. I had taken it from a mezzanine, but as the mezzanine was no longer there, I couldn't replicate the angle. The modern lounge was still a grand space. It had been extended and the pillars repositioned. Steps linked the lounge to the reception area. As I was trying (unsuccessfully) to match the original photo, a waiter came over to see what I was doing. His name was Ladion. I showed him the old

1987: Hotel Adriatiku's Stalinist rigour.....

2017: ...has been compromised by lift shafts and an extra storey.

photo and he immediately spotted a metal tray and a sliver of counter in the bottom left-hand corner. He thought that would have been part of the bar. He pointed to a yellow panel halfway up the wall. That, he said, was where I had taken the original photo.

We'd planned to walk into town, but the rain set in. So we sat by the window, watching the clouds scud across the bay. The hotel was quiet and another of the waiters came over for a chat. Ermal was twenty-eight, a local man whose family had lived in Durrës for generations. As a young child, Ermal had lived near the hotel; he was eight when it had been burned down in 1997. Its original shape must have been imprinted on his brain, because when I showed him the photos it was as if a switch had been thrown. He looked at the pictures as if he was trying to think himself back to his childhood. He told us, not without pride, that Hotel Adriatiku had been the first hotel in Albania built for foreigners. Now he had a job working here and he could talk to guests without fear.

Ermal's parents had told him that life during communism had been hard. If a policeman heard you complaining that you didn't have enough bread, he'd say, "You want bread? We'll give you bread in prison." In the hotel, there'd been plenty of bread, there'd been plenty of everything. So his family had mixed feelings about the place. It was both a source of pride and a source of envy: why should all these foreigners have food while Albanians went hungry? In the 1980s after Hoxha's death, more tourists began to visit Albania and they stayed at Hotel Adriatiku. For many Albanians, this was the first time they had seen other Europeans in the flesh. Ermal's family took comfort from their presence, because it meant that Albania was no longer cut off from the rest of the world.

The rain eased and we went outside. One of the photos showed Hotel Adriatiku from the south. Most of the picture was sand, but half-hidden among the palms and pine trees were two other hotels. Ermal knew them both. They were Hotel Durrës and Hotel Iliria. Both had been demolished.

Ermal was proud of his city, but he wasn't happy with the way it was changing: "Albania has had so much money from the EU it should be like Switzerland. It has the sea and mountains and lakes, but still Albanians are poor." Under communism, he said, people had not been free to do as they wanted. But under capitalism, it was no better. Albanians had been cheated; they'd been made promises about better lives, but the promises hadn't been kept.

Durrës town: relics or redevelopment?
1987

It was a short ride from the hotel to the town. The intercom clicked. "Ladies and gentlemen, good morning. Today, we shall visit Durrës town, an important city in Albanian history. We shall visit the Museum of Antiquities, and then we shall go to the amphitheatre where you will have some free time to walk around."

The road ran along the coast past hotels, chalets and apartments - all holiday accommodation for Albanian workers, all at this time of year deserted. At the crossroads where the road branched to Tirana there was a Young Pioneers camp. We passed gypsies, the women wearing orange headscarves. A short wait for a diesel train shunting trucks into the port, then past a crowded railway station. Behind the station there were spotlights and gun emplacements. "No photography, please," said Edi as we passed the Enver Hoxha naval base. In the small square by the entrance was a bust of Hoxha.

Then things started to go wrong. The road was blocked. Usually when this happened, our driver blew the horn and tried to bully the obstruction out of the way. But on this occasion he waited quietly, and we soon saw why. Four green army trucks were parked in the square with a queue behind each tailgate. As our coach inched through the crowd, Edi told us that the men were signing on for their two years of compulsory military service. This, he said, was the constitutional duty of every Albanian over the age of eighteen, "so that everyone, male and female, is able to defend our country". As well as receiving a military training, soldiers also had to work in the fields and on construction projects. In the socialist state, Edi said, it was important for the army to strengthen its connections with the people.

I think Edi had been caught unawares by the Sunday call-up, but he dealt with it calmly. Albania was far from alone in having conscription, and if we had been in Greece or Italy, we wouldn't have paid it much attention. But when you're beginning to suspect that your tour is designed as much to hide as to reveal, incidents like this carry extra weight. We all felt that we'd just seen something we weren't supposed to have seen.

2017

In 1987, Durrës was Albania's second largest city with a population of 72,600. The farms on the plain around it grew cereals, vegetables, cotton and rice. Durrës was also an industrial centre that produced radios and televisions, tyres, cigarettes, plastics and chemicals. The Albturist guidebook suggested that anyone wishing to get better acquainted with Durrës' industry should walk up the hill that overlooked the city:

> From here we get a view of the tall chimneys of the Rubber Factory, of the Factory for Synthetic Products, of the Cigarette Factory, whose wide variety of cigarettes may be found in the foreign markets, too. Gigantic cranes are constantly at work by the railroad station next to the port where a large number of steamers load and unload their cargoes day and night.

A lot had happened since 1987. When the old regime collapsed, most of Durrës' industry went with it. There'd been riots in December 1990, and the city attracted international attention in 1991 and again in 1997 when tens of thousands of Albanians had converged on the port, trying to flee the chaos. When controls on internal migration were lifted, thousands of people came to the larger cities in search of a better life. Durrës' population ballooned to more than 100,000. The city had to reinvent itself. It had to do it quickly and the beach was crucial to its plan.

In 1987, Dag and I were struck by the large numbers of bunkers along the beach and the trenches in the forests. Walking now with Kirstie, most of the bunkers had gone. The trenches had been filled in when trees had been felled to clear space for new hotels. As for the seafront, it had changed beyond recognition. It would be wrong to eulogise the communist-era beach as some kind of pristine wilderness. It wasn't; all along the shoreline there'd been shacks, Zog-era villas and communist-era cabins and apartments. They were there in the old photos.

The real difference between then and now was in the size and density of the development. Prior to 1990, Hotel Adriatiku had been the biggest building on the bay. Now it was just one of hundreds of hotels in a development that stretched more than 15 kilometres south to Qerret. One of the few places where you could get a measure of how the beach had been before 1990 was in the restricted zone south of Hotel Adriatiku, where forests and sand dunes had survived. A notice on the fence said, "NDAL! Rezidencë Qeveritare", "HALT! Government Residence". But since the end of communism, parts of the restricted zone had been turned into holiday accommodation. You could now stay in Melissa Residency, which had been a government retreat. Further south had been Kampi i Pionierëve, which reopened in 2006 as Tropikal Resort. Its refurbished bungalows were at one time dormitories for the Young Pioneers.

At the end of the beach by the harbour, a footpath joined the main road and brought us to the train station where those day-trippers from Tirana would have disembarked. In May 2012, I'd been in Albania with our son Joe and we'd caught the 8.40 from Tirana to Durrës. A one-way ticket cost 70 leks, about 40 pence. The carriage windows had been smashed during the 1997 disturbances, but the train was clean and the seats comfortable. As we waited to depart, the guard paced up and down the platform. He had a whistle on a green ribbon around his neck and a grey pouch slung over his shoulder. A lurch and a jolt as an elderly diesel unit was attached to the coaches, and then we were off, trundling through Tirana's northern suburbs, sounding a klaxon at unmanned crossings, of which there were many. Wheels scraped on the tracks, making a sound that was half-swish, half-squeal. The guard came through and snipped our tickets with a small pair of scissors.

The stations were no more than halts: Vorë, Sukth, Shkozet. For a time, a muddy path ran alongside the railway. People were walking or riding bicycles. Beyond Vorë, the city apartments gave way to houses with gardens. There were even some fields. It was hard to know how fast we were going, but it couldn't have been much more than 20 miles an hour. Cars and buses on the motorway were all going faster. We were travelling in a relic of the old world paid for by the Soviet Union and built by youth volunteers. We thought even then that without investment, the line was doomed. Sure enough, it closed the following year.

For reasons that weren't clear, the station now was in far better repair than it had been in 2012. The coaches along the platform were graffitied and their windows broken, but the station itself had been repainted in grey and yellow and an indicator board listed the stations you could go to: Pogradec, Elbasan, Vlorë, Shkodër and Tirana. In the waiting room, posters advertised the delights of Albanian Railways. There was no timetable.

Rruga Egnatia runs from the station to Durrës' south-facing waterfront. It's a busy commercial street, but along it you can find remnants of its previous incarnations. A fine neoclassical building with columns and balustrades had a crossed rifle and pickaxe on its pediment. Opposite the harbour, next to a new Orthodox church, was one of Durrës' finest Eclectic buildings. It had opened in November 1925, one of the first branches of Banka Kombëtare Tregtare, the National Commercial Bank. A plaque on the wall noted that on 6 October 1943, guerrilla units from Durrës and Tirana had raided the building and had taken "a large amount of food items" that were needed by the National Liberation Army.

Past the docks, you come to the castle and its Byzantine walls where a statue commemorates "Hero i Popullit Mujo Ulqinaku" who was killed in 1939 by Italian invaders. Next to him is the derelict shell of Hotel Volga. Italian-designed, it opened in 1940 and was stylish enough to rival Hotel Dajti in Tirana. Known originally as Grande Albergo dei Dogi, the communists renamed it Hotel Volga in honour of Albania's friendship with the Soviet Union. In a waterfront park is one of Albania's most dramatic Socialist Realist *lapidars*, Monumenti i Rezistencës: a soldier on a stepped pedestal with rifle raised above his head urging his comrades into battle. Near the partisan, four classical columns had been re-erected on a concrete plinth. By the pillars, modern statues (already crumbling) of two Illyrian warriors stood ready for combat.

The complexity of modern Durrës had been laid out for us along one short stretch of road.

1987

The archaeological museum was on the seafront. There were pillars and palm trees in the garden and a pile of cannon balls. Inside, it was full of Albanians, all jostling to get a view of the exhibits. On a strip of parkland facing the sea, old men sat on benches. The air was cool but there was still some warmth in the sun. A short uphill walk brought us to the amphitheatre. The road looked new, still dirt, lined with apartment blocks and villas. And it being a sunny Sunday, washing hung from every balcony - shirts, socks, underwear, lives hung out to dry. In one of the flats, a young couple were painting the window frame. The street was broad and straight, and seemed to be a favoured place to stroll: pairs of old men in jackets and sunglasses; girls walking four abreast with arms linked; middle-aged women with handbags. Then an army truck nosed its way up the street and everyone moved out of the way.

Only partially excavated, the amphitheatre was squeezed between crumbling but still-handsome Italianate villas above and a cluster of small houses below, whose backyards were crammed with all manner of useful bits of wood and metal and garden tools. The guide told us that the amphitheatre had only been discovered a few years ago by accident, in 1966, when someone was digging foundations for a new house, which explains why half of it was still buried. Exposed water pipes and cables ran across the upper tiers. The Byzantines used the corridors beneath the amphitheatre as burial chambers, and we were shown their chapel and its frescoes of saints and angels. We were told that an earthquake had struck Durrës in the fourth century AD, and stone from the amphitheatre had been used to rebuild the town. As we clambered over the ruins, men watched us from the fenced walkway above the amphitheatre.

I climbed to the top tier and then carried on up the road. It was the first time I had been on my own. Further up, the path became smooth and steep, except that it was no longer a path. It was a culvert and it brought me to one of the bastions of the old castle. I could see across the bay to the hotel; in the harbour below a Jugolinja cargo ship was waiting to be unloaded. I had a strong feeling I shouldn't be here. Someone was watching. I turned and saw a soldier behind coils of barbed wire. I didn't hang around. I half-slid, half-ran back down the culvert and rejoined the group.

2017

The Albturist guide described Durrës' archaeological museum as "one of the richest museums in the country". It drew special attention to its collection of Illyrian tombstones, "yet another proof of the role the Illyrians have played in the life of the city". I had a photo of its exterior which showed the gardens and some classical pillars. But it didn't matter where I stood; it was impossible to make a match. I showed the photo to one of the curators who told me that this was a new museum that had opened in 2002. The old museum was a couple of blocks away, near Monumenti i Rezistencës. When the old regime collapsed, the villa which had housed the museum had been returned to its pre-war owners. It had been looted in 1997 and the building damaged, so the Bashkia had decided to build a new one.

The new building was air-conditioned and had captions in English and Albanian. We wandered round a fine collection of pillars, marble heads and truncated bodies, barnacle-encrusted amphorae, displays of red and black pottery, stelae and mosaics. The upper floor was to house a medieval collection that had yet to be organised.

The old museum was in a sorry state. Surrounded by new apartments, it was the only surviving villa along that section of the seafront. In its day, it must have been a handsome building, an austere 1930s, Rationalist villa with square windows and balcony. Now it was derelict. Its roof had collapsed and its façade covered with graffiti. Its rubbish-filled interior was used by drug addicts and prostitutes, to the annoyance of residents.

From the seafront, Rruga e Epikadave led up to the amphitheatre. This was the road Dag and I had walked up in 1987. The street had been transformed. Now asphalted and lined with tall apartment blocks, it had been absorbed into the new city. By contrast, the amphitheatre had changed little. One of the old photos showed collapsed brickwork near the entrance to the underground chambers. That had been fixed, but the arena itself was still grassy and unexcavated. Religious context had been restored. To the south, a minaret rose above a parade of neoclassical villas. To the north was Xhamia e Madhe.

When I'd clambered up the culvert in 1987, I'd taken three hasty shots over the town. Stitched together they made a panorama of Durrës, from the harbour all the way round the bay to Hotel Adriatiku. But finding the way to the castle wasn't easy. We got lost and ended up on the hillside near King Zog's summer villa. People had different ideas about the road we should take. We followed a track that branched off Rruga Anastas Durrsaku and then petered out among houses. I shouted to a man that we were trying to get to the castle. He shouted back that the road was blocked. He explained that someone who'd been living in London had come back to Durrës, had built a house and then put a gate across the road. It was particularly irritating for the man we were shouting to because the gate blocked access to his house. He kindly let us climb over the fence into his garden, asking us not to trample on his vegetables. At the back of his house, we crossed a ditch and could then get back on the path. It was worth the effort. And there was still a concrete culvert running down the hillside.

This part of Durrës had been the heart of the ancient city. It was where most of the Roman monuments were: the amphitheatre, the forum and thermal baths. It was the area encircled by walls at the beginning of the sixth century by the Byzantine emperor Anastasius who was born in Durrës. The bastion where we were now standing, Kulla Anzhouine, was part of an Angevin fortification from the early fourteenth century. When the Ottomans took control of Durrës in 1501, this was where they built Xhamia e Fatihut to honour Sultan Mehmet Fatihu, Mehmed the Conqueror. The mosque is one of the oldest in Albania.

After independence, the area formed the core of the modern city. The central square was laid down in the late 1920s, shortly after Zog had declared himself Mbreti i

Shqiptarëve, King of the Albanians. The Bashkia with its distinctive square clock tower was inaugurated in 1929. The Italian-designed Xhamia e Madhe followed two years later. A Palace of Culture and the city's Prefecture were added by the communists.

The old photos show the city centre in the final years of the communist regime. Three streets converged on the harbour; all were lined with villas. There were some communist-era apartments along the seafront, but in the main the houses were either late Ottoman or early twentieth century. Xhamia e Fatihut's minaret had been demolished in 1967, but its tiled roof was visible on the curving street that ran through the old town.

At the centre of the image, directly below the castle, was what looked like a neighbourhood within a neighbourhood, where a number of villas were grouped together. To the left was the Bashkia, which stood out as much for its Rationalist design as its size. In the old photo, it was painted white. Next to the Bashkia, partly obscured by trees, were the remains of Xhamia e Madhe which been damaged by the 1979 earthquake. A fig tree had taken root in the bastion. Clumps of trees were dotted around the town. Sections of the Byzantine walls were smothered in foliage.

Beyond the town was the harbour. The guidebook's reference to "gigantic cranes" was accurate; there were more than twenty of them along the seafront. Near the western end of the harbour was a large building occupying several blocks. It was the Telat Noga Cigarette Factory, founded in 1924 and taken into state ownership in 1945.

The communist-era city was already an awkward composite of historical periods which sometimes overlapped - the thermal baths only came to light when the authorities started digging the foundations for Pallati i Kulturës. But since 1990, redevelopment on a huge scale has added another layer to the city. Durrës has become a city of apartments, and although by global standards they are not that high, even a twelve-storey block will seem enormous in such a low-rise environment.

In the old photo, the Bashkia had been the largest building. Now it was dwarfed by apartment blocks. There were at least a dozen of them on the eastern side of the main square. More were being built on the coast; from the castle, it looked like a whole new high-rise suburb. The biggest of the lot was the tower block next to Banka Kombëtare Tregtare. Its skeletal superstructure dominated the town. The Orthodox church next to it looked miniscule.

But despite everything, the core of the original settlement around the amphitheatre had survived. Some of it was even being refurbished. Villas were being restored. Xhamia e Fatihut had reopened with a new minaret. To the left of the Bashkia, now painted red, Xhamia e Madhe had been rebuilt with an eye-catching yellow dome.

The one major casualty was the Telat Noga Cigarette Factory. It had closed in 1996, but the building was still standing when Joe and I came to Durrës in 2012. I'd taken photos of a frieze on the wall commemorating a strike by "the working class of Durrës" on 12 July 1940. It wasn't a particularly accomplished piece of art - stern-faced workers shaking their fists and carrying banners saying "Down with Fascism" - but it was undeniably a part of the city's history, as was another plaque listing the names of nineteen factory workers who had died during the National Liberation War. The factory had been demolished in 2013. In its place was the Albanian College which offered students a private secondary education in English. It was an overblown, neoclassical building with a semi-circular portico supported on six Corinthian columns. Looking down from the castle, its most striking feature was its dome, about the same size as the one on Xhamia e Madhe.

1987

"Ladies and gentlemen, we have about forty minutes before we must leave for the capital of our country, Tirana. We will now go to the centre of Durrës where you may have a walk."

1987: Durres was a low-rise city. The Bashkia on the left, one of its biggest buildings,

2017: …is dwarfed by apartment blocks that have transformed the city skyline.

We were dropped in the main square by the Palace of Culture, where tonight a Finnish folk group was going to perform. A bust of Stalin stood in the garden. We clambered out of the coach, and before we knew it we'd been absorbed into a huge crowd that filled the square and spilled into the surrounding streets. It was weird. Albanians and foreigners were sharing the same space, but you felt there was some kind of invisible barrier between us. Both groups had been fed myths that sowed mistrust. In our eyes, this was the urban proletariat, the workers in whose name the state ruled. To them, we were degenerate capitalists hell-bent on destroying socialist states like Albania. I'll be honest, it was intimidating.

A road led off from the square. By Western standards, it was bleak - a broad, straight avenue lined by apartment blocks. But there were trees along the pavements, and it was car-free. People were strolling, mostly men walking with friends. A few were on bicycles. Despite the numbers, the street was quiet, just a subdued hum of conversation. Although it was Sunday, everything was open. Near the theatre was a *gjellëtore*, a restaurant run by NTUS, presumably a state organisation, and several snack bars, *bufe*, where parents could buy drinks and ice creams for their children. Further along the road was a cavernous *birrari* with plate-glass windows and net curtains, then a shop selling *artikuij kulturore* which included musical instruments, copper trays and woollen shoulder bags. Three young girls with violin cases on their way to (or from) a music lesson were loitering outside. Set back from the road between crumbling apartment blocks was an open-air cinema, Kinema Iliria, its exits secured by sheets of corrugated iron. At the far end of the street was a *farmaci*.

Now we were actually at street level, the crowd seemed less dense. The people looked poor, but they were not badly dressed. Most of the men wore jackets and flared trousers; some had stripy jumpers. It wasn't so much our clothes that set us apart as what we were carrying: camera bags, leather satchels and backpacks. When we regrouped at the coach there was animated chatter about going into a shop and buying a bar of chocolate or having a drink at the *bufe*. Someone asked Ilir why in a country that prided itself on its equality there were so few women on the streets. Ilir shrugged: "We try, but some customs are deeply rooted and are difficult to change."

2017

In 1987 the square, now called Sheshi Iliria, had been an austere space. It was framed by Pallati i Kulturës at the northern end and the Bashkia at the southern, with the Prefecture and ruined Xhamia e Madhe on the western side. To the east were some run-down, once-handsome 1920s villas. The square's single embellishment (excluding Stalin's bust) was a fountain in front of the Bashkia. It was a simple structure: two bowls - one large, one smaller - surmounted by an urn. It had been designed by Zog's official architect, Kristo Sotiri, and was erected shortly after the completion of the Bashkia.

As post-communist Durrës began to take shape, the Municipality decided that the square needed a make-over. In 2008, tenders were invited for ideas that "would give force and quality to the whole urban and metropolitan structure". The following year the Municipality announced that an Italian company, Michele Crò, had won the commission. Their plan was to integrate old and new. The square would have palm trees and benches. But it would also be flexible enough to stage events, especially in the summer. On the western side, a flight of steps would link the square with the amphitheatre.

The first stage was completed by 2011. But when work began on relaying the main part of the square, it became clear that Kristo Sotiri's fountain was not part of the plan. The fountain had been a cherished part of city life for eighty years and citizens mobilised to protect it. Activists formed a protective cordon around the fountain. A banner read: *Mos e Shembni Shatërvanin e Durrësit*, Don't destroy the fountain of Durrës. The campaign to save the fountain became a more generalised protest about the way Durrës was being developed. It seemed to many that the city's archaeological inheritance was being lost to what Albanians call *betonizimi*, when everything gets smothered in concrete. The protests continued for four years. Then on the morning of 10 January 2015, Durrës woke to find that the fountain had been removed under cover of darkness. The Municipality explained that the crane used to remove it was so large it would have caused traffic jams if the work had been done during the day.

Before we left the centre, I wanted to try to find the street Dag and I had walked along in 1987. Two roads ran north from Pallati i Kulturës: Rruga Aleksander Goga and Bulevardi Dyyrah. The photos showed a cobbled, tree-lined street of the kind you would find in any Albanian town, but we did have a clue - a plaque outside the shop selling *artikuij kulturore*. Only half the plaque was in the photo and it was too small to read, but it was something to look for. Bulevardi Dyrrah seemed the likelier of the two streets, so Kirstie and I set off in search of the plaque.

The road had been re-laid. There were new pavements. Apartments had new windows and refurbished façades. Shop fronts had been modernised. We didn't find the plaque. We reached a crossroads, and a building caught my attention. It was a stylish, 1930s corner block with a rounded façade. A similar block on the other side of the road had been refurbished and a glassed-in penthouse added. But this one had hardly changed. In the old photo, the building was cream. There was a *farmaci* on the ground floor and washing was hanging on the balconies. In its modern form, the building had been painted a brighter yellow with the insets around the windows a contrasting grey. The farmaci had become a convenience store, but structurally it was unaltered. There was even washing hanging on the balconies.

We walked back along the beach and stopped to eat at a *piceri* called Liburnia Vitaminaga which jutted out into the sea on wooden piers. It, or something very like it, had been there in

1987: Locals mingle outside an elegant 1930s corner block…..

2017: … that has hardly changed. There is even washing on the balcony.

1987. It had been revamped with a new entrance and dining area, but it still felt very old school. It belonged to a version of Durrës that was rapidly disappearing.

It was dark by the time we got back to Hotel Adriatiku. Its name, stars and logo were illuminated over the entrance. We strolled through the lobby and along a corridor where a selection of Marubi prints were displayed: soldiers posing with rifles; a sophisticated young woman reclining by a brazier; a view of Durrës harbour at the turn of the century - and then some grittier images: tailors at work stitching by hand; women and children working in a sweet factory.

Hotel Adriatiku has tried to document its own history through photographs. A website gallery had several images of the hotel during communism. One was of the lounge and mezzanine balcony where I must have stood to take my photo. Another showed a larger-than-life portrait of Enver Hoxha over the hotel entrance. In the picture, Hoxha is smiling, his right arm raised in greeting. In his left hand, he's carrying his trilby and a bunch of lilies. I said to the receptionist that I had some old photographs of the hotel: would they like to add them to their gallery. The following morning, I got an email from Nevila Dudaj thanking me for the photos.

5: Berat
ENVER/NEVER

1987

From Durrës, we turned inland through fields where peasants were at work. Maize stalks were being cut and loaded onto ox-carts. Fields of red and yellow peppers shone in the sunshine. In the corner of a muddy field a boy minded a flock of turkeys. Caterpillar tractors were preparing the fields for winter wheat. A work party dug ditches. Horses pulled carts. We had to stop for a moment while a bullock cart dumped mulch by the roadside.

My Albturist map marked a low mountain range between Tirana and the coast. It was bisected by a river, the Erzen; the road followed the river through the hills. On a rise to our left, we saw radio aerials and I wondered if, when I was at home listening to Radio Tirana, that was where it was coming from. Beyond the pass the plain opened up again and there were ranks of squat, grey bunkers, hundreds of them protecting Tirana from seaborne attack. Edi told us that the bunkers had been built in the 1960s and 1970s, when Albania had feared foreign invasion. But, he added, keen to turn a negative into a positive, we shouldn't assume that Albania was an isolated country. Currently Albania had diplomatic relations with 108 states - but not with the Soviet Union, the United States, Israel, South Africa or Britain.

For the next two nights we were staying at Hotel Tirana, one of the newest and best-equipped hotels in Albania. It was on Scanderbeg Square, at the centre of Tirana. After supper,

Dag and I went out for a walk. A cold wind was blowing. Then we heard music. It was coming from a restaurant near the hotel, but curtains over the windows muffled the sound and prevented all but a glimmer of light escaping. Two Albanians, shadows in the darkness, were standing with noses pressed to the glass. One of them turned to us and mimed putting a ring on his finger. Through cracks in the curtain we could see the bride, veiled and in white, dancing with an older man. Sometimes she disappeared behind the curtains; when she reappeared she was distorted by rivulets of condensation running down the glass.

It's an early start: today we're off to Berat. It's less than a hundred kilometres away, but Edi says it will take us about two and a half hours. Before breakfast, there's time to tune into Parla Tirana for the headlines. Top story: Albania is hosting this year's Balkan Weightlifting Championship with athletes from Bulgaria, Greece, Yugoslavia, Romania and Turkey taking part. A trade protocol has been signed between Albania and the Democratic People's Republic of Korea. Youth delegations from the Dominican Republic, Scandinavia and Tanzania are visiting; some of the Tanzanian delegation are interviewed in English and say how much they're enjoying their stay.

Downstairs in the foyer, there were kitbags everywhere. Some of the weightlifters were staying at the hotel; a fleet of buses was waiting to take them to the Partizani Palace of Sport. On a table by the reception, a pile of press releases in English had been left for interested foreigners. I took a set, fourteen pages of typed news about Albania, but no time to read them right now because Edi is already counting heads.

We retraced our steps to Durrës, then turned south. For a few kilometres the road hugged the coast. In the pine forests that backed onto the beach, you could see lines of defensive trenches. A single-line railway ran alongside the road. In Kavajë, overnight rain had turned the central square to mud. We overtook a lorryload of naval recruits on their way to

Vlorë. They were standing in the back of the lorry singing and waving carnations. Then it was out into the country again along the main road to the south, a single strip of tarmac. To the west was the plain, an unbroken expanse dotted with bunkers and criss-crossed with drainage channels. Edi told us that before liberation, much of the plain had been swamp and had now been drained. In this region were some of Albania's largest state and cooperative farms. Some of the farms were so big they had their own kindergartens and schools, hospitals, libraries and shops.

In an olive grove, peasants were harvesting with nets spread beneath the trees. They had planted a red flag in the ground with all their stuff around it in an untidy jumble. A bullock cart loaded with fodder trundled along the road, the animals yoked to a roughly hewn wooden beam attached to their necks. Sacks of cotton had been stacked at the roadside. Men crouched by tobacco drying racks were having an early lunch.

We watched these rural scenes unfold, framed by the coach window like a film. Then someone asked: why do we only stop in towns? Why can't we stop in a village for a change and walk in the countryside? Edi's answer was that villages didn't have cafés large enough for a group of our size, so we were surprised when, a few moments later, the bus came to a halt and we were told we could get off.

We had stopped by one of those characteristically large fields. This one was growing cotton. Women with white headscarves and red cardigans were up to their waists in cotton plants, picking the bolls and putting them in sacks. On the eastern skyline you could see oil derricks. We piled off the bus and started walking towards the women. As we got closer, cameras primed, the women stopped picking and stared at us. They must have wondered what on earth was going on. We took photos and then rather self-consciously milled about in the field while the women continued to stare. I was glad to get back on the coach.

We were approaching Berat. On the outskirts was an enormous industrial complex. It was the Mao Ce Dun

Textiles Combine which employed more than 7,000 people, mainly women. Next to the Textiles Combine was a food processing plant that produced wine, bread, oil and pasta. We drove in through suburbs of decrepit apartment blocks. Then something almost magical happened. We turned the corner and suddenly there were beautiful old houses on both sides of a steep river valley. Although they were crammed together on the hillside, all had windows overlooking the river. Some of the larger houses had more than a dozen windows. This was why, said Edi, Berat was called the City of a Thousand Windows. Because of its beauty and historic importance, the government had declared it a "Museum City".

2018

At Ura Vajgurore, the road turns south past the military airport at Kucovë, known during communism as Qyteti Stalin. It was, said the Albturist guidebook, an important oil producing centre. It must have been somewhere along this road that Edi had stopped the coach. The combination of cotton, sheep and oil had been another of those defining images of communist Albania. As we sped towards Berat on a fine new road, we passed remnants of the old order: cooperative farm buildings, rusting greenhouses and housing blocks for the collectivised peasantry.

It is still the case that the approach to Berat is underwhelming. The first thing you see are the derelict remains of Kombinati i Tekstileve Mao Ce Dun; its saw-tooth roofs run for more than half a kilometre by the side of the road. Bankrolled and equipped by China, the plant was completed in 1968, just at the point when Sino-Albanian relations were beginning to sour. In a world where big was good, the bigger the better, the combine was regarded as one of the major achievements of the Fourth Five Year Plan (1966-70). Propagandists drooled over its statistics. Five factories spread over forty hectares turned raw cotton into more than five million metres of fabric a year, a tenth of all Albania's textiles. The combine produced a range of eighty articles in 585 designs using 1,013 different colour combinations.

The factory closed in 1991. Since then, grand plans have been put forward to regenerate the site. It could be turned into an arts complex, a performance space, a textiles museum, an industrial museum. So far, the most creative use has been to build a luxury hotel, the White City, on the combine forecourt. It's a jarring juxtaposition of old and new.

I had taken some photos of the suburbs from the coach. One of them showed a street and garden with trees and benches, and five-storey apartment blocks. All the women were wearing cardigans, presumably made at the combine. On the corner had been a billboard with the slogan: "Glory to the shining and immortal works of Comrade Enver Hoxha". The slogan had been removed long ago but the apartments were still there, overtopped by a newer, taller block. The Hoxha slogan had been replaced by an advert for the White City Hotel.

Closer to the centre, a minaret rose above the trees - which wouldn't have been there in 1987. But the Martyrs' Cemetery would have been, and so would the *lapidars* along the road. They were in good condition, their communist insignia picked out in red, black and gold. One commemorated Berat's liberation on 13 September 1944 and showed armed partisans, guns at the ready, brandishing a red flag. Near it, an enormous Albanian flag made of concrete was supported on an upright shaped like a rifle. The *lapidar* commemorated the formation of the Margarita Tutulani Battalion in September 1943. A third *lapidar* was older. Erected in 1935, it showed a group of fighters on horseback. The inscription read "Dëshmorët e Kombit", Martyrs of the Nation. Four names had been added in 2012 to mark the centenary of Albanian independence.

1987

The coach dropped us in the central square outside a padlocked mosque. It was market day and members of the cooperative peasantry and urban proletariat were fraternally elbowing their way onto battered articulated buses. Many clutched hessian sacks or boxes tied up with string. As the buses departed, they belched out clouds of blue smoke. Brightly dressed schoolchildren waved cheerily and shouted, "How are you?"

Berat felt more relaxed than Durrës or Shkodër. It was down at heel, but along the river at least, there'd been an attempt to spruce things up. Formal gardens with flower beds, palm trees and cacti ran along the riverbank, and there were benches where you could sit and enjoy the view. There was also plenty of socialism. Among the flower beds, we spotted Lenin's unmistakable profile. A bronze tableau in the centre of the square showed a crowd gathered around a table where a man, presumably Enver Hoxha, stood with his fist raised. A dark-haired woman wrapped in a red Albanian flag had been painted on a wall. There were more pictures and slogans around the edges of the square. One said PUNA, which I now knew meant "work".

After coffee at Hotel Tomorri, we were free to wander. Dag and I walked up the main street and indulged in a little window-shopping: trainers and ping-pong balls from Czechoslovakia in a sports shop; a "jazz" drum kit on sale for 2,000 leks, about £160, in a music shop. In the market hall, stalls were selling apples, pears, peppers, onions, carrots, wine and spirits, and bottles of tomato purée. Posters on the walls gave dietary information about the nutritional benefits of aubergines and peppers.

On our way back to the hotel, we fell in behind a group of elderly men. They were stocky and walked slowly with shoulders hunched as old people often do, but what caught our attention were the worry beads dangling from their fingers. Even more interestingly, they were speaking Greek.

And then I wondered if that was one of the reasons why Berat seemed such a lovely town. It reminded me of Greece.

We had lunch at the hotel - *avgolemono* soup (very Greek), salad, meat and a sponge dessert topped with artificial cream. After we'd eaten, I asked Edi about Berat's population; were they different, I wondered, to people in other parts of Albania? "Yes," said Edi, "they are smaller." It was an uncharacteristic answer. He seemed irritated, but I tried again: "I saw some old men walking with worry beads, I'm sure they were speaking Greek." "That is your impression," he answered. He wasn't going to be drawn and I let it drop.

2018

Kirstie and I had booked into a hotel in Mangalem on the north side of the Osum river. During the National Liberation War, Berat was a communist stronghold and communist-era symbols were still embedded in the cobbled *kalldrëm*: a pickaxe and rifle picked out in white stone; a communist star with a book at its centre and four hammers, one at each corner.

A short walk along Berat's main street, Rruga Antipatrea, brought us to the central square where we had been dropped in 1987. It was a large space with civic and religious buildings around its edges. The Lead Mosque had been restored with Turkish money and expertise. In 2014, a new Orthodox cathedral dedicated to St Demetrius had been built next to it. On the other side of the square was the Prefecture, the Bashkia and the privatised Hotel Tomorri.

Another, smaller building was tucked into the corner of the square. It was marked on my Albturist map as Muzeu i 22 Tetori, the Museum of 22 October. This was the building that had had the painting of a dark-haired woman wrapped in an Albanian flag on the wall. The painting was called *Shqiponja*, The Eagle, by Zamir Mati and had been one of the most reproduced images in communist Albania. The building was important and had been given Category 1

1987: Closed in 1967 during the atheist campaigns, Berat's Lead
Mosque....

2018: ... has been restored and is open for worship.

protected status in 1961. Originally a cinema, it was where, on 22 October 1944, Albania's Provisional Government had been declared.

In his memoir, *Laying the Foundations for the New Albania*, Enver Hoxha gives an account of that tumultuous week in October 1944. Berat had been liberated the previous month, and by mid-October the communist leadership felt confident enough to bring thousands of its fighters into the town. As the partisans marched in, "men and women, old folk, mothers with children in their arms, boys and girls, pioneers welcomed us with songs and protracted cheers. For hours on end, the singing and cheering continued."

On the morning of 20 October, the Anti-Fascist National Liberation Committee assembled at the cinema. Outside, partisans formed a guard of honour. Inside, despite the best efforts of the chairman to keep order, "enthusiastic people" continued to cheer. Hoxha describes the cinema "decorated with flags, flowers and laurel wreaths. On the curtain at the back of the stage there was a very big flag of Albania, lovingly embroidered, and on both sides of it the slogan 'Death to Fascism - Freedom to the People'."

Discussions continued for two days. Then, on 22 October, the chairman called the meeting to order: "Let us vote on the proposal that the Anti-Fascist National Liberation Committee should be turned into the Provisional Democratic Government of Albania. All in favour raise their fists." Hoxha continues: "Everyone stood up with their clenched fists raised high." That was the scene depicted on the bronze tableau that Dag and I had seen in 1987.

The tableau survived the transition to capitalism, perhaps because of Berat's support for the communist cause. It was removed at some point after 2005. Most of the *lapidars* in Albania celebrate the PLA; maybe the fact that this one featured Enver Hoxha so prominently had something to do with its removal.

Kirstie and I walked back to Mangalem through the gardens by the river. This was where Dag and I had seen the bust of Lenin. He had gone, but other communist-era busts and *lapidars* had survived, including one of "Heroinë e Popullit" Margarita Tutulani, whose name had been commemorated on that *lapidar* in the new town. In 2013, the gardens had been overhauled. Bulldozers broke up the old flower beds and new footpaths were laid. A large piece of uncut marble celebrated the renovation.

1987

Berat's glory is its castle; it sits on a rock high above the town and river. The path was steep so the coach took us all the way up to the gates and parked next to a monument to Batalioni Antonio Gramsci, Italians who fought with Albanian partisans during the National Liberation War. A cannon poked out through the wall above the main gateway. Inside, near a small *bufe, LAVDI PPSH (Glory to the Party of Labour of Albania),* had been written in white stones on the bank.

Houses, some small, some large and all with tiled roofs, lined the main street. Narrow alleyways twisted and curled up the hillside. Some alleys led to the ramparts where there were spectacular views of the river and flood plain; others terminated abruptly in front of high stone walls. To the west, *ENVER* had been carved in huge capital letters into the mountain.

It was a beautiful place, so quiet that it seemed deserted. And then, in the manner of Greek villages, you notice a face at a window or a door closing quietly as you approach.

We were taken to see some frescoes in a Byzantine church whose dark interior was crammed with scaffolding. Then to the Icon Museum, opened the previous year in a large eighteenth-century church. Our guide was a dark-haired young woman who smiled a lot and told us that most of the icons were painted in the sixteenth century by Onufri, or by his son Nikolla. Onufri, she said, was a great national artist whose paintings helped to form a national Albanian art. No mention of his subjects or inspiration. An incense censer with eggs in its supporting chains hung from the ceiling, and there were intricately carved wooden seats around the walls. Someone with a morbid sense of humour had painted a skull and crossbones on the altar screen.

Children asked for pens and chewing gum, and dived for cover when anyone pointed a camera in their direction. A tall, thin-necked and toothless man told us in Italian that he was aged seventy-three. When one of our group volunteered that she was seventy, he crossed his arms over his chest in respect and we all laughed. Someone had an English-Albanian phrasebook and the children, getting bolder, found questions like, "what is your name, please?" or "do you have children?" and we could say, "we are very glad to be in your beautiful country".

It's a curious thought that in days past, this castle would have been at the heart of political and economic power. Nowadays, to come up here is to escape from the noise and activity on the plain. As we straggled back to the bus, silence returned to the citadel. An old man, head bowed, walked slowly across the courtyard and past the *LAVDI PPSH* stones. The silence became more intense and then we heard an engine, quiet at first then getting louder. A truck was coming up the hill. It stopped outside the gate for half a dozen men to jump down and start loading logs into wheelbarrows which they pushed into the citadel - a reminder that winter would soon be here. The truck had Chinese symbols on its bonnet.

2018

In 1987, Dag and I had been driven up to the castle; this time, Kirstie and I walked. Workmen were relaying the cobbles. They were crouched down, bedding the stones in sand and then chipping them to size with hammers just like the ones we'd seen in the pavement in Mangalem.

At the castle entrance, I showed the photos to the man in the ticket office who seemed amused that anyone should have visited Albania during communism. "Enver Hoxha", he said, almost with a chuckle; and then, "Enver Never!" After the fall of the old regime, that enormous *ENVER* across Mali i Shpiragut had been changed to *NEVER*.

I took some matching photos in the courtyard where *LAVDI PPSH* had been picked out in white stone. Traders had hung woven rugs and pieces of embroidery on the walls. CDs of traditional music were for sale. I tried to line up a wider shot of the street, but a car was in the way. The driver was sitting in it with the door open and engine running. I took the photo anyway, with the car in the foreground. When the driver got out, I showed him the photo and explained what I was trying to do. He introduced himself: his name was Vladimir. He took the photo from me and looked at it closely. Then an elderly friend came by and he looked at it too. It was the people they were interested in, not the buildings: people who'd been caught by chance in a foreigner's photograph more than thirty years ago. In the photo, an old man was sitting on the step outside the *bufe*; they thought it was Lika. Then they looked at the doorway on the other side of the street. Although there was only one doorway in the photo, there were in fact two doorways next to each other. Two brothers had lived there; they were Vladimir's uncles. Then Vladimir noticed a woman standing in the doorway holding a baby. It was hard to tell, but he thought it might have been his grandmother.

I asked Vladimir if he'd like a copy of the photo. He did, but before that would we like to drink a coffee with him? His house was down a narrow *kalldrëm*. It had a small garden full of flowers. Steps led up to a veranda with a fine view over the roofs. The veranda was cluttered with scraps of electrical equipment. A hefty pair of binoculars was on the table.

Vladimir was in his early fifties. He went off to make coffee, and when he came back he told us a bit about his life. During communism, he'd trained at Technical School as a builder. When the old system collapsed, he went to Athens. He worked on building sites until he'd made enough money to come back to Berat. He showed us his sitting room; he'd done all the work himself. It was beautifully finished with a glass-fronted cabinet for family treasures. Downstairs next to the kitchen was a room he rented out. It was simply furnished with two beds, but deep inside the house it was cool even on the hottest days. He asked how much we were paying for our room in Mangalem. I said €30. Vladimir said we could have his room for €13.

I asked about life now, and it was the familiar story. There was little work; it was hard to make enough money to live. Here in the castle, there were about 150 permanent residents. In the old days, there'd been enough children up here for the castle to have its own school. As Albanians left, foreigners were buying properties: Italians, Germans, Greeks.

After we'd drunk our coffee and *raki*, Vladimir got out a magnifying glass to look at the pictures in more detail. He told us that the *bufe* had burned down. At the back of the *bufe* there'd been a yard where the old men played cards and dominoes; the *bufe* used to give them sausage and *raki*. Earlier in the summer, some young Kosovars had stayed in his room. They had asked Vladimir where the clubs were. There was nothing for young people in the castle. Soon, said Vladimir, it would be only old people left.

Always keen to reinforce the connection between modern Albanians and ancient Illyrians, the Albturist guidebook emphasised the castle's Illyrian foundations. In the second century BCE, the settlement had been known by its Illyrian name, Antipatrea; its castle had been the stronghold of an Illyrian tribe, the Dasaretes. The guidebook notes that the large stone blocks in the walls date from this period, but as it stands today the castle is mainly Byzantine, the result of a major reconstruction overseen by Emperor Michael Komnenos in the early thirteenth century. Within its walls, there were around twenty Byzantine churches, many dating back to the time of the rebuilding. The castle was taken by the Ottomans in 1417 and they added two mosques:

Xhamia e Kuqe, the Red Mosque, and Xhamia e Bardhe, the White Mosque.

When the communists declared Berat a "Museum City" in 1961, they gave four of the castle's churches and both its mosques state protection as Category 1 Cultural Monuments. In 1986, the Cathedral was redesignated as Muzeu Kombëtar Onufri, the National Onufri Museum, to showcase icons painted by Onufri and other Albanian artists. This was the museum Dag and I had visited in 1987.

Despite its atheism, the state allowed religious art to be displayed so long as it was framed as national art. Nationality was more important than religious faith - the fact that these artists painted religious subjects was due to the social conditions of the time, for which they were not responsible. Commentators, including Enver Hoxha, stressed the naturalism of Onufri's painting: "It has human forms of real people", Hoxha wrote, underlining Onufri's sympathy for a nascent proletariat.

I'm not sure which church had had its interior crammed with scaffolding, but it must have been either Kisha e Shën Mëri Vllahernës. the Church of St Mary Vlachernae, or Kisha e Shën Nikollës, the Church of St Nicholas. Both were small; both were frescoed. I think on balance it must have been Kisha e Shën Mëri Vllahernës because I had a photo of its exterior. I showed the photo to a man and woman who had a souvenir stall near the churches. They had the keys to both of them, and this time Shën Mëri was free of scaffolding. The walls were covered in frescoes: biblical scenes, then lines of saints and martyrs, some gloriously dressed in Byzantine robes. The frescoes had all been painted in the late sixteenth century by Onufri's son, Nikolla.

At the southern tip of the castle, beyond the mosques and the beautiful Kisha e Shën Triadhës, the Church of the Holy Trinity, was a viewing point overlooking the river. A man had set up a stall under a tree and was selling fruit wrapped in paper cones. I said I'd been here in 1987 and showed him the photos. He pointed to a row of stone arches:

during communism, he said, that had been a prison. And that - pointing to what looked like a crumbling Ottoman mansion - that was Kisha e Shën Gjergjit, the Church of St George. We were getting used to seeing churches that had been used as warehouses or sports halls, but this was on a different scale. It was one of the most brutal transformations we'd come across. In the 1980s, the upper part of the church had been demolished. Using the ground floor as a base, the communists had built a *pika turistike*, a tourist centre, on top of the church, designed to look like a traditional Ottoman mansion. The restaurant was derelict, but the church beneath it had been reconsecrated and in 2015 had been declared a Category 1 Cultural Monument. This hybrid building was an extreme example of how the past continues to infiltrate the present.

I bought a cone of plums, which the man washed before handing them over. The wet cone disintegrated and the plums fell on the ground so they had to be washed again. I was wary of being caught in a never-ending loop of washing and rewashing. But the plums were sweet and juicy.

On the way out, I took some matching photos by the castle entrance. I had three from that first visit. One was of that truck parked outside the gates delivering wood. You could see the rough track up to the castle and the unchecked undergrowth around the walls. A tree was sprouting from the battlements. This afternoon, workmen were setting out a new approach road. Kerbstones were already in place; coils of plastic drainage pipe were being buried. The tree had been removed from the battlements and railings installed along an exposed section of wall. These comparisons remind you how neglected and run-down everything was in 1980s Albania. There's a lot of catching up to do.

The *lapidar* commemorating the partisans and the Antonio Gramsci Battalion was on a traffic island. I remember being impressed that Italians had fought alongside partisans, and even more impressed that they had named themselves after a cultural theorist. The *lapidar* was a simple structure:

four concrete columns topped by communist stars. A frieze around the uprights depicted a battle scene and the heads of three fighters. In the old photo, the hillside behind the monument had been bare; now there was a large, pseudo-Ottoman restaurant on it called Nova.

The frieze was pockmarked by a cocktail of weather and pollution, but even so, the *lapidar* remained integral to the landscape. There are thousands of such monuments spread across the country, all erected by a regime that was swept away more than thirty years ago. But despite their political provenance, they have become an accepted part of the historical record. By default, they also serve as a measure of how far Albania has come since 1990.

My other photo was a view down Rruga Mihal Komnena, the cobbled path between castle and town. In the old photo, the suburb between the Osum river and Rruga Antipatrea - called Lagja 30 Vjetori - was a residential zone dominated by apartment blocks. To the left was the dome and minaret of Xhamia e Plumbit, the Lead Mosque; it kept its minaret during communism because it had Category 1 protection. To the right was Albturist's Hotel Tomorri.

Post-communist additions have transformed the skyline. Xhamia e Plumbit and the new Orthodox cathedral were so close to each other that, from a distance, they looked conjoined. Those monolithic suburbs had been broken up with new buildings. The oddest one was Hotel Merko, a glass-fronted tower with a rooftop loggia that had sprouted from a parade of apartment blocks. Behind Hotel Merko was Hotel Tomorri. Both were dwarfed by a domed building that until recently had been the Universiteti i Beratit. Its mission to be a "regional development force" was terminated when its president was accused of selling degrees. The building was sold, and two years later it reopened as Hotel Colombo. Older citizens might have recognised the name: in pre-communist Berat, Colombo had been a byword for luxury. A CIA Information Report on Berat from 1953 described the hotel as "about the largest building in town except for the

1987: This *lapidar* outside Berat's castle….

2018: …continues to be a reminder of the old regime.

hospital". In his memoir, Hoxha recalls that partisans who descended on liberated Berat in 1944 and had a little cash to spare "spent it on tobacco, a razor blade or to drink coffee like 'lords' in the Colombo Hotel".

1987

We still had some time before we had to go back to the coach, so Dag and I crossed the river on a pedestrian bridge. The river was low and young men were playing football on the riverbed. Ducks and hens pecked in the dirt. Then a flock of sheep came along and stopped to graze. From this side of the river, we had a fine view of the castle and houses which clung effortlessly to the hillside. Small shops and cafés lined the waterfront. Some were open with awnings and chairs outside; most were shuttered. Another bridge was downriver. Concrete railings had been added, but it was still a handsome structure.

We walked along the riverbank, then took a cobbled path up into the settlement. Like their counterparts on the other bank, these mansions also had hefty wooden doorways and thick stone walls. They were less densely packed, with broader paths and even some small squares. But they were in a very poor state of repair. Windows were broken; whitewash had gone grey. On one mansion, a downpipe had broken off at chest height and green slime was dribbling down the wall. At the centre of the neighbourhood was an Orthodox church. It was locked, its roof partly collapsed. Beautiful as Berat was, you got the impression that, despite its status as a "Museum City", its preservation wasn't the government's top priority.

2018

The settlement on the south side of the Osum river was Goricë. It was scruffier than Mangalem and more relaxed. Derelict houses rubbed shoulders with restored Ottoman and neoclassical mansions. Several of the mansions had wall plaques recording that they had been bases for LANÇ, the National Liberation Army. Margarita Tutulani, whose statue we'd seen in the park, was born in Goricë. She was tortured and then killed in July 1943. She was only eighteen and became one of Berat's most lauded martyrs. Her name and the names of nine other martyrs were recorded on Goricë's riverside *lapidar*. There were also several Orthodox churches in Goricë, the largest of which was Kisha e Shën Spiridhonit, the Church of St Spiridon. It was almost certainly the one Dag and I had seen in 1987. It was a large church with a nave, portico, narthex and bell tower. It had been the first church in Berat to reopen when restrictions on religious observance were lifted in 1990.

Two elderly men sitting by the door signalled that it was OK for Kirstie and me to go inside. We had a look around and then I asked one of the men what had happened to the church during communism. He took me by the arm and we went back inside. He pointed to the north wall - could I see the line? There were frescoes below, bare plaster above. When the church was closed in 1967, it was turned into a depot for building materials; the communists had put it another floor to increase storage space. The frescoes below had survived, but the frescoes in the upper room had been destroyed. There were no frescoes on the south wall because of damp from a leaky roof. So now that thin strip of fresco on the north wall was all that remained. I asked about the balcony, which looked more like a mosque than a church, and the man said that it had been for women. During the Ottoman occupation, even in Christian churches, women had to sit separately from the men. That was also why the church had no cupola, because those too had been banned by the Ottomans.

We walked along the riverbank towards the bridge, Ura e Goricës. I had the old photos with me, and as we walked the old image came into focus. Of course things had changed: houses refurbished, the road resurfaced. But of all the neighbourhoods we'd seen in Berat, this felt the least touched.

The same parapet wall with the same distinctive concrete triangles ran along the riverbank. There was the same line of shops and warehouses by the bridge. Men were reroofing a warehouse, and you could smell the hot bitumen. The bridge itself had been cleaned and was now pedestrian only, but it still had its communist-era balustrade. I lined up the photo. You could just make out *NEVER* on the hillside.

On the other side of the river, people were waving from one of the bastions. Then we noticed a familiar name written in capital letters on the brickwork: *ENVER*. He still seemed to have his supporters.

The hotel where we were staying in Mangalem was up a narrow *kalldrëm*. It's quite possible that Dag and I had walked past the house in 1987. It was run by Nasho and his wife Bia. When we got back, Nasho invited us to have a drink with him. Nasho made his own red wine from grapes that came from the mountains; made without machinery, without chemicals. It was, he said, *primitiv, organik, pastër* (pure). He poured us each a glass and we toasted in English and Albanian: cheers, *gëzuar*. The wine was light, tart and very drinkable.

Nasho was a natural communicator. He spoke expressively in Albanian, supplementing language with gesture; when comprehension faltered he moved to French, and if that failed there was always Italian as a back-up. He took down a black and white photograph from a shelf, a portrait of a man with an extravagant moustache. It was Nasho's great-grandfather, Jani, who, Nasho told us, had been a poet and patriot.

Jani Vruho was born in a village near Berat in 1863, when Albania was still part of the Ottoman Empire. When he was eighteen, he emigrated to Egypt. He went to Cairo where there was already a large ethnic Albanian community. Jani did well, making money as a trader and using his wealth to support the Albanian *Rilindja*, the Awakening. He began writing and publishing patriotic newspapers. He was a friend of Fan Noli, who would later (and very briefly) become Albanian prime minister. King Zog regarded Jani as such a menace that he sentenced him to death *in absentia*. Jani never returned to Albania. He died in Cairo in 1931. Later, a Berat neighbourhood was named after him.

Jani's role in promoting Albanian consciousness was praised by the communists, and like his grandfather, Nasho's political sympathies were on the left. That didn't mean he agreed with everything the communists did, but some things were better then than they were now. Education was one. During communism, education was highly valued. Children took it seriously; teachers didn't take *bakshish*. If children wanted good marks today, they just bribed their teacher. Talking about children and schools reminded Nasho of *brigadat*, the brigades. We must have seen the *brezaret*, the hillside terraces that had been dug by youth volunteers. Here in Berat, children had worked on the *kalldrëme*. Nasho thought the idea of young people contributing like this was a good thing.

On the downside, the communist system and its leader, Enver Hoxha, had been *paranojak*, paranoid. He gave us some examples. When the state built new roads, they built them with lots of curves - Nasho wiggled his hand like a fish to demonstrate. They did this because Hoxha had seen a film starring Alain Delon in which a plane had landed on a straight road; so to stop enemy planes landing on Albanian roads, they were all built *poshtë e lart*, back and forth. Albania is a small country, but you can imagine how long it took to get from one end to the other with roads like that. In the vineyards, farmers had been told to put metal spikes on the posts supporting the vines, so if enemy parachutists were to invade, they'd be impaled.

Once, when Hoxha visited Berat, he suggested building a new bridge over the river. There was, said Nasho, already a perfectly good bridge, but because it was Enver Hoxha's idea, it had to be built.

And now? Is life better? Nasho agreed that Albania was now free, but there was also poverty. During communism, everyone had been poor. But now there were very rich people and very poor people; and along with poverty, Albania now had a problem with *krim i madh*, organised crime.

One of the personal consequences of Albania's poverty was that both his sons had gone to America. If he or Bia wanted to see them, they had to get a visa. Visas were expensive and hard to get. You go to the office and fill in the paperwork. You pay €100 and then they refuse your application. €100 is a lot of money; it's what an Albanian pensioner gets each month.

Before we went to our room, we drank a toast - *për të ardhmen e Shqipërisë*, to the future of Albania. We chinked glasses and Nasho mimed blowing up a balloon and then bursting it with a pin - bang!

We had accounted for all but two of the old photos. Dag and I had come back to Berat in 1988 as part of a tour of the south, and I had a photo of a monument that had been erected that year. It celebrated the inauguration of a pipeline which brought drinking water to Berat from a village called Bogovë:

1988
Përurohet Ujësjellësi i Bogovës
Dhuratë e Partisë Popullit të Beratit

1988
The water supply of Bogovë is inaugurated
A gift from the People's Party of Berat

A frieze with dancers and musicians on one side and young men and women holding garlands on the other had been mounted on five concrete supports. A curtain of water fell from the frieze into a trough below. We found the monument next to a children's funfair by Hotel Tomorri. I took some photos and then we went for a coffee at the hotel.

Hotel Tomorri had been rebranded "HT". Because it was so close to the funfair, its terrace had become a favourite spot for families to come and eat ice cream. Inside, despite an extensive make-over, the reception area preserved the best of its communist décor: marble floors, a fine curved wooden reception desk, a staircase with modernist metal railings. And plenty of pot plants.

That left just one photo of a five-storey, brick-built apartment block set back from the road behind an arched entrance. The block was communist, but the arches were stylish and looked older, possibly part of a neoclassical parade. My assumption was that it had to be somewhere near Mangalem and the main square, because that's where Dag and I had walked - unless I'd taken it from the coach, in which case it could be anywhere.

We found it on the pedestrianised section of Bulevardi Republika, where people came for the evening *xhiro* or stroll. You would have thought that something as obvious as a row of arches would be easy to spot. Not so. A combination of sun umbrellas, a new roof and a metal trellis had done a good job in hiding them. The central arch, the largest of the three, opened onto a courtyard, as it had in the photo. The two smaller arches had been closed in and turned into tiny cafés. Albanians have a flair for finding commercial advantage in the smallest of spaces. I showed the photo to the waiter, but he wasn't interested. He had people to serve.

When we got back to the hotel, Nasho was sitting on the doorstep. He wanted to know where we'd been. I showed him the old photos, and he leafed through them; it was interesting to see what caught his attention. In the photo of the apartment blocks and the Enver Hoxha slogan, a blue *traktoraki* was coming down the road. Apart from a truck parked by the apartments and a man on a bicycle, it was the only vehicle. "That's my friend," said Nasho, and although you couldn't see the driver, I suppose there weren't many little blue tractors in Berat in the 1980s, so you probably knew who drove one.

Nasho also lingered over the photos with buses in them. In one of them, people were clambering onto a battered articulated bus; another bus was parked by it. Those were local buses, said Nasho, adding that there'd only been two in Berat, so I'd managed to capture the entire fleet. Other buses were parked in the square. They looked more roadworthy, and Nasho said they were long-distance buses. He looked at the people waiting to board. There were a lot of them, but no-one he recognised.

Then, as often seems to happen, a friend walked past. This man, said Nasho, was a historian and had worked at the museum. They looked through the photos again; this time they concentrated more on the buildings and monuments. The photo of the water feature caught Nasho's friend's eye. He read out the inscription. What I hadn't noticed earlier in the day was that part of the inscription had been chiselled off. The line reading *Dhuratë e Partisë Popullit të Beratit*, A gift from the People's Party of Berat, had been removed. The full inscription was in the old photo.

There was more discussion about the exact location of Lenin and how close he'd been to "Hero i Popullit" Hajdar Tafa, whose gilded bust we'd seen in the riverside gardens. Then their attention switched to a photo Dag had taken near Hotel Tomorri. It showed our Albturist coach parked in the main square next to a two-storey neoclassical villa. That had been the local PPSH headquarters, Nasho said. There had also been a prison in the building, and when you looked closely at the photo, you could see bars across a ground-floor window. The building had been demolished and replaced by the new Prefecture.

All this talk about communism gave Nasho an idea. He wondered if we'd like to meet a friend of his called Avdyl, who had been the First Secretary of the Communist Party in Berat. I said yes, where might this meeting take place? Nasho said that Avdyl always went to the same café on Rruga Antipatrea, about ten minutes' walk from the hotel. He said he'd give Avdyl a ring. The next morning after breakfast,

Nasho drew a map. He didn't know the name of the café, but it was run by a man called Niko. It was near Hotel Gega. If we passed a *rrapi*, a plane tree, we'd gone too far. Avdyl would be expecting us around eleven.

Rruga Antipatrea is Berat's main thoroughfare. It runs from the Textiles Combine, through Sheshi Teodor Muzaka to the Regional Hospital. In Mangalem, it passes some of Berat's finest buildings: Xhamia e Beqarëve, the Bachelor's Mosque, with a beautiful painted exterior; the remains of Kurt Pasha Vrioni's *serai*; and a religious complex with a mosque, a *tekke* and *han*, all being restored by Turkey. Beyond the main square, the road continues through a residential zone still dominated by communist-era four- and five-storey apartment blocks. Structurally speaking, it can't have changed much since 1990.

We walked past Hotel Gega, and although we thought we were looking carefully, we reached the plane tree without finding Niko's café. I phoned Nasho for more precise directions. If I couldn't find the café, his advice was to ask in another one: they'd know which one Avdyl went to. We retraced our steps, but there were at least half a dozen cafés, none with names. So we ended up loitering outside each one, hoping that Avdyl was looking out for us and would make himself known.

Eventually, a balding man with a scrubby beard and lined face came over to greet us. We sat down at a table and Avdyl asked when I had first visited Albania, what did I think of it, how many times had I been since. I asked how he knew Nasho. Avdyl said that they came from the same neighbourhood and had become friends. He told us that, like many of his generation, he spoke Russian. He'd also been to Syria, a long-time ally of communist Albania.

These days, Stalinism is a hard sell, but Avdyl had not given up. In June 1991, PPSH, the Party of Labour of Albania that had ruled since 1944, rebranded itself as the Socialist Party. Hoxha loyalists regrouped and formed PKSH, Partia Komuniste e Shqipërise, the Communist Party of Albania.

Almost immediately, it ran into trouble. One of the first pieces of legislation passed by Sali Berisha's Democratic Party after its election in March 1992 was to ban PKSH. The ban was eventually lifted by the Socialist Party in April 1998.

In 2003, Avdyl tested the water. He stood as an independent candidate in Berat's mayoral election. His strategy was to remind voters of what he had done for Berat as First Secretary of the Communist Party. One of his biggest achievements had been to bring drinking water to the town in 1988. He didn't get elected.

In 2007, another Stalinist party was launched. It called itself PPSHr, Partia e Punës së Shqipërisë e Riorganizuar, the Party of Labour of Albania Reorganised. PPSHr quite deliberately used PPSH imagery in its logo: a communist star, hammer and sickle, ears of wheat. It promoted itself as a Marxist-Leninist movement that wanted to re-establish a "proletarian democracy" that "satisfies the interests of the masses". Avdyl's name appeared on a list of PPSHr candidates standing in Berat's local elections in 2013.

Avdyl was quite open about his admiration for Enver Hoxha. On Martyrs' Day in 2014, he and other communists had gone to the Martyrs' Cemetery in Tirana. They had taken placards of Hoxha with them, but were prevented from showing them. Avdyl was critical of the exhumation of Hoxha's body in May 1992; he thought he should be returned to the Martyrs' Cemetery.

Avdyl's influence was all over the photos. They were snapshots of the Berat he'd worked to create. This was his vision of the city: its gardens and public spaces, its monuments and statues, its housing, its water feature with an unexpurgated inscription. The bust of Lenin was there because Albania had followed a Marxist-Leninist path, and he explained about the bronze tableau. When I asked what had happened to it, he just said that it was *prishur*, demolished. He tutted at the weeds growing around the water feature. He liked the photos of the gardens along the river. Berat, he said, had been *qyteti i trëndafilave*, a city of roses. Now they had taken away most of the flowers and had planted trees. Avdyl preferred the flowers.

Whatever you think about the old regime, not all its servants had been evil. It must have been painful for Avdyl to see his life's work discarded. You got a strong sense of a man who had taken pride in the neatness and orderliness of his town, and you can understand why he was so attached to the gardens. Apart from being aesthetically pleasing, their formality was an idealised reflection of the social order where everything was controlled and harmonious. Then he got up; he said he had friends to meet. We shook hands and off he went.

6: Sarandë, Butrint and Ksamil

"The Green Crown of the Riviera"

Sarandë: "the place for honeymoons"
1988

This time Dag and I flew. Direct flights from England were new; they'd been negotiated by Voyages Jules Verne, who were offering tours to what it called "Europe's last frontier". The Albanian leader, Ramiz Alia, had spoken of his willingness to normalise relations with Britain; these flights were being cited as evidence of a diplomatic thaw.

We touched down at dusk at Rinas Airport where a single strip of lights marked out the runway. As we landed, the plane's wheels thrummed on the hexagonal concrete blocks. In the terminal, soldiers in green uniforms and peaked caps collected, inspected and then stamped passports. We boarded our Albturist bus and were taken to Hotel Tirana in Scanderbeg Square. Tomorrow, we'll be heading south to Apollonia, Gjirokastër, Sarandë and Butrint.

While we waited in the foyer the next morning, I picked up a set of press releases. The lead story was a round-up of events from around the world celebrating the eightieth anniversary of Enver Hoxha's birth. Trades unions in Sao Paulo had held a commemorative meeting. The Japan-Albania Friendship Association had shown a film, *Long Life to Enver Hoxha.* In Italy, Professor Mario Proto from the Italy-Albania Friendship Association had praised Hoxha as the "bearer of the loftiest ideals of the socialist society, deprived of the sentiments of bourgeois individualism". Other stories were less strident. A preview of a Balkan conference to be held in Tirana next spring concluded that "This meeting will be another effort to create and carry forward the spirit of confidence and understanding between the Balkan countries." Another article highlighted the growth in foreign language dictionaries. This was partly a response to the "cultural and scientific requirements of the working masses". But it also indicated increased levels of interest among "foreign scholars, friends and tourists who visit our country".

We left Tirana at 8.30 a.m. and by 2 p.m. we'd reached Gjirokastër - five and a half hours to cover 230 kilometres. Albania is a small country, but from inside it seems to expand. That's partly due to the roads (narrow) and terrain (mountainous), so you have to go slowly. But it's not just about speed - or lack of it. Albania is a kaleidoscope of images. So far today we've seen mountains and rivers, ancient castles and modern cities, agriculture and industry. The visual intensity is exhausting.

Another two hours on a winding road brought us to Sarandë, "the place for honeymoons" our guide Pepi told us, adding that the state provided special hotels for newly-weds. We were staying at Hotel Butrinti, about a kilometre from the town centre. After supper, Dag got talking to the hotel manager. He offered us glasses of *fernet* and asked Dag about the CND badge he was wearing. Dag explained about the Campaign for Nuclear Disarmament. Then he unpinned the badge and gave it to the manager. The manager thanked him and returned a few moments later with two lapel badges which he presented to us: a red flag with a black double-headed eagle and a gold star between its heads.

In the morning, from our balcony we could see the whole of Sarandë. The Jules Verne brochure compared it to a "tiny, well-kept Greek port". That was wide of the mark. Even the tiniest Greek harbour is all noise and bustle, especially in the early morning when fishing boats arrive and depart, bikes buzz along narrow streets and music spills out of the cafés. Apart from some members of our party who were having a pre-breakfast dip, Sarandë was eerily silent. Corfu was only a few kilometres away, and in the clear morning light you could pick out coastal settlements. One of them must have been Kassiopi, where sixteen years ago I'd sat on a beach looking across the water at Agioi Saranta.

2019

It was mid-September, still hot, but the reception area was cool and spacious. By the desk, the hotel's name and logo were displayed on a marble block. Along a corridor, where in the old days there had been cabinets for handicrafts and books by Enver Hoxha, there were now Greek amphorae dredged from the sea, Roman ceramics, Ottoman brassware and assorted weaponry from the early twentieth century. It was hard to believe that thirty years ago Dag and I had been sitting here in a smoky lounge drinking *fernet* and swapping lapel badges.

Hotel Butrinti had been built with foreign tourists in mind. When it opened in 1973, it was regarded as one of Albania's most prestigious hotels. Three owners and two renovations later, it still had five stars. The prices were ridiculous at €147 a night, but the important thing was the balcony. I'd taken two photos from here in 1988, one in the morning, one at dusk.

In the morning photo, you can almost *see* the silence. There were no boats in the bay and no cars on the road. The only traffic was a truck and a tractor. The photo reminds you what a compact settlement communist Sarandë had been. Behind the fishing harbour, apartment blocks spread up the hillside; *New Albania* described them as "the tiered seats of an amphitheatre". Then it was just scrub and bare mountain all

1988: Sarandë, once a small seaside town, …..

2019: … has become a major holiday resort with hotels lining the waterfront.

the way to the summit. Those "broken teeth" I'd seen from Kassiopi were on the headland - it's called Kodrra - on the far side of the bay: five-storey apartment blocks interspersed with smaller blocks with tiled roofs. On the foreshore below them was Sarandë's commercial harbour. You could also see buildings from earlier periods. On Kodrra next to what had been a flour mill was a single-storey Ottoman building with an arched façade. Along the waterfront by the fishing harbour was a 1930s parade with a red-tiled roof.

Like other coastal settlements, Sarandë has expanded massively since the end of communism. Old buildings have been repurposed and new apartments erected. Green spaces have been eaten up. An Orthodox church has been built next to the 1930s parade. A fifteen-storey tower block looms over the harbour. You fear that sometime soon the mountain will disappear under concrete. But even so, many of the old landmarks have survived. The Ottoman building by the harbour has been restored and absorbed into a hotel. The Bashkia plans to turn the old flour mill into a cultural centre. The 1930s parade is still there. Against the odds, so is another 1930s villa next to the harbour.

During communism, that villa was Bar-Lulishte Butrinti. It was famous for its music. A virtuoso clarinettist, Astrit Gega, used to play there with his band. Those unable to pay for a seat inside could listen to the music from the gardens. The villa is no longer a café, but it's instantly recognisable because it's one of the very few unmodernised premises along the seafront. The last time I walked past it there was washing on the balcony, so someone was living there, and the garden below it was a riot of purple bougainvillea. The villa is still owned by the Bashkia. In 2019, an attempt to auction it was blocked by the courts. Two years later, the council was forced to intervene to stop the floor collapsing. It would be nice to think that the villa's survival owes just a little to its special place in Sarandë's folk memory.

Butrint: a wondrous place
1988

After breakfast, Pepi gave us the day's itinerary: a visit to the archaeological site at Butrint, lunch at Ksamil and then in the afternoon time to explore Sarandë.

The road to Butrint followed the coast. Just beyond the hotel was the Martyrs' Cemetery. Its stairway and graves, white on an otherwise virgin hillside, must have been visible all over town. South of Sarandë, the hills had been terraced, the mazy rows of olive trees like contour lines made real. The terraces, Pepi told us, had been dug by young volunteers who'd come from all over the country to take part in "youth actions". And then one of those sights you're not supposed to see: a prison under construction. It was definitely a prison. Dag managed to take a photo of look-out towers and high brick walls.

We crossed a river onto a plain where tractors were ploughing and cows chewed on maize stalks. The river, said Pepi, was the Bistricë. It used to flow across the plain but there was a problem with flooding so it was canalised and it now emptied into the sea. Across fields, we could see smoke billowing from a chimney. A pumping station straddled an irrigation channel. Then reed beds fringed a lake: the Lake of Butrint, an expanse of shimmering water with mountain ranges rising on its eastern shore. A tiny village perched on an outcrop above the lake looked like the imaginings of a Romantic artist.

Butrint was a bewitching place. The old town was on a peninsula at the southern end of the lake, and although it was an important archaeological site, first impressions were not archaeological. Butrint seemed in danger of being overrun by vegetation. Undergrowth pressed in on the ruins; tendrils twisted around blocks of stone; trees sprouted from ancient walls. The air was sweet with pollen and shimmered with insects. Nature was doing her best to reclaim what was hers, and she had a powerful ally.

The town is surrounded by water. Water had nourished the vegetation that had made the site so attractive to its first settlers. Water had protected them and they in turn used it to beautify their city with ornamental fountains and baths. Rising water levels in the late fourteenth century had forced Butrint's citizens to abandon the settlement. Now, water flowed through the city. It had flooded the amphitheatre and Temple of Asclepius. The ruins of the Gymnasium were reflected in its own unofficial lake. Water encouraged other settlers: frogs, water snakes, turtles and terrapins. The humidity was perfect for mosquitoes.

We sat for a few moments in the amphitheatre, looking down on the stage where frogs were chirruping in water clotted with algae. At the Baptistery, a wondrous mosaic of animals and birds was protected under gravel. We passed the roofless Basilica, its walls still standing to full height. Then we came to the Lion Gate, so called because the carving over the doorway shows a lion attacking a bull.

The path began to climb. We stumbled over broken masonry and ducked under trees until we reached a gateway. It opened onto a courtyard that had been part of a Venetian castle. The courtyard was getting a make-over. New paths and gardens were being laid; new trees, including a mature palm, had been planted. Marble pillars stood in the flower beds. The castle walls had been restored and the donjon repointed. You might (and we did) moan quietly that it was a bit of a botched job, especially when the rest of the city had been left (quite rightly in our view) to continue its battle with nature. But the view was stupendous.

To the west, a broad channel connected the Lake of Butrint to the sea. At the channel's mouth, a castle sat on low ground, surrounded by marshes. Corfu was less than two miles away. To the south, on the other side of the channel, there was a smaller, triangular castle. Beyond it, fields - pale green strips alternating with dark, muddy earth - stretched across the plain. An irrigation channel with sluice gates at its mouth took water to the fields.

To the north was a tiny harbour, just big enough for a battered old tug that looked as if it had been welded together from scrap metal. Some men climbed aboard. The engine rumbled and the tug backed slowly out of the harbour, taking care not to collide with a rickety fish pen. Then it headed off up the lake.

2019

On 25 May 1959, Soviet leader Nikita Khrushchev flew into Tirana on a Tupolev Tu-104. For the next twelve days he toured Albania and was greeted warmly by the crowds. But his denunciation of his predecessor Joseph Stalin had not gone down well with the Albanian leadership. The ideological gap between Moscow and Tirana was widening, but Hoxha wanted Khrushchev's visit to be a success. He thought Khrushchev might appreciate a bit of downtime, so he arranged a visit to Butrint.

On 1 June, Khrushchev and Hoxha boarded a Russian warship at Vlorë and sailed down the coast to Sarandë. A film crew was waiting for them on the quayside. After fraternal hugs and kisses, the motorcade set off down a new asphalt road built specially for the visit. Khrushchev jauntily doffed his hat to the crowds.

As Kirstie and I set off for Butrint, the road was busy with construction vehicles and coaches ferrying visitors to and from the hotels. There was no sign of the prison Dag had photographed, or of the terraced hillsides that been such a feature of the landscape. Since 1990, almost all the terracing around the city has been abandoned or has disappeared under suburbs.

The road sweeps round the corner and you cross the canalised Bistricë almost without noticing. When the canal opened in July 1959, Enver Hoxha officiated at its opening. He noted in his Diary that the canal was "one of the largest reclamation schemes on the Vurg plain". A section of the old road bridge was visible next to the new. That was where Hoxha had stood (minus the concrete railing) to cut the ribbon. Back then, the headland bisected by the canal had been bare scrub. Now it was crisscrossed with access roads for hotels and apartments. When the redevelopment finally peters out south of Çukë, the landscape looks much as it had done in 1988. The land is still intensively farmed with large fields that have not been broken down into individual plots. And the irrigation system still seemed to be working; the pumping station Dag had photographed was still there astride a drainage canal.

At Butrint, there had been changes: a larger car park; a new hotel by the entrance; more boatmen offering trips along the Vivari Channel to Ali Pasha's castle. Inside the park, there was a handicrafts stall, better signage and, in a nod to health and safety, wooden handrails and ramps had been installed. But Butrint's unique atmosphere had survived. It was still a wondrous place.

But it didn't impress Khrushchev. The Albanians had done everything they could to ensure that his visit went smoothly. They had laid a new crazy-paved path around the site. Fearing that Khrushchev might be stung by bees or bitten by water snakes, the authorities burned all the beehives and poisoned the snakes. The party visited the amphitheatre and halted briefly to admire the Lion Gate. But when Hoxha tried to explain to Khrushchev why the Albanians held Butrint in such high regard, Khrushchev became irritated. According to Hoxha's account of the visit in his memoir, *The Khrushchevites*, Khrushchev replied, "Why do you employ all these forces and funds on such dead things! Leave the Hellenes and the Romans to their antiquity!" Hoxha corrected Khrushchev. It wasn't just Hellenes and Romans who had shaped Butrint. Another "ancient culture" had flourished here: the Illyrians. "The Albanians," Hoxha explained, "stem from the Illyrian trunk." To which Khrushchev replied, "Why are these things of value to you? Do they increase the well-being of the people?"

Hoxha thought Khrushchev was an ignoramus. He claimed to have overheard Khrushchev and the Soviet Minister of Defence discussing a plan to turn Butrint into a naval base that would have wrecked the old city. Hoxha wrote: "It made my flesh creep to hear them talk like this, as if they were masters of the seas, countries and peoples." It all sounds a little too synthetic, a recollection of two pantomime villains hatching a dastardly plot. Whether true or not, the story fed into the communist narrative of little Albania facing down a bullying Soviet Union.

On that first visit with Dag, Butrint had been defined by water. This time, it was wind. It hissed through the trees and whipped up eddies of dust. It blew ribbons of eucalyptus bark across the path, and dry leaves crackled underfoot.

Kirstie and I followed in Khrushchev's footsteps. The first building we came to was the amphitheatre. In my old photo, the stage was under several inches of water and a wooden walkway provided access to the seats. Now, the whole stage had been boarded over and the walkway replaced by a ramp. Beyond the Agora we came to the Gymnasium where there had been classrooms and designated spaces for exercise and relaxation. In the central courtyard were the remains of a nymphaeum and bathing pool. In the old photo, the whole courtyard was flooded. This afternoon the water was where it should have been, in the bathing pool.

Near the circular Baptistery, its mosaics protected under sand, was the Great Basilica. I had taken a photo of it in 1988. The trees around it were metres taller than they had been, but the Basilica was the same, except for one small detail. A pillar had been placed in the sanctuary to create an altar. The path continued along the outer wall, past the Lake Gate and then to the Lion Gate. Even Khrushchev who was not a tall man had to stoop to get through it.

Dag and I must have stopped briefly just before we entered the citadel, because I had some photos of that tiny harbour. Thirty years on, I had to scramble through undergrowth to

1988: The stage of Butrint's amphitheatre, once a haunt for frogs and terrapins, ...

2019: ...has been boarded over and access improved.

get to the same spot. I climbed onto a bluff and for a moment wondered if my memory had failed. Half a dozen fishing boats were moored along the shore, but the harbour and buildings had vanished. Now there were only trees. They were growing all along the shore, right down to the water's edge. Hoxha often spoke about man's relationship with nature. In a speech given in 1968, he said that in order to build Socialism, the Party had to make the broad masses "capable of knowing, mastering and applying the laws of nature properly, and of turning them to the material advantage of man and society". Nature plays a long game. In Butrint, it was getting its own back.

Inside the old town, surrounded by walls and forests, Butrint feels enclosed, even a little claustrophobic. It's only when you reach the citadel that you can appreciate the town's spectacular setting. The citadel is only 43 metres above sea level, but the views stretch for kilometres: south over Fusha e Vrinës, east towards mountains, west along the Vivari Channel. Corfu fills the western horizon.

The citadel had been fought over by a succession of invading forces: Greeks, Romans, Slavs, Angevins, Byzantines, Venetians, Ottomans. Nowadays, its most prominent feature is its Venetian castle. The castle was reconstructed by the Italian Archaeological Mission in the 1930s. The Mission then was led by Luigi Maria Ugolini, a citizen of Fascist Italy, and his reconstruction was controversial. The old castle was dismantled and replaced with what one expert[1] on Butrint has called "a picture-book Italianate donjon": a crenellated stone tower with arched windows and an external staircase to access the upper floor.

When the communists came to power, they accused Ugolini of exploiting archaeology to validate Butrint's role in Rome's foundation myth. Aeneas had stopped at Butrint

---

1 R. Hodges and A. Paterlini, *A Short History of the Butrint Foundation's Conservation Programme at Butrint, Albania: 1994–2012*, p. 257. Online at: https://www.academia.edu/7702316/A_Short_History_of_the_Butrint_Foundation_s_Conservation_Programme_at_Butrint_Albania_1994_2012_by_R_Hodges_and_A_Paterlini

(Buthrotum) on his way to Italy after the Trojan War and had met its ruler, Helenus, the son of King Priam of Troy. The communists complained, with some justification, that building a Venetian castle in the citadel amounted to cultural appropriation. The communists themselves weren't averse to using archaeology for ideological ends. Hoxha's insistence on establishing continuity between the Illyrians and modern Albanians turned the excavations at Butrint into an ideological project. It was the job of Albanian archaeology to find the evidence to support the hypothesis.

But they didn't knock the castle down. When we were here in 1988, the courtyard was being refurbished. Thirty years on, the flower beds were green with unkempt shrubs and a large conifer overtopped the tower. The palm tree had been felled. In its place was a rustic sun shelter, but it was more than compensated for by the other trees. The greenery changed the space; it softened it, made it more welcoming.

I'd taken photos up here in 1988. Back then, all the land around Butrint had been consolidated into a state farm based at Vrinë on a wooded rise to the south. The Albturist guidebook was fulsome about the improvements made by the state farm: "the old mosquito feeding swamps and marshes" had been drained and "degenerate and badly kept forests" uprooted. Vrinë today, it said, was "a veritable granary" of fields and pasture. In the main, it was still fertile land; there were new citrus groves, and meadows had been cut for hay. But because the pumping systems had not been maintained, fields close to the shore had reverted to marshland and were too salty for cultivation.

We sat on the wall overlooking the sea. The wind had dropped but there were still a few scuffs on the water. In the fading light, the Vivari Channel had taken on a silvery sheen and Corfu across the strait was a misty purple. It was a calming scene, a huge natural canvas. Butrint had lost none of its power to enthral and I could have quite happily sat there until darkness - except that it was closing time. Guards were blowing whistles and ushering visitors to the exit.

Ksamil: how not to develop a tourist industry
1988

We piled back into the coach and retraced our steps to Ksamil, "the only town in the world without a graveyard," said Pepi. Ksamil was the newest town on the Ionian coast. It had been built by the youth, who had also provided much of the labour for terracing and harvesting.

Ksamil's tourist restaurant was on a headland overlooking citrus groves and the sea. But for all its natural beauty, Ksamil was an unprepossessing place: just a few apartment blocks, a cultural centre and a tourist complex. A couple of decrepit buses were parked in the town centre, presumably to ferry people to and from Sarandë.

2019

Ksamil was always workaday, but since 1988 it has changed beyond recognition. An article in *New Albania* dubbed the region the "Green Crown of the Riviera". It described how more than 80,000 young people had "toiled to embellish and transform the Ionian coastline and convert the steep hillsides into fertile and scenic areas". Altogether 2,700 kilometres of terrace had been scraped from the rock. As you drive into Ksamil today, you see hillside terraces; but most of them are uncared for. The main impression is of entering a construction site. The old centre, known as Katër Pallatet with its four apartment blocks, is still there along with a socialist-era statue of dancers in traditional costume. But rapid and uncontrolled development has turned Ksamil into a ragged sprawl.

Ksamil was originally settled by Muslim Chams from Varfanj (now Parapotamos) near Igoumenitsa in Greek Epirus. They were forced to leave when the border between Greece and Albania was finalised in 1913, splitting a region called Chameria that had been inhabited by ethnic Albanians.

The foundations of the communist-era settlement were laid in the mid-1970s. Following a PLA directive to "Take to the hills and mountains, and make them as beautiful and fertile as the plains", sixty families from Maliq and Sheqeras, both villages in eastern Albania, were resettled at Ksamil in the four apartment blocks in the village centre. As the population grew, more blocks were built on land near the shore. There was also a *kinoteatër*, a tourist facility and a brigade headquarters to coordinate work on the terraces.

Those first families were chosen for their agricultural experience. But it was a hard life. The land was stony and difficult to cultivate. Some families couldn't cope and had to leave. When a family left, the state replaced them so that work on the terracing could continue. It was also tense. Ksamil is close to the Greek border. In April 1967, a military junta seized power in Greece and the threat of invasion was taken seriously. Soldiers patrolled the beaches, and a curfew was imposed. After 6 o'clock, no-one could leave or enter Ksamil.

As well as its permanent residents, the village also had to accommodate the thousands of young *aksionistë* who came every year to work on the terraces. These "actions" were political as well as economic. They were promoted as a way of breaking down divisions between intellectuals and workers, between town and country, between lowlands and highlands. As the rhetoric of the time had it: "In glorious work at the service of socialist construction, our young men and women are imbued with the lofty norms and virtues of communist ethics, they are tempered so as to become worthy citizens of our new socialist society."

By 1990, when the old regime was crumbling, Ksamil's population stood at around 3,500. Almost everyone was employed on the land. But unlike other regions of Albania, Land Law 7501, the legal vehicle for land redistribution, was not applied in Ksamil. That explained the large fields around Çukë and Vrinë; the question was, why had they been exempt? A World Bank report issued in 2007 suggested it was because "the land was considered to be valuable". But there were plenty of other equally "valuable" regions in Albania, not least Fusha e Thumanës or Bregu i Matit, both of which had been broken up into private plots.

It turned out that Ksamil's particular "value" was touristic rather than agricultural. According to Mero Baze, a journalist based in Sarandë, the Democratic government elected in 1992 wanted, not unreasonably, to develop Ksamil as a tourist resort. That was easier to do if the land was not broken up into small plots. So Ksamil's collective farm continued to function under foreign management until May 1994. Pay was good, and the fact that the farmers had not received land only became an issue when the farm closed. At that point, Ksamiliots realised that not only had they lost their jobs, but they had no land of their own because they had missed out on land redistribution.

Ksamil's economic problems were exacerbated in September 1992 when fires destroyed hundreds of hectares of citrus and olive groves. The source of the fires was never properly explained; conspiracy theories started to circulate suggesting it was Greek sabotage aimed at snuffing out Ksamil as a rival fruit producer. More damage was done in the violence following the pyramid scandals in 1997, and many people emigrated. When a degree of stability had been restored, the government's plan to develop Ksamil as a tourist destination was taken as a green light for a building free-for-all. Developers from all over Albania descended on the village and it became notorious for its land grabs and illegal building. In the space of a few years, Ksamil mushroomed from a village of about twenty apartment blocks to more than 400 buildings. In an effort to impose some kind of legal order, the Socialist administration declared at least 250 buildings illegal, and in the early 2000s a number of demolitions were carried out.

The policy was reversed in 2006, when the incoming Democratic administration passed a law conferring retrospective legality on more than 200,000 illegal buildings across Albania. The effect was to trigger another wave of illegal building, particularly in Ksamil. More demolitions followed in 2012 and 2014 when the Socialists were returned to power.

One demolition in particular received a lot of press coverage. In April 2014, three illegal buildings on one of Ksamil's islands were dynamited; the explosion was so powerful that it caused part of the cliff to collapse. This was very embarrassing for the authorities, because in 2002 Albania's National Agency of Protected Areas had added the islands to its list of protected places. The application of one set of rules made a mockery of another set, both of which should have been protecting places like Ksamil.

As well as these belated attempts to regulate development, the authorities have still to deal with long-standing issues of land redistribution as specified by Land Law 7501. Farmers have gone to court and have lobbied local politicians to get what they see as their rightful share. So far, they have been unsuccessful.

This toxic cocktail of corruption and obfuscation has made Ksamil a case study of what happens when powerful forces collide. At the end of his article, Mero Baze writes that "the pearl of Albania has been plunged into illegality, chaos and urban ugliness". The agent of this "massacre" is the Albanian state. Ksamil, Baze concludes, has become "a desert".

Sarandë: shopping, Albanian style
1988

Days are short at this time of year, and as soon as we'd been dropped at the hotel, Dag and I set off into town. A broad esplanade lined with pines and palm trees ran around the coast to the centre, where there were gardens with benches and statues. One was of women harvesting oranges; two were reaching up for the fruit while a third held the basket.

We were walking by the fishing harbour when two crop-headed boys approached us. Dark-skinned and full of confidence, they spoke Greek and said their father was a government chauffeur. They asked if we were Greek and if we had any paper or pens. We gave them each a biro. Nearby, a stage had been set up with lights and cameras; the boys said it was for a Greek-language film that was being shot in Sarandë.

The town's main streets rose in tiers behind the harbour. Broad flights of steps linked the tiers. One flight went to Sarandë's theatre. By the entrance, a billboard read: Socialist Culture a Great Active Force for the Advancement of the Fatherland (*Kultura Socialiste Forcë e Madhe Aktive për Përparimin e Atdheut*). On the roof, its letters silhouetted against the sky, was *Lavdi PPSH*.

At the top of the steps, we came to what seemed to be the main street. In front of us was a large building fronted by palm trees. Two policemen in blue uniforms and peaked caps stood outside. A rooftop slogan read: Glory to the works of Comrade Enver Hoxha (*Lavdi veprës se shokut ENVER HOXHA*). Over the entrance, a full-length portrait of Comrade Enver in a silver-grey suit smiled down on passers-by. His right arm was raised in greeting. Then we had to jump smartly out of the way to avoid being run down by the local cycling team.

The street opened onto a pleasant square with trees and villas. The setting sun gave the buildings a mellow orange tinge, and you got a fleeting sense of what Sarandë must have been like before communism. A handsome 1930s villa had a picture of Ramiz Alia on its façade and *Rroftë PPSH* on the roof. There was no signage, but when we got closer we realised it was a bookshop. Inside, there were the usual piles of books by Enver Hoxha and Ramiz Alia, but the difference here was that many had been translated into Greek. I bought a Greek version of a speech Hoxha had made in November 1984 to mark the fortieth anniversary of Albania's liberation. On the front was a suited, bespectacled ENBEP XOTZA.

We continued up the steps into one of the newer neighbourhoods. They were mostly five-storey apartment blocks; some had been rendered, others were bare brick. Dirt tracks ran between the blocks. Before communism, this must have been a desirable part of town and a number of older stone mansions had survived. Some even had gardens. Despite the density of the housing, it was surprisingly green. There were trees along the tracks and ivy had colonised derelict buildings, smothering windows and cascading off roofs. Through a gap we could see down to the main street where a slogan, *LAVDI MARKSIZEM LENINIZMIT*, glimmered in the gloom.

As the light faded, Sarandë came back to life. Shops had reopened and people were strolling and chatting. They were mostly civilians but there was also a smattering of soldiers in green caps and uniforms. We passed a tailor's where women were bent over sewing machines making up suits from paper patterns. Outside a shoe shop, policemen were struggling to control an excited crowd. Someone told us it was pay day and it had coincided with a delivery of new shoes. And sure enough, a young woman emerged from the shop on platform shoes with hefty heels, the kind of footwear that had been fashionable in London fifteen years previously.

On the drive yesterday, Pepi had explained a bit about prices and wages. An average worker earned around 650 leks a month, about £60. A "higher cadre" who had more responsibility got up to 750 leks. Wage levels also reflected education and length of service. Although Albanians are poor by Western standards, they don't pay tax and food prices are subsidised: a kilo of bread costs 2 leks, a kilo of sugar 8 leks, a kilo of meat about 15 leks. Luxury items like TVs and cassette players were, as Pepi put it, "a little bit expensive". Those shoes were definitely a luxury item. They cost 290 leks, about £25, getting on for half a month's wage.

I bought a paper cone of sticky caramel sweets in a grocery store. Behind the counter were bags of flour, bottles of pickled peppers, tomato purée and a variety of jams - plum, apricot, orange - selling for 5 leks a bottle. Further down the street, women were queuing for olive oil; very sensibly, you brought back your empty bottle and it was refilled from a barrel. There was plenty of fresh fruit and vegetables: leeks, peas, beans, apples, quinces. When you had made your purchase, the vegetables were wrapped in newspaper. We went into a clothes shop where people were looking at shirts: plain ones cost between 50 and 60 leks; striped ones up to 110 leks. Cardigans were even more expensive at 260 leks. If you wanted to make your own clothes, you could buy material by the metre; the most expensive was tartan at 180 leks.

As we walked back to the hotel, we passed another revolutionary poster - there were a lot of them in Sarandë. This one showed a young woman with a pickaxe across her shoulders standing among hills that had been planted with fruit trees. The slogan read: Our Youth are Inspired by the Needs of the Fatherland (*KU KA NEVOJE ATHDHEU MOTIV I RINISE SONE*). A young man passed us with a cassette player on his shoulder playing music that sounded suspiciously like reggae. Then we heard pinging. In a small act of rebellion, youths with catapults were firing stones at the road signs. In the bay, spotlights on the water were a reminder to any would-be defector to think twice before planning an escape.

2019

Although modern Sarandë is no longer the little town it once was, its seafront is still delightful. The promenade is lined with cafés, restaurants and souvenir shops. There are gardens and lots of statues, communist and post-communist.

That sense of continuity is also noticeable in the town. Sarandë's two main streets, Rruga Flamurit and Rruga Skënderbeu, were laid down in the 1930s during King Zog's reign. Both continue to be the core of the modern settlement. Zog's influence remains strong. As well as the streets, Zog built the harbour, the promenade and parades of villas along the seafront. Sarandë was renamed Zogaj in his honour. Development brought an increase in population. A census taken in 1927 recorded 810 residents. A decade later numbers had swelled to 1,800. When the communists took power, Sarandë became an administrative centre with a Bashkia, Communist Party offices, a theatre and Post Office. The Post Office is on Rruga Flamurit and still has its communist-era symbol above the entrance: a fusion of bugle, lightning bolts and a five-pointed star. Next to the Post Office is the Archaeological Museum. It was built in the 1960s when excavations for the Post Office uncovered a fine fifth-century Roman mosaic floor. Rather than move the mosaic, the authorities built a museum over it and preserved the original 1930s street plan.

I had two photos that must have been taken in Rruga Flamurit or Rruga Skënderbeu. In one, a crowd has gathered outside a Këpucë Sandale, a shoe shop. The other shows two cobblers. Both shops have signs saying Riparim Këpucësh (Shoe Repairs) and a set of initials, NRSh, which stood for Ndërmarrja e riparim-shërbimeve (Repair-Service Enterprise). The shops look run-down. Curtains hang from broken fittings. A chunk of concrete is missing from over one of the doorways. By 1988, Albania's economy was in crisis. You can see the neglect in the photos.

Both Rruga Flamurit and Rruga Skënderbeu are short streets, and you would have thought it would be easy to find the old shops. It wasn't. Because the streets were terraces, there was little to distinguish one shop unit from another. Renovation on Rruga Flamurit made it even more difficult. Crumbling brickwork had been restored. Every shop had a full-length plate glass window and a red awning.

We eventually decided that the best match for the two cobblers were a *farmaci* and a *foto* shop on Rruga Flamurit. True, the modern façades were rusticated - they weren't in the original photo - and the plasterwork above the shop fronts was more ornate. But it was hot and easy enough to persuade yourself that these changes had been part of the renovation.

The shoe shop had definitely been on Rruga Skënderbeu. Unlike Rruga Flamurit, Rruga Skënderbeu had not been renovated. It was even a little bohemian, a street in transition,

1988: The shops are different....

2019: ...but otherwise, the street is much as it had been thirty years ago.

close enough to the shore to benefit from the tourist boom, but far enough away for traditional businesses to survive. Boutiques with names like New York Collection, Anima and Paranoia shared the street with a paint shop, a shop selling second-hand electrical appliances and a motor parts store. I was sure that Këpucë Sandale was now Hackett London. The shop had replicated Hackett's logo of two furled umbrellas and a bowler hat. (Hackett has a number of overseas branches, but there's no mention on its website of any outlets in Albania.) The unit to the left was derelict. The one to the right had been a Kinkaleri, a haberdashery. It now sold office equipment, but if you looked closely, you could see the imprint of the old communist lettering across the front.

Rruga Flamurit and Rruga Skënderbeu converge on what is now Sheshi Nënë Tereza. It's a paved, triangular space with a park on its northern side. We were looking for two buildings: the one with that outsize portrait of Enver Hoxha and the old bookshop. After about a hundred metres, we came to the Bashkia. Trees made it hard to see the whole building, but it seemed to be the same size and shape as the one in the photo. The façade wasn't quite the same, but it wouldn't be surprising if, at some point since the end of communism, the building had been upgraded. I took a couple of photos and we moved on.

We were now looking for the bookshop. According to a tourist map we'd bought, there was a bookshop only a few metres from the Bashkia. We walked up and down the street, but all the developments were new and we saw nothing remotely resembling the building in my photo. We stopped at the new bookshop; if anyone was going to know where the old one was, it would be someone with an interest in books.

A woman came to talk to us. I showed her the photos and she went through them, sorting them into two piles: *ekziston* and *nuk ekziston* - it exists, it doesn't exist. The bookshop and the Enver Hoxha building went onto the *nuk ekziston* pile. Of the others, she confirmed that the shoe shop had been on Rruga Skënderbeu. She pointed to the window above the Kinkaleri - she lived there, that was her apartment. She

1988: Sarandë's Communist Party HQ was demolished....

2019: ...and became a Friendship Park. The palm trees survived.

was less certain about the cobblers, but she thought that one of them was now a café called Bar 21, also on Rruga Skënderbeu. I said we'd go and have another look. The mural of the young woman with a pickaxe was also on the *ekziston* pile. The mural, she said, had been by the harbour, opposite what was now Bar Limani.

So what about those *nuk ekziston* photos, where had they been? She pointed back up the street to Sheshi Nënë Tereza. The building with the portrait of Enver Hoxha wasn't the Bashkia. It had been the Communist Party headquarters. It was *prishur*, destroyed, and the site had been turned into Parku Miqësia, Friendship Park. The bookshop was also *prishur*. It too had been in the square. Where it had stood there was now a bank; we couldn't miss it because it had a *fasade xhami*, a glass façade.

Suddenly we could see what had happened. It was astonishing, a total transformation. A branch of Credins bank with a blue glass façade had replaced the bookshop. But it wasn't just the bookshop that had been demolished. All the buildings in the photo had gone. The mansions to the left had been replaced by a glass and concrete tower belonging to the American Bank of Investment. And then there was the park where the Communist Party building had been. I realised with a lurch that the steps up the park were the same as the ones in the photo. The wall and palm trees that had been in front of the building had also survived.

The steps were disquieting. I couldn't work out if they were innocuous or malevolent, but once you knew what they were they exerted a kind of fascination. It was tempting to invest them with symbolic significance. What went through the minds of older citizens when they saw them? Did they choose to avoid them, wary of the memories they might stir up? Or had they been deliberately left there, proof that the old regime was well and truly dead?

We stopped for something to eat at Taverna Leo on the steps opposite the theatre. It was run by a man called Almet, and when we'd finished, I showed him the old photo of the theatre. It took a few moments for it to sink in. First surprise, then amusement. He flicked through the photos and then took me inside to a back room where some policemen were having a late lunch. They were very friendly and asked me to join them for a beer. I spread the photos on the table and their response was like Almet's: momentary blankness, then recognition as something clicked, a recalibration, a shift of gears, and the old world came back into focus. The photos made them laugh in a *can you believe it?* kind of way, *was it really like that?* The older policeman knew most of the places and was keen to show off his knowledge. He read out the slogans on the theatre and Communist Party building; they were clearly familiar to him and they rolled off his tongue, almost like incantations. Even the portrait of Enver Hoxha only raised a wry smile. There seemed to be an acceptance of what had been.

Almet had been hovering while the policemen looked at the photos. When I got up to go, he clambered onto a chair - Almet was not tall and liked his food - and took a wooden plaque down from the wall. It had an Albanian eagle stencilled on it and he gave it to me. Reciprocity. I had shown him the pictures, I had to be given something in return. As we walked out, Almet took me by the arm and said in a low voice, *Shqipëria nuk është e mirë*, Albania isn't good. He'd been running the restaurant for ten years, but he'd had enough. He had plans to join his son in Greece and start a new life.

We found Bar Limani on the seafront and started to walk along Rruga Jonianet which runs along the shore. The street had become a prime target for redevelopment. Many of the 1930s villas had been demolished to make way for hotels, but not all of them. On the corner opposite the Lion Gate Hotel was an ice-cream bar called Kayak. It occupied the ground floor of one of the old villas. The mural had been on its wall.

In the old photo, the parade was run-down but still handsome. It had a rusticated ground floor, plaster mouldings along the roofline and terracotta roof tiles. Since then, it had been adapted for the new economic order. As well as the ice-cream bar, the upper floor had been converted into a holiday apartment with a protruding balcony that distorted the profile of the original building. And there was still a mural on the wall, not a woman with a pickaxe, but goggle-eyed minions eating ice cream. Thirty years on, the wall was still doing the same job.

Kayak was owned by a man called Xaris. His dad was Albanian, his mum Greek, but he identified as Greek. He had opened his shop in 2012 when "things had settled down". He'd called it Kayak because he was a keen kayaker. Xaris was five in 1988 when the photo had been taken, but he said he remembered the mural. I showed him the pictures of Rruga Flamurit and Rruga Skënderbeu. He remembered them too, except he called them Street 1 and Street 2. He pointed across the bay to all the redevelopment. It was hard to remember that until 2000, with the exception of Hotel Butrinti and Varrezat e Dëshmorëve (the Martyrs' Cemetery), all that had been mountain and olive groves.

When the old regime collapsed, Xaris' parents had started a mussel farm in Ksamil, but it hadn't worked out and they'd gone to Athens. Xaris spent summers in Sarandë and winters in Greece with his parents. He liked summertime Sarandë; when business was slow he could swim and kayak. The water was clean and cold where the Bistricë river flowed into the bay.

And what about relations between ethnic Greeks and Albanians in Sarandë? Sometimes there were difficulties, he said, and left it at that.

I asked if I could take a photo of him and his shop, and Xaris posed with a chocolate ice cream. Then he asked if he could have a picture of the mural. He thought his mum and dad would like to see it.

The photo of the cobblers was still niggling, so we took another stroll along Rruga Flamurit. It was late afternoon and Sarandë was stirring after its siesta. The *foto* shop had reopened; its owner was sluicing down the pavement outside.

When he'd finished, I said I had a photo of his shop from 1988. He studied it for a few moments and then summoned his granddaughter who had better eyes and could read the signage. After a chat with his granddaughter, he turned to us and said it wasn't his shop. He thought my picture was of the barber's further down the street, and just so there was no confusion, he came with us to explain. The barber was in mid-cut, but he stopped to look at the photo. The other customers came over to look and the man whose haircut had been interrupted swivelled round so he could see too. There was a lot of discussion and slowly a consensus emerged, led by the man in the chair. We were in the wrong street. We needed to go up a level, to Rruga e Skënderbeu and look there. I wasn't convinced but we took the advice.

We'd already been up and down Skënderbeu several times. Its shops and houses were a random lot of varying heights and designs, and we hadn't seen anything that matched the photo. We looked again. Opposite Hackett London was a row of two-storey villas. Two units had been modernised with new windows and a third-floor extension. The others were in their original state. The more I looked, the surer I was that the modernised units had been the two cobblers. The downpipes matched. The windowsills matched. The wall brackets for holding flags matched. One of the units was a clothes boutique. The other was a café. The woman in the bookshop had been right. It was Bar 21.

It was a steep climb up to the newer neighbourhoods. I had three photos taken somewhere up here. One showed apartment blocks and a stone villa with a rough track running up the hillside. Another was much the same, except it had washing hanging from a lamp post. The third was a view across rooftops with the slogan, *LAVDI MARKSIZEM LENINIZMIT*, in red letters. Given all the new building, there seemed little chance of finding the spots where I'd taken the photos, but I tried to think it through. It was likely that Dag and I had used one of the flights of steps between Rruga Skënderbeu and the two higher roads, Rruga Onhezmi and Rruga Lefter Talo. So we concentrated on the areas around the steps; but each time I thought I'd found a match, something didn't fit: the wrong balcony, the wrong street plan, seemingly the right apartment but in the wrong place. We needed help.

A restaurant on Rruga Lefter Talo had been built onto the front of an old villa. There were some empty tables so we stopped to eat. After the meal, I got out the photos and showed them to the young man who'd brought us our food. His name was Emmanouel. He was twenty-six and for several years had worked on ships sailing out of Otranto. He spoke very good English. The restaurant, he said, was a family business named after his dad, Haxhi. His mum did the cooking, he looked after the restaurant, and his dad.... well, these days, Haxhi spent a lot of time in front of the telly. For most of the evening, he'd been glued to a Hits of the '80s Channel. Eventually, Emmanouel persuaded Haxhi to look at the photos. Haxhi put on glasses which had a little light attached to them. But even after close scrutiny, he couldn't say for sure where they'd been taken.

Haxhi had been born in 1958. As a young man, he was a champion swimmer, the second best in butterfly in the whole of Albania. In 1976, he represented Albania in games held in China. When he began working, he became a driver taking mussels and eels from Sarandë to Tirana. The refrigerated lorry he drove had been imported from West Germany. I asked how long the journey took. There and back was between twelve and thirteen hours. He'd leave early in the morning, get to Tirana by mid-day and then drive back to Sarandë. It was hard work - he mimed turning the steering wheel on the winding roads - and you got very little money. I said there were places closer to Tirana where there was fishing, Vlorë for instance. Haxhi became momentarily intense and told Emmanouel to translate. He wanted to tell us that there were currents in the Corfu Channel that made the water around Sarandë ideal for fish: the best fish in Albania, he said, came from Sarandë.

6: SARANDË, BUTRINT AND KSAMIL

As the tables emptied, Emmanouel's mother, Eva, emerged from the kitchen. As well as Emmanouel, she had two daughters. One was still in school and had just started learning English; the other worked in a Special Needs day school in the town. Eva's sister had moved to Scotland; she was toying with the idea of sending her younger daughter to finish her education there. She'd need a visa and visas were expensive. But all in all, life was certainly better now than it had been during communism. Back then, said Haxhi, you could be jailed for saying "this beer isn't good" and your family could be moved somewhere far away. On the other hand, society was more level. Everyone had work, education was good, crime was low.

Back at the hotel, I took some photos of Sarandë and Kodrra. The promenade had become a glittering ribbon of light. The Orthodox church gleamed under floodlights. Below us was the Finix Night Club and its neon logo, a naked woman lying on her stomach with her legs in the air. It was a far cry from Sarandë in 1988. In the old photo of Kodrra, its apartment blocks were silhouetted against the sky and lights shone from their windows. Since then, those older blocks had been submerged in an arc of new building that peaked at the crown of the hill and then fell away on each side. In the main, the new builds were for visitors not residents. Out of season, most of them were empty. Having been one of the brightest neighbourhoods in communist Sarandë, modern Kodrra was almost dark.

The next morning we had one last go at the three unmatched photos. We walked back along Rruga Skënderbeu to Bar 21. Two men were sitting having coffee. I explained about the old photos, and they invited us to join them. One of them, Artan, owned the motor parts shop opposite the café and had lived in Sarandë all his life. His friend Arti was from Lushnjë. The two of them looked through the photos. So much, said Arti, was *ish-*, ex-: *ish-biblioteka*, *ish-riparim këpucësh*, *ish-kafene* next to *ish-biblioteka*. Arti didn't like the speed or degree of Sarandë's redevelopment; it had grown too much too quickly. He reckoned the town's resident population was about 30,000. In summer it swelled to 200,000, an almost sevenfold increase. "It was," he said in English, "too many people." And then in winter, most of the apartment blocks and hotels were empty, so whole neighbourhoods were like ghost towns.

While Arti was talking, Artan had been studying the photos and he was sure he knew the location of one of them. The photo of the apartment blocks, stone villa and track had been taken from the *shkallë* linking Rruga Telat Noga and Rruga Lefter Talo. He showed me where it was on the map. He thought the other two photos had been taken lower down the same *shkallë*. Armed with our new intelligence, Kirstie and I carried on up the hill. It took a few moments to make sense of the junction. A narrow asphalt road continued up the hillside – that was the track in my photo. On the left, the stone villa had grown upwards and outwards. It now had an upper floor and a front extension with balconies facing the street. We would never have found it if we hadn't been told where to look, and I marvelled at Artan's visual memory. We never found the other two.

Himarë: a community under threat 2019/2021

Xaris reckoned that around 40 per cent of Sarandë's population were ethnic Greeks. The percentage was higher up the coast where three villages - Himarë, Dhermi and Palasë - had Greek majorities. The largest of the three was Himarë with a population of around 2,500. It seemed a good place to go for a Greek perspective.

Himarë is about fifty kilometres from Sarandë. We booked into a guest house in Old Himarë; in the morning our host, Oresti, sat with us on the terrace and gamely answered our questions in a mixture of Greek, Albanian and English. He lent us a *Tourist Guide of Himarë*, produced by Himarë's

Bashkia, which sketched in the region's history from a Greek point of view. It highlighted Himarë's independence from Ottoman rule and its hostility towards the Albanian state. Only days before Albania's declaration of independence, a Himariot soldier, Spyros Spyromilios, took control of Himarë and held it until the Greek army arrived in November 1912. For a few months in 1914, what was now officially southern Albania declared itself the Autonomous Republic of Northern Epirus. When Greek forces returned in December 1940, Himariots greeted them enthusiastically. In December 1945, Himarë boycotted a plebiscite to legitimise the incoming communist government. Local leaders were arrested and Greek schools closed. So how had things changed since the end of communism? Had life become easier for Albania's Greek communities?

Oresti knew a lot about his village. His family had always lived in Himarë. His ancestors had been farmers growing wheat, grapes and olives. The house had been in his family for three hundred years. During communism, their land had been confiscated and farmed cooperatively, but they had been allowed to keep the house. When the system changed in 1991, because there was no written record of the family's land holdings, they were unable to claim full restitution. But they were given two small plots: one with olives, the other with lemons and mandarins.

One morning, Oresti asked if we'd like a tour of Old Himarë. He took us along the southern edge of the village, through arches and along a vaulted passage. He showed us a hole in the wall made by a shell fired from an Italian warship during the Second World War. Spyros Spyromilios' mansion overlooked the bay. It was derelict and padlocked, but the gate had disintegrated and it was easy enough to get inside. It was a huge place with rooms for family and servants, its wings linked by stone stairways. In a courtyard, there was an oil press with a cogged wheel and three hefty millstones. Oresti told us that the last of Spyromilios' direct line - a mother and her son - had been living in the house in the early years of the last century. During the Liberation War, the son had been a partisan and was killed in the fighting. After 1991, the house had been returned to the family. Oresti said that they were trying to sell it: the last price he'd heard was €80,000, but that was a few years ago and he thought the price had probably gone up since then.

Some houses, like Oresti's with views over the olive groves and the sea, had been converted into holiday accommodation. But the main part of the village was on the eastern side by the church where there were some small shops and cafés. Oresti thought that about forty houses were occupied all year round. During communism, more than a hundred families had lived in the old town. It had had its own school - you could see it behind the Alpet filling station. Oresti had been to school there; he reckoned there'd been about 150 pupils. Nowadays, Greek-speaking children went to the school next to the church.

There were a huge number of churches in Old Himarë. In the late fifteenth century, Himarë had been at the centre of what the booklet called the Autonomous Keravnian Commonwealth. It became a magnet for Orthodox Greeks and every family settling in the town had built their own church. When the Greek missionary saint, Kosmas of Aetolia, visited Himarë at the end of the eighteenth century, he counted at least a hundred and fifty churches. Kosmas advised Himariots to stop building churches and concentrate on schools.

Most of the churches were derelict, some barely recognisable as churches at all, but a few had been given state protection and were being restored. I asked Oresti what had happened to them during communism. He said that most of the ones in the old town were too inaccessible to be useful. Some had been vandalised during the atheist campaigns in 1967. The main church by the school, the Church of All Saints, had been used as a warehouse. It had reopened in 2006. Oresti added that there were only two Orthodox priests for the whole of Himarë.

To the west of the castle, a deep ravine, Kanioni i Vishës, was where the Greek army had halted its advance in 1940. More recently, the canyon had acted as a firebreak, protecting Himarë during forest fires earlier in the year. Oresti said that one of the effects of the fires had been to detonate unexploded ordnance.

When we got back to the guesthouse, I showed Oresti the old photos of Sarandë. He didn't comment directly on them, but they gave him a context to talk in more general terms about the Greek community. When the borders opened in 1990, many of Albania's ethnic Greeks emigrated, or found work in Greece and began sending back remittances. Albanian Greeks had Greek passports and could claim Greek pensions. Oresti had a Greek passport; he went to Greece to get his (free) Covid jabs.

Open borders have had contradictory effects. On the one hand, increased numbers of Greeks coming to live and work in Albania have increased awareness among Greek Albanians of what it is to be Greek. At the same time, mass emigration has reduced Greek influence within Albania. The community was shrinking. Only Himarë, Dhermi and Palasë had the numbers to maintain Greek language and culture. Qeparo, fifteen kilometres to the south, had once had a Greek majority but most of its Greeks had left. If you visit Qeparo today, said Oresti, you're unlikely to hear any Greek being spoken.

We got another Greek perspective from Spiros, who ran a guesthouse on the outskirts of Himarë. When I showed him the photos, his first reaction was surprise: surprise that we'd been able to visit Albania, surprise that we'd been able to take photos: "wasn't someone with you? didn't they try to stop you?" He was even more surprised by the photos of the apartment blocks; he couldn't believe we'd been allowed to wander without supervision.

Then he started looking more carefully at the images: "Oh man, we were so poor!" Spiros was particularly interested in the clothes. He was convinced that the woman outside the bookshop was Greek because her cardigan had a V-shaped pattern on the shoulders. You didn't get that kind of knitwear in Albania. Spiros reckoned that relatives had sent it from Greece. One of Spiros' cousins had been accused of being a spy and had been jailed by the communists. Eventually the Albanian government agreed to swap him for an Albanian spy being held in Greece. Spiros remembers the man coming to visit them in 1988. The thing that stayed with him was not the fact that he'd been a spy; it was his clothes: "he was dressed differently", said Spiros. Before he left, Spiros' family persuaded the man to leave them his clothes.

In 1988, Spiros had been fourteen. He said that young people like him admired foreigners, but if you talked to them it could land you in trouble. Everyone was watching everyone else; one in three people were "snitches". I said we had been into shops in Sarandë and bought things. Spiros said that in every shop, a member of Sigurimi, the state security service, would be working there too, and that shopkeepers were told how to talk to foreigners if one came in.

Then he became a bit more positive. Albania had been poor, he said, but it was also beautiful. The air was clean, there were no cars, there were flower gardens, it was safe for kids. All the kids played together, they enjoyed football or did gymnastics, there was no rich or poor, just people from the town or from the country. In that sense, he said, old Albania would have been a good place for his kids to grow up.

Although both Spiros' parents were Greek, he'd been born in Shkodër. This was because his mother's family had a "bad biography". When the Liberation War began, some members of the Greek community, including Spiros' maternal grandmother, joined a guerrilla organisation called MAVI which stood for Metopo Apeleftherosis Voriou Ipírou, the Liberation Front for Northern Epirus. MAVI had links with EDES, a right-wing resistance group active across the border in Greek Epirus. When the communists came to power, his mother's family were exiled to the north.

Spiros' father had trained as an engineer and was sent to Vau i Dejës to work on the hydroelectric scheme. Vau i Dejës is close to Shkodër. His mum and dad met "because Greeks have a way of finding other Greeks". Spiros had been born on Christmas Day. His mum wanted to call him Christos, but the name was forbidden. There were specific names the Greek minority could use, so he was named Spiros. He showed me a grainy black and white photo of himself and his sister which he had on his phone.

The family spoke Greek at home, but all Spiros' schooling was in Albanian. The authorities, Spiros said, wanted everyone to think and talk in Albanian. It was a way of suppressing the Greek community; they wanted to deprive them of their language. "Bastards!"

Schoolchildren could go to libraries and read books about the old times, but really it was a propaganda society - "propaganda was so deep". Every week students had classes in "political information" where they were told about problems around the world, particularly in the Middle East and Gaza. At the end of the lesson, students were told that "Albania was the only free and happy country". Spiros conceded that maybe the older generation believed the propaganda, especially those who had fought in the National Liberation War. But for younger people like him, they could see through it.

Of course, things had improved since 1990. Greeks now had their own schools and their own political party. But Spiros was uncomfortable with the way post-communist Albania was going, especially the attitude of Albanians towards Greeks. He thought this was a particular problem in Sarandë and Himarë where the Greek population had never been officially recognised. In Albanian eyes, said Spiros, Himariot Greeks are ethnic Albanians who happen to speak Greek. Respect was important: "Albanians don't show Himariot Greeks enough respect."

I asked if he'd ever thought about going to live in Greece. He pulled a face. Himarë, like most of Albania, was suffering from depopulation. Spiros had a Greek passport, but he had his business here in Himarë and it was doing OK. He had an Albanian wife who taught at the Albanian school in the village. His main concern was his kids' education. He could send them to a Greek school or an Albanian school, but neither was much good. The Greek school had teachers from Greece, but they were poor quality: "who wants to come from Greece to work here?"

Then he laughed. If he was ever feeling nostalgic for the old days, he looked at North Korean films on YouTube. Maybe one day he'd go there to see the statues and propaganda. They were even stricter than Albania and treated their leaders like gods. Imagine if Enver Hoxha's son was in charge of Albania now...

7: Dropull and Gjirokastër
"Two Friendly Peoples"

Dropull: beauty and mistrust
1988

As the road zigzagged up and out of Sarandë, it passed a marker stone: Tirana 280 kilometres. We won't be going that far today, we'll spend the night at Fier, but we still have a long drive ahead. I got a seat by the window, notebook open, and for the first part of the journey scribbled away, pen slipping as the coach lurched. I noted that new olive groves had been planted on the hillsides above Sarandë and that inland there were animal stockades, more olive terraces and bunkers galore. The plain was gridded with irrigation channels. We passed the grey concrete tanks of a fish farm on the Bistricë river. I noted that the river had been canalised and that the water flowed swiftly along a concrete channel next to the road. The river was also used for hydroelectric power with pipe-runs on the hillside.

Without a proper understanding of the way Albania functioned, it became even more important to wring as much information as I could from the landscape. I felt obliged to record it, absorb it and then interrogate it. But it was an impossible task. How do you decide what to record and what not to record? Maybe it's better just to sit back and let the landscape wash over you.

The plain narrowed and the road entered a wooded gorge. We began to climb. Through trees, we glimpsed a small lake that Pepi called Blue Eye. Its surface was smooth as a mirror. We were now deep in the mountains and still climbing. To our left was a vast, misshapen bowl, chaos on a grand scale, a jumble of vegetation and orange sandstone carved by wind and rain into outlandish shapes. Across the valley, PARTI ENVER had been cut into the hillside. Then the road began to descend, gently at first and then more precipitously. It clung to the mountain edge, twisting back and forth. Tilted rock strata, seemingly frozen at the moment when they were about to break free and crash onto the valley floor, added to the sense of vertigo. Almost unbelievably, a laden donkey train was inching its way across the rock. And at every corner, just when it seemed that the road was going to stop in mid-air, we got glimpses of the Plain of Dropull. It was extraordinarily beautiful, a patchwork of pale green fields and brown earth laid out with mathematical precision. Everything about it - its flatness, its fertility, its regularity - contrasted with the mountains we'd just crossed. As we descended hairpin by hairpin, the river unfroze, trees started to move in the breeze, and we could see that the plain was dotted with bunkers. There were dozens of them arranged in defensive lines along the borders of the fields.

2019

Kirstie and I left Sarandë after breakfast, as our Albturist group had done in 1988. But that was as far as similarities went. The marker stone at the foot of the hill had long gone. The olive groves above Sarandë had disappeared under hotels and apartments. They spilled over the ridge at Gjashtë and down onto the plain. Strung along the road were warehouses to feed the building boom. Everything you needed was right here: bricks, steel mesh and girders, wood, tiles, sanitary equipment, air conditioning units, water tanks, windows, solar panels. It wasn't until we got to Vrion, about six kilometres inland, that the development tailed off.

The old cooperative fields had been broken down into smallholdings with greenhouses and vineyards. On the outskirts of Çlirim, a *Kantina e Verës* specialised in local red wines. There was also a lot of fallow land. Terraces had fallen into disrepair. A concrete water channel, supported on stilts to span a shallow valley, had cracked. Stagnant ponds had formed where irrigation channels had silted up. But the canalised Bistricë still ran swiftly next to the road and it still powered two hydroelectric plants, privatised in 2013 and now run by a Turkish company, Kurum.

Until 2022 when a new road linking Sarandë to Gjirokastër had opened, this road over the pass at Qafa e Muzinës had been Sarandë's main connection with the interior. It was narrow, steep and had to carry a lot of traffic. You could easily get stuck behind a truck struggling with the gradient, and because it was so busy, it was difficult to stop. I photographed the *PARTI ENVER* mountain from the car. Then we pulled off at Muzinë for a better view of Blue Eye. I couldn't match the old photo exactly, but from where we were standing we could see along the lake to the sluice gate at its southern end.

Qafa e Muzinës is a dramatic and barren stretch of road. In September 1943, a battle was fought here between Partisan battalions and a German Alpine division. A *lapidar* opposite a disused petrol station commemorates the clash. Then the road begins its descent to Fusha e Dropullit, the Plain of Dropull. In 1988, I was so blown away by the view that I took four photos, which back then was an extraordinarily profligate use of film. It's still one of my favourite views in southern Albania. As we descended, Kirstie hung out of the car window and took a burst of photos. By chance one was almost an exact match.

Then we had another bit of luck. About two-thirds of the way down, there was a lay-by where the view matched another of the old photos, one looking south towards the

Greek border at Kakavia. In the old photo, the plain stretches into the distance until it's absorbed in a blue haze. In the foreground you can see three large bunkers on the corner where the road branches to Sarandë. At least thirty smaller bunkers had been sited along field boundaries. One of the large bunkers was still there. The other two had been demolished; a pile of rubble looked like the remains of one of them. Most of the smaller bunkers had gone too. These days, two features above all dominate the view. At Glinë, on the far side of the valley, there's a sleek new bottling plant. And there's the motorway to Greece, cutting a broad path across the plain.

Although the border at Kakavia technically reopened in January 1985 as a "transit point", it remained closed to most Albanians. Border restrictions were lifted in May 1990, and by mid-1991 more than 3,000 people a day were crossing into Greece. By the end of the year, it was estimated that more than 100,000 Albanians, many of them ethnic Greeks, had left. There was another surge during the 1997 disturbances as Albanians crossed the border to escape the violence.

The border post couldn't cope with such large numbers and in the autumn of 1997, when the unrest had subsided, Greek and Albanian governments agreed a plan to modernise the border post and build a new highway from Kakavia to Gjirokastër. The highway was paid for by the EU and built by Greek contractors. It was completed in 2001. Since then, Kakavia has become one of Albania's busiest crossing points, used by transiting trucks as well as local traffic.

The highway has brought benefits to both countries, but when it opened, some ethnic Albanians regarded it with suspicion. Rather than seeing it as a step towards ending Albania's isolation, it was regarded as a salient - a Greek highway promoted by a Greek government giving Greece direct access to southern Albania and its ethnic Greek population. In the words of an academic[1] who has made a study of the highway, it became "incorporated within the nationalist tensions of the region". Those tensions had been fuelled by more than forty years of rhetoric from both sides of the border. Greece accused Albania of mistreating its ethnic Greek population. Hoxha railed against "Great-Greek chauvinism" and the Greek nationalists - he called them "Vorio-Epirotes" - who wanted Vorio Epirus (Northern Epirus) to be absorbed into Greece. Even now, thirty years since the fall of the old regime, it doesn't take much to rekindle that legacy of mistrust.

1988

On the plain, we could pick up speed (relatively speaking). In the foothills to the west we passed a string of villages that looked almost untouched by collectivisation. We could see Orthodox churches - or more accurately, buildings that had once been Orthodox churches. These, said Pepi, were the villages of the Greek minority. Pepi tells us that the villages have their own Greek-language schools and Greek-language newspaper and that they are loyal citizens of the state. We were frequent visitors to Greece; I'd been going ever since that first visit in 1972. Whenever Albania was mentioned, I tended to sympathise with the Greek view that Albania's Greek minority were harshly treated. Looking at these villages now, I'm not sure who to believe.

2019

I had pictures of two villages, both taken from the Albturist coach. When I got home, I just labelled them as "Greek minority village - Plain of Dropull". Road signage along the

---

1 Dimitris Dalakoglou: *The Road: An ethnography of the Albanian-Greek cross-border motorway* (2009), p.138.

highway was good, with placenames in Albanian and Greek. We drove slowly looking for matches, and soon enough we found the first one. It was Lugar/Λιουγκαρη.

Lugar was, still is, a pretty village. In the old photo, there is a mansion at the village centre and an Orthodox church to the south. Cooperative barns and warehouses overlook the fields between village and road. In modern Lugar, the mansion has been reroofed and the bell tower restored. There were new houses with blue plastic water tanks on the roofs. One of the farm buildings had been demolished and replaced by concrete pillars for a yet-to-be completed building. But the other ones were still there, partly hidden behind a new warehouse.

The second photo was of Goranxi/Καλογοραντζή about ten kilometres further north. It was bigger than Lugar with more than twenty mansions and a large Orthodox church. Goranxi had been the administrative centre for a cooperative farm. In July 1956, Enver Hoxha paid a visit. There's a photo of him surrounded by villagers in his memoir about Greeks and Albanians, *Two Friendly Peoples*. In a speech, he told villagers that "the Party gave them freedom, the land, schools in their mother tongue and all the rights which they enjoy today". He advised the traitors and their henchmen to stop agitating because "you no longer have teeth to bite what you call Vorio-Epiros".

Since 1988, many of the mansions had been refurbished, but the general look of the place had not changed that much. In my old photo, the land by the village entrance had been used for grazing and wood storage. It was now a garage and HGV depot.

Derviçan: a showcase village

There were 99 officially recognised Greek minority villages in southern Albania; 41 of them were in Dropull. Derviçan/ Δερβιτσάνη was one of the largest. During communism,

1988: The ethnic Greek villages of Dropull have been hit by large-scale emigration...

2019: ...and survive largely on remittances.

it had a population of around 1,800 and was a showcase community where visitors were brought to see how well the authorities treated the Greek minority. Bill Bland went in 1984 and was impressed by the new Palace of Culture which had an art gallery, a library and a restaurant, plus a theatre with seating for 470 and a revolving stage.

Since then, migration has reduced Derviçan's population to around 500, but it was still a functioning community with shops, cafés and a Post Office. It had a newish secondary school that was opened in 2010 by Sali Berisha. But plaques around the village showed how involved Greece had been in the town's post-communist renewal. The central park had been refurbished by SFEVA/ΣΦΕΒΑ, an Orthodox Greek pressure group that lobbied on behalf of Albania's ethnic Greeks. A statue of a woman from Derviçan in traditional wedding dress was a gift from American Greeks. On the north side of the square were two communist-era buildings. One was Derviçan's Palace of Culture which still functioned, restored with Greek money in 2000. Next to it was what used to be the Communist Party offices. A minimarket occupied the ground floor, while the upper floor was derelict.

As we walked around, people called out to us in Greek. They wanted to know where we came from and what we were doing. A group of elderly men sitting outside the Palace of Culture pointed to a plaque on a column by the entrance steps. I went to have a closer look. It celebrated 1821, the year of Greek independence.

Derviçan's main church was dedicated to the Dormition of the Virgin Mary. Inside, we were greeted by a woman who wanted to tell us about its history. She spoke in Greek and told us that services had been held here until 1967 when, like all religious institutions in Albania, the church had been closed. It had first been given to Derviçan's Communist Youth. Then it became a fertiliser warehouse. When the church reopened in December 1990, the service had been taken by Father Mihalis, the same priest who had taken the last liturgy before the church had been shut in 1967. Most of the interior fittings were new, but two frescoes had been recovered from the old church. One was St Eleftherios, the patron saint of childbirth. The other was a full-length portrait of St Kosmas of Aetolia who had told the Himariots to build more schools

Away from the main square, Derviçan had many elegant mansions with slate roofs and balconies. Some had been patched up, others left to rot. New houses filled the gaps, some flaunting the wealth of their owners with fancy balconies and pediments. A man stopped to tell us that one of his sons was an artist in Athens. He showed us a plaque by a doorway with a date, 1931, recording when the house had been built. The door was locked, and the man told us that the property belonged to a Greek family who had emigrated.

The road ended at the top of the village. We stopped by a garden planted with onions, potatoes and aubergines. There were wooden feeding troughs along the roadside for sheep. A man came out of the house. He saw us admiring his garden and asked if we'd like to join him for coffee. His name was Gregoris. He was sitting with an older friend, Michaelis, on his balcony which had a stupendous view over the plain. To the right of his house was a deep ravine. He said that during the winter it had been filled with snow.

I had the old photos in my pocket and they instantly recognised the two villages. I asked about the old road to the border. You could see a single strip of tarmac on some of the photos, but it didn't seem to continue south. Michaelis assured me that it had done. He knew, because in January 1991 hundreds of people from Dervitsani had gone to Kakavia and crossed into Greece.

Gregoris served us coffee, walnut *gliko* and small glasses of *tsipouro*. I said it was easier for me to speak Albanian and he didn't take offence. Both men had Greek passports. Michaelis told us that his two children were in Athens. His son was a dentist; his daughter was training to be a teacher. Gregoris' children were still living in Dervitsani; they had recently been to London and he showed us a picture of them posing by Tower Bridge. Right now, their wives were on holiday in

Nafplion with other women from Dervitsani. It was a bit of a joke in the village: how were the men supposed to cope while their wives were away?

Michaelis had retired, but Gregoris was still working; he was only fifty, a baby compared to his friend. He drove a digger and was working on the road improvements around Gjirokastër. Although Gjirokastër was only a few kilometres away, most villagers preferred to cross the border and go to Ioannina. Healthcare was better, they could use the university hospital; in the shops things might be a bit more expensive, but there was a lot more choice.

I asked about relations with Albanians. Gregoris said that Bulo on the other side of the valley was an Albanian village. So were Kordhocë and Lazarat. But there was no problem. He pointed to his garden where he had fresh vegetables; he could make *tsipouro* from his vines. Life wasn't perfect, but broadly speaking things were OK.

Gjirokastër: Enver Hoxha's long shadow
1988

From the plain, Gjirokastër didn't seem anything special. There were the usual apartment blocks and factories: food processing and knitwear, said Pepi, leather and cigarettes. We turned off the plain and roared up the hill into the main square. A banner strung along the front of the hotel read: Glory to the Shining Works of Comrade Enver Hoxha (*Lavdi Veprës së Ndritur të Shokut Enver Hoxha*). On the castle walls above the hotel was another slogan: *LAVDI PPSH*.

After lunch, we set off up a cobbled street. At the crossroads was an extraordinary triangular building, narrowed to accommodate the convergence of the roads but topped with a square upper floor which created an overhanging roof. I'd never seen anything like it. The building was at the centre of the old bazaar. Like everywhere in Albania, the bazaar was run-down, but that only added to its authenticity. You felt it had hardly changed since Ottoman times.

There had been some small efforts to smarten it up. Metal signs, ornate by Albanian standards, hung outside the shops. There was a *pastiçeri*, a tailor, a tobacconist and a shop selling schoolbooks. Men lounged against the shop fronts on the sunny side of the street and watched us go past. There was that sense again of an almost physical wall between us and them. At the bottom of the hill was a hard currency shop with tourist gifts - carpets, dolls, silverware and carved wood as well as cameras and cassette players. A crowd had gathered to admire a large red motorbike parked outside, available to anyone with a pocketful of pounds, francs, lira or marks. There were a lot of people hanging around.

As we continued up the hill, Pepi told us that Gjirokastër was famous for its mansions. Most of them had been built in the nineteenth century, but some were earlier. They had been lived in by Ottoman landowners and merchants. Some looked more like fortresses than homes, with massive stone walls and slate roofs. Further up the hillside, where the need for defence was less pressing, the architecture was more domestic. These mansions had arched entrances and shady balconies. Each mansion was unique. That was why, said Pepi, the state had declared Gjirokastër a "Museum City".

A cobbled street that traversed the mountain flank brought us to the Museum of the Anti-Fascist National Liberation War of Gjirokastër. The museum was in a mansion with a stone porch and a balcony jutting out over the road. There was another reason why this mansion was so important. On 16 October 1908, Enver Hoxha had been born here.

As well as the history, the museum gave us a chance to see inside one of these amazing mansions. For a few leks, I bought an English-language booklet about the museum with the inevitable quotation from Hoxha on the opening page. This one praised "the invincible fastnesses of the people who were fighting fiercely against fascism". The room where Hoxha was born had latticed shutters over the windows and an ornate fireplace. Upstairs, displays told the story of Albanian resistance to "fascist aggression". There was a radio that was used in secret during the war and a compass that had belonged to the "Hero I Popullit" Asim Zeneli. And there was plenty of Hoxha memorabilia: family photos; his pen, rifle and boots in a glass cabinet; one of his walking sticks hanging from a shelf.

Sometimes in Albania you have to pinch yourself and remember that this is 1988. This year back home, Tim Burton has directed *Beetlejuice* and the Hollies' *He Ain't Heavy, He's My Brother* has just been Number 1. In Albania, they are still reliving the Second World War.

2019

As you leave Derviçan, a sign over the road says *Καλό ταξίδι*, have a good trip, a last reminder (if one was needed) that you'd just been in a Greek village. The road followed the Drinos valley and we were soon in Gjirokastër where roadworks slowed traffic to a crawl.

Before we went into the old town, I wanted to go to the Martyrs' Cemetery. Gjirokastër's was next to the hospital. Overlooked by new apartment blocks and surrounded by trees, it would have been easy to miss. Rather than a declamatory public space, this cemetery felt more like a secret garden. It was exceptionally well kept. Grass had been mown and bushes trimmed. Each headstone had an asymmetric border painted a bright revolutionary red. The *lapidar* was a slim column supporting a broader concrete upright painted red. At the top was a black Albanian eagle and a five-pointed communist star. A horizontal slab had been etched with faces. The faces were idealised but sufficiently personalised - a woman with braids, a man with moustache - to make you think they were portraits of once-living people. The faces had been so lightly etched that they seemed to hang in the air like wraiths.

7: DROPULL AND GJIROKASTËR

Perhaps because of its unique connection with Enver Hoxha, Gjirokastër had a larger than usual number of *lapidars* spread through the town. On the outskirts, you are met by a stern-faced partisan carved from a block of stone. The caption below him reads:

Qyteti i gurtë mbeti në shekuj kala për liri.
This stone city has remained for centuries a fortress for freedom.

By the main square, a relief depicts a troupe of dancers and musicians - during communism, Gjirokastër had been famous for its folklore festivals. In the square, a *lapidar* commemorates Bule Naipi and Persefoni Kokëdhima. Both were partisans; both had been hanged in July 1944. A statue of Çerçiz Topulli stands outside Hotel Çajupi. Topulli fought against the Turks in the early years of the twentieth century and was declared "Hero i Popullit" by the communists. Outside the "Asim Zeneli" Gymnasium, a bas relief commemorates a skirmish between students and fascist occupiers in March 1942. Another, shaped like an obelisk, is dedicated to "the pioneers of Albanian education".

These were prestige monuments, declarations of the victory of communism. But Gjirokastër also had smaller, more domestic *lapidars* that commemorated people from specific neighbourhoods who died during the Liberation War. One in Dunavat depicted a partisan, but all the others were simple columns. There was one in Palorto near the Gymnasium. Wreaths had been laid at its base and a few people had gathered around it, old and young. Some of the older folk had communist lapel badges; others were wearing red neckties. A man came over to us and started to tell us about the *lapidar*. He was bright-eyed and wiry, with a straw hat to protect him from the sun. He spoke quickly and it was difficult to understand what he was saying. Then his granddaughter joined us and explained that her grandfather wanted to tell us about Fato Berberi, whose name was on the *lapidar*.

Fato was a student at the Gymnasium. She had long hair, and when the National Liberation War started, she cut it off and joined the partisans. She gave her hair to her grandmother and told her that when the war was over, she would come and reclaim it. Unfortunately, Fato was captured by the Fascists and hanged in August 1944. She was only seventeen. After her death, the government made her a "Heroinë e Popullit". The girl told us that her grandfather belonged to a Veterans Association; they had all come to remember Fato and the seventeen other students from the school who died during the war.

Clearly these *lapidars* were still potent, and it wasn't just the older generation who'd come to pay their respects. If there was one place in Albania where you might expect to find communist diehards, it would be here.

In 1993, Hoxha's mansion, which had housed the Museum of the Anti-Fascist National Liberation War, was rebranded as Gjirokastër's Ethnographic Museum. I had a photo of the cobbled street and museum entrance from 1988. Apart from the sign by the door that now said Muzeu Etnografik, little had changed. What we hadn't been told at the time was that the original nineteenth-century mansion where Hoxha was born was burned down in 1916 by the Greek army. When it was rebuilt in the 1960s, it incorporated design features copied from other mansions in the city.

I had the old museum leaflet with me. As we went from room to room, I could chart what had changed. Wall maps and diagrams illustrating the deployment of partisan brigades had been taken down. So had information about the founding of the Communist Party in Gjirokastër. Socialist Realist paintings on the first floor had been replaced by braided jeleks. But some of the old museum's less contentious exhibits had found a place in the new one. A collection of walking sticks had made the transition. So had scale models of some of the city's mansions. The old radio was still on display, but without its original label.

And within the displays there was no shortage of communist iconography: a wooden panel with a double-headed eagle and communist star; a tapestry with PPSh embroidered into it standing for Partia e Punës e Shqipërisë, the Party of Labour of Albania. Hoxha's boots and rifle had been removed - in their place were distaffs and embroidery - but Hoxha himself had not gone away. Two portraits of him were displayed by the entrance. One, heavily airbrushed, showed Hoxha as a young man. The other was a photograph of a portlier Hoxha as General Commander of the National Liberation Army.

Although Hoxha's original home had been burned down, the mansion that replaced it continues to be intimately associated with him. This was the house (or something like it) where he had been born and where he lived until he was eight. Was that enough to justify the portraits on historical grounds? Or was it a financial decision? Had enough time elapsed for Enver Hoxha to become a commodity, someone whose presence among the displays had commercial value?

In 1988, when our group was shown the room where Enver Hoxha was born, family portraits of Hoxha's mother, Gjylo, his father, Halil, and his uncle Hysen hung on the walls. The portraits had been replaced by muskets but otherwise the room was exactly as it had been. Even though the family home had been rebuilt as a grand Ottoman mansion, the sign over the doorway still described it as "Living Room, the birth room of Hoxha".

Enver Hoxha lived in Gjirokastër until he was nineteen. Many years later, he published a memoir, *Vite të vegjëlisë* (Childhood Years), which gives a romanticised account of his early life. Hoxha remembers cold winters and hot summers. He remembers a friend called Elmaz whose parents had a house with a shady terrace where the two boys did their homework. Hoxha had an older friend called Sotiri who drove an ox-cart. He describes his excitement at going to the market at Roskovec where Sotiri bought baskets of red grapes. On the way home, Enver ate so many he was sick.

On another occasion, Hoxha recalled how he had earned 25 leks by copying legal documents for a relative who was a lawyer in Fier.

The memoir has remarkably little to say about Hoxha's family. When he was still young, his father, Halil, and his older brother, Beqir, went to work in America. Hoxha's uncle Hysen oversaw his upbringing and schooling in a household which Enver shared with his three sisters. There is only one reference to his mother, Gylo. Hoxha mentions the Greek occupation several times, but there is only a single reference to the family home being burned down and no mention of where they went afterwards.

When we came out, I lined up a matching shot of the exterior. A young man was watching. He had a stall outside the museum where he sold old photos, communist-era books, T-shirts and tourist trinkets. I could see him looking at my photo. Then he saw the booklet: "Where did you get this?" It sounded almost accusatory.

Kavjol was nineteen. He was born in 1999, too late for even the briefest personal experience of communism, but he seemed fascinated by it. He was studying Economic Tourism at Gjirokastër's Eqrem Çabej University. Kavjol thought it was important to get a good education, but the facilities were poor. What made it worse was that most of his friends had gone to Tirana; there weren't many young people left in Gjirokastër and this was a big problem for him.

Kavjol knew a lot about Gjirokastër and the Hoxha mansion. He said that many of its holdings had been sold in 1990 when everything collapsed. I asked if he had ever been in the museum, and he said no. When potential customers came past he broke off our conversation and launched into a spiel based on his photos to give them a potted history of the town. He had an impressive selection of images, from Scanderbeg to Ali Pasha; from Ismail Qemali, Albania's first Prime Minister, to King Zog. He had at least five pictures of Enver Hoxha: as a young soldier, meeting the people, with his family, as an elder statesman in winter coat and trilby. He also had a picture of the enormous statue of a seated Enver Hoxha that had been inaugurated in 1986. In his photo, Hoxha's widow Nexhmije and other family members are standing in front of the statue.

I asked Kavjol where he'd got the Hoxha photos. They were, he said, mostly from books or from friends. His grandfather had a book of old postcards, but to Kavjol's annoyance he wouldn't let him copy any of them. He flicked through my photos, as if assessing their worth. He was interested in the ones with communist slogans, but the image that really caught his attention was the one of the museum. He had several communist-era pictures of the museum on his stall, but my shot was slightly wider and included the space in front of the building. In my picture, the space was empty. Now it had been built on; the house opposite the museum had used it for an extension. Kavjol gestured towards the house. They'd also put in a new window which irritated him. I said that I thought the old town was protected. "Ha," he said, "this is Albania."

I bought two of Kavjol's photos: one of Nexhmije in front of Hoxha's statue and a view of the city before the statue was erected. Kavjol thought the latter photo had been taken in the 1970s. At the centre was a neoclassical building with an arched façade. It was still there; it housed Gjirokastër's Court of Appeal. Next to it was the Palace of Culture built by the communists on the site of an old mansion – Museum City protection went only so far. The Palace of Culture had then been demolished to make way for the statue. When the statue was demolished in 1991, the site was returned to its original owners and became a restaurant.

I asked Kavjol if he'd like any copies of my photos. He didn't have a phone and he ran off to get a friend who had one. He laid the photos out on the pavement and his friend took pictures of the ones he wanted.

Shtëpia e Skëndulit, the Skënduli House, is one of Gjirokastër's finest mansions. It was built in 1826 by Skënder

Skënduli, an Ottoman administrator and landowner. After the communist takeover, the family continued to live in the house until 1981, when it was appropriated and turned into the Ethnographic Museum. The house was returned to the family in 1993 and they were now trying to make a living by showing people around it.

The current owner, Nesip Skënduli, was the eleventh generation of the family. He was an enthusiastic guide who spoke in a mixture of Italian and Albanian. The tour was heavy on numbers. The mansion, he told us, had forty doors, sixty-four windows, nine chimneys, seven fireplaces, six toilets and four bathrooms. The number of chimneys was significant; the more a building had, the higher the social status of its owner. On the ground floor, a huge cistern collected rainwater; it had a capacity of 130 cubic litres, equivalent to 130,000 litres of water. The larder was next to the cistern, so perishable goods could be kept cool. Down steps beneath the house, there was a bunker to protect the family in times of war.

We had not been taken to see the Ethnographic Museum in 1988, but I had a photo of its exterior - we had passed it on our way to the Hoxha mansion. After Nesip had finished his tour, I showed him the photo. By now Nesip had been joined by his grandson, Kristian, who spoke good English and helped with translation. The photo seemed to make Nesip angry. He told us that when the state had taken the house, they hadn't looked after it. The roof had leaked and some of the wall paintings had been damaged or whitewashed. He ran back into the house and a few moments later returned with a bulging pink folder which contained documents about the house.

Nesip was looking for a photograph. When he found it, he laid it on the wall. The photo had come from the National Film Archive in Tirana and showed his house with a double porch, two doorways set at right angles to each other. In my photo, ivy had smothered one of the doorways, but in Nesip's you could see them both. It was a handsome structure, an impressive entrance to an impressive house. At some point after 1988, the communists had decided to build a house on the corner next to the mansion. To make space, they demolished the porches. Volunteers had helped reconstruct the current entrance in the side alley, but it didn't compensate for the loss of the original porch. Although the family had got their house back, Nesip was still bitter at the way he and his house had been treated.

The Skënduli family had not supported the communists. They had owned 100 hectares of good farmland in the valley which had been taken from them and given to a cooperative. The land had not been returned. Nesip's argument was that if he had the land, he would have more income to look after the house. Otherwise, he had to rely on visitors paying 200 leks to look around. I asked about UNESCO and Gjirokastër's status as a World Heritage Site. Nesip laughed. His view was that the listing meant nothing without financial support. He didn't like the present government: it wasn't working for the people, there was corruption… It was the familiar litany of complaints. I put the rest of my photos on the wall but he wasn't interested. When his grandson Kristian read out the slogan on Hotel Cajupi - *Lavdi veprës së ndritur të Shokut Enver Hoxha* - Nesip made a dismissive gesture and busied himself with his paperwork. He didn't want to be reminded of the regime that had deprived him of his house and land.

One of Kavjol's photos was of children with hammers and chisels laying cobblestones. When Gjirokastër was declared a Museum City in 1961, renewing its cobbled streets became a national priority. Laying cobblestones is slow and laborious, and to speed up the process, the authorities - as they had done in Berat - decided to involve schoolchildren. They declared an *aksion* and every afternoon after lessons the children became *gurskalitësit e vegjel*, little stonemasons, and were set to work relaying the *kalldrëme* around their schools. The *aksion* continued from 1971 until 1980 when the authorities finally acknowledged that laying cobblestones was skilled work best left to craftsmen.

Gjirokastër is often called "the city of stone". The Albturist guidebook describes its mansions as "strange creatures with stone legs, stone body and stone head". Ismail Kadare called his wartime memoir about growing up in Girokastër *Kronikë në gur*, Chronicle in Stone. The city's *qilima guri*, its carpets of stone, have been celebrated in verse. They are one of the city's most distinctive features, especially in the old bazaar where white stones have been used to create diamond patterns.

I had some photos of the old bazaar. One is a view up the street to that wondrously eccentric triangular building. You can just see ENVER in the sky above a fortification to the west. In modern Gjirokastër ENVER has gone, shop fronts have been modernised, there are cars in the street and benches along the narrow pavements. But the cobblestones with their diamond patterns are still there, a tangible link between communist and post-communist eras.

I had other photos from around the bazaar. One was of the cobbled road to Dunavat as it climbs past Xhamia e Pazarit. On the mosque wall you can see part of a *Këndi i Fletrrufëve*, a red noticeboard where citizens made self-criticism or were publicly criticised. Another photo showed the Post Office; a grey Russian Pobeda with a distinctive sloping back was parked outside.

Although the physical layout of the bazaar hadn't changed since 1988, the mood could not have been more different. It was now a relaxed and friendly space, but from an Albanian perspective it must have seemed that the bazaar was no longer theirs. The old men continued to do what they had always done: they sat chatting over small cups of coffee in their favourite café. And there was one grocery store with fruit and vegetables displayed on the pavement. But for the most part, the shops catered for tourists. They had been converted into cafés, snack bars and souvenir shops.

One of the positive effects of tourism has been to boost traditional crafts. Along Rruga Gjin Bue Shpata, which leads to the castle, there was a shop selling rugs and carpets. In

1988: Most of the shops in Gjirokastër's Ottoman bazaar….

2019: …have been converted for the tourist trade.

the same street, a stonemason carved images of Scanderbeg, Albanian eagles and Gjirokastër itself, the stone city replicated in stone. Next to the stonemason was a woodcarver, a gentle soul called Petrit, where we bought souvenirs: an Albanian eagle and an ear of wheat (which might or might not have been communist-inspired).

As we walked around, I tried to show the old photos to shopkeepers. They were polite but for the most part reluctant to enter into discussion. In the capitalist economy, they didn't want to miss the chance of a sale. But even a cursory glance tended to elicit the same response. Back then, the streets were quiet, there were no cars and it was safe to walk in the road. Now, the constant stream of buses and cars passing right through the centre of the bazaar was damaging and unpleasant.

We needed to change money. Near the mosque was a photocopying shop that also advertised "exchange". The shop was small and almost empty: a desk with a drawer for currency, some shelves for stationery, a photocopier and bags of herbs for sale on the windowsill. It was run by Coli. His friends called him *Coli ne pazar*, Coli in the bazaar. We changed €100 and as there was no-one else waiting, I got out the photos. Coli put on his glasses.

He looked first at the ones of the bazaar. The shop next to his was in one of them: it had been a *Rroba*, a clothes shop; now it was a restaurant. Coli was a realist. Things had to change. He had a foot in both camps: the locals came for the photocopier; the tourists, like us, came to change money. Both tourists and locals liked herbs.

I said that when we had been here, there'd been a lot of men just hanging around, you could see them in the photos. Coli said that after work, men who lived in the new town came up to the bazaar for a beer. It was part of their evening *xhiro*. I asked where they would have been working. There were lots of factories in the new town, said Coli. During communism, he had worked as a technician in the shoe factory. It had been part of a *kombinat* that employed 600 people. The shoes were good quality; they were made of leather with rubber soles. His description made me think of the young woman in Sarandë with her new pair of shoes. I asked what had happened to the factory. When communism ended it was taken over by a Greek company who ran it until 2000. Then it closed.

Coli broke off for a moment to do some photocopying. When it was quiet again, he continued looking through the photos. He told us that there'd been a terrible fire in the house next to the Post Office; two children had died in the blaze. The house had never been rebuilt.

The photos set him off on a more general reminiscence. In his view, education had been better then: "we didn't have calculators (picking up the one on his desk), we had to do it all in our heads". I asked about foreign languages, had he ever been to Russia? No, but he had learned some Russian at school. Other students learned English or French: "we had to go to school; if we didn't our families would get fined, they could even lose their jobs." In Coli's eyes, you had to balance the good and the bad. On the good side, people had free education and hospitals, they had work and food. On the bad side, the government was strict, you couldn't travel, people were poor.

He got up and went to the shelf at the back of the shop. He came back with a black and white photograph which he gave me. It was a view of Gjirokastër, looking south towards the castle. The town mosque was in the foreground. It had lost most of its stone tiles and a communist-era building, now demolished, filled the space below the portico. But its minaret was still standing. Coli wasn't sure when the photo had been taken, but when religion had been banned in 1967, the mosque and minaret had avoided destruction because they were cultural monuments. The mosque had been used as a training hall by circus acrobats. It reopened in 1991 and was currently being restored.

The process of renewal continues. When we came back to Gjirokastër in 2021, the main square had been cordoned off while Hotel Çajupi was upgraded and an underground car park dug. Work had begun on a new ring road, prompting

UNESCO to warn the city not to damage its historic core. The scaffolding had been removed from Xhamia e Pazarit. Best of all, the bazaar had been pedestrianised.

1988

When we came out of the museum, the city was in shadow. It was as if someone had gone crazy with a spray gun and sprayed everything grey: grey houses, grey roofs, grey shale, grey mountain. At the bazaar, we took a cobbled path up to the castle. From here we could see the whole monochrome city ranged across the hillside. Beyond roofs to the north, a monumental stairway led up to a circular platform at the centre of which was a huge marble statue of an enthroned Enver Hoxha.

The castle was on a ridge to the south side of the city. In gloomy recesses along a vaulted entry passage were a selection of Italian and German field guns. A statue of a partisan stood guard; he was heavily armed with rifle, pistol and bullets around his waist. Upstairs, there were more guns and weapons, part of the collection of the National Museum of Arms. In one gallery, dominated by a statue of Enver Hoxha in military uniform, there was a gruesome reconstruction showing how partisans had breached German defences by laying animal skins on the barbed wire. In another gallery, a Socialist Realist tableau depicted a partisan grappling a German soldier to the ground. Scattered around the tableau were German helmets, guns and grenades. It was an unsettling mixture of brutality and triumphalism.

After the galleries, we were taken to see the cells where partisans had been tortured. We looked down long corridors closed off with rusting metal gates. Dag said the castle was bringing back memories of his own incarceration during the Second World War.

In pride of place on the battlements was an American spy plane shot down in the 1950s. It had "US Air Force"

1988: Enver Hoxha's statue has been removed....

2019: ...but the view from Gjirokastër's castle is still spectacular.

written in large letters on its nose. Then we crossed through an arch into an open space where chairs had been set out in front of a stage. Only a few weeks ago, there had been a folklore festival here. A medallion behind the stage showed a troupe of dancers. Across the top was written *Festivali Foklorik Kombëtar*. It was a magnificent, almost primeval location. Like the rest of the town, the castle and clock tower were now in shadow, but on the eastern side of the valley the mountain peaks were still bathed in soft orange sunlight. Undulating foothills on the plain had become bright islands marooned in a sea of shadow.

2019

Kirstie and I took the same path up to the castle. As it climbs, the views become bigger and wider. I had taken photos from here in 1988. In one picture, washing had been spread out to dry on hedges and bushes. Two of the buildings in that photo were now hotels. In another photo, a couple are sitting by a fire in a yard at the back of a stone-tiled house. The house was not much changed, except that it now had water tanks on the roof, a satellite dish and a sign asking people not to park in front of the gate. From the ramparts, the view stretches across the town and up the Drinos valley. We had photographed Hoxha's outsize statue on its outsize plinth from here. The statue had gone, but the plinth was still clearly visible.

Because of its status as a Museum City, by the 1980s there were at least seven museums in Gjirokastër covering the Albanian Renaissance, the National Liberation War, education, ethnography and archaeology. The biggest museum was in the castle: Muzeu Kombëtar Armëve, the National Museum of Armaments, was inaugurated in 1971. The armaments in the vaulted gallery are part of that original museum. Its purpose then, as it continues to be, is to celebrate communism's victory over fascism. The partisan still keeps guard, sleeves rolled up, rifle at the ready. On the terrace, the American spy plane is still there, although over the years it has been cannibalised and there's not much of it left apart from the fuselage.

In 2012, a new museum opened in the castle called Muzeu i Gjirokastrës, the Museum of Gjirokastër. Financed by the Albanian government and private donors, it is one of the very few museums in Albania with the resources to develop a post-communist historical narrative. It begins with an Early History section and then moves on to the five centuries of Ottoman rule, including a display about Ali Pasha. A side gallery profiles some of the foreign travellers who visited Gjirokastër: Evlia Çelebi, François Pouqueville, Lord Byron, Edward Lear. Then it comes to the modern period, including the dictatorship. In a town that seems to have such an ambivalent attitude towards Enver Hoxha, it was instructive to see how the museum tackled the half-century of communist rule.

A photo collage gives an overview of twentieth-century life with plenty of images from the communist period: children laying *kalldrëme*, traditional dancers and singers, bunkers, family portraits, sports events, a political rally, Ismail Kadare and so on. At the centre of the display is an image of Enver and Nexhmije Hoxha strolling through the old town.

In terms of historical influence, it's hard to argue with the placing of that image, but even so, you felt it must have taken some courage to put it there. A collection of displays describe life in communist Gjirokastër: the socialist economy, the concept of *punë vullnetare*, voluntary labour, political prisoners and the bunkers. Another display explains what happened in 1967 and reproduces a Socialist Realist painting of the humiliation of an Orthodox priest. At the core of the section is a display called "Communism and Enver Hoxha". It calls Hoxha "Gjirokastër's most notorious son" and describes how the regime held onto power by "cultivating an atmosphere of constant fear and uncertainty, even amongst those loyal to it… Thousands of people were killed, imprisoned, sent into exile or to labour camps for the slightest offences." An image below the text shows stonemasons working on Hoxha's statue.

The text is even-handed, critical where it needs to be but always restrained. Whoever wrote and designed this part of the exhibition deserves praise for trying to do something that even now, thirty years after the fall of the regime, is extremely challenging.

Then you go upstairs and it's as if the clock has been turned back. The galleries on the upper floor are a continuation of the old National Museum of Armaments. Everything on display is communist: sculptures, weaponry, art. At the far end of the gallery is an extraordinary representation of Mother Albania. Her head and torso are fully formed, but her lower body is inchoate. She seems to be emerging from the earth, as if Albania itself is giving birth to her. She is pointing with her right arm, but the arm is more like a rocky promontory than bone and muscle. In her left hand she holds a rifle. At her feet are two small figures: one a priest clasping a bible and looking anxiously over his shoulder; the other a truculent-looking figure in military greatcoat and peaked cap, an oppressor carrying skulls. At the centre of the room, Odhise Paskali's "Partizani fitimtar", The Victorious Partisan, still stands triumphantly over a cowering German soldier.

This was the same exhibition that Dag and I had seen in 1988, and judging from the state of the galleries - crumbling plaster, ill-fitting windows, damp walls - there'd been no attempt to modernise it. There was one difference. Enver Hoxha had been removed: no statue, no quotations, no displays. But apart from that, the communist narrative was undisturbed. The time lag is as much economic as political. Historical revisionism is costly and potentially controversial. When you're trying to rebuild a country, museums are not a priority. It's easier and much cheaper to leave them as they are. So by default, many of Albania's museums have become time capsules memorialising the old regime. The unique thing about the castle at Gjirokastër is that *both* versions of history are represented in the same building - then and now juxtaposed.

As we walked down from the castle, we could hear music. It was coming from the stadium near Xhamia e Pazarit where a folk festival was being held. On stage was a troupe from Gramsh, eight men and four women in traditional costume. They were polyphonic singers. Their singing was spine-tingling: melodic lines converged and diverged. Sometimes when voices clashed it was almost atonal, the dissonance underpinned by a held note that acted as a drone. It catapulted me back forty years, to when I'd first heard polyphonic singing on Radio Tirana.

Enver Hoxha was a fan of Albanian folk music. He called it a "priceless asset" and criticised those who had an "openly scornful stand towards folklore in general". A few years before he died, Hoxha had been guest of honour at a Youth Congress in Fier. He was talking to one of the delegates and happened to mention a song he had heard many years ago. He thought it was called "Bukuroshja e Strumit", The Beauty of Strum, but it was so long ago he had forgotten the words. When the Party Committee in Fier heard about the conversation, the Party Secretary ordered his music experts to go and find the song. They went to Strum, a small village on the plain east of Fier, and found nothing. But Hoxha was *Komandanti* and *Komandanti* didn't make mistakes. So they decided to create a song. As no-one had any idea what Hoxha remembered or thought he remembered, and no-one dared ask, it was a high-risk strategy. The musicologists came up with a song that drew on other folk tales from the region. It told the story of a beautiful girl who collects water from a spring. She carries a pot on her arm and has smiling lips. The singer implores the girl to lift her veil so he can see her beauty. He begs her to speak, but she remains silent. "Bukuroshja e Strumit" was performed at Gjirokastër's folk festival in 1984. It was well received and has become part of the folk repertoire. The song is one of the stranger impacts of the past on the present, testimony to the enduring power of a dictator. If it hadn't been for Hoxha's fading memory, there would have been no song. Dictatorship can still intrude into public life in unexpected ways.

After breakfast the next morning, we went back to our room to pack. We'd made friends with one of the hotel's staff, a woman called Donna. She was waiting for us in the corridor. Donna spoke very good English. She prided herself on her knowledge of England and was a big fan of the *Forsyte Saga*. She said how much she'd enjoyed meeting us, and that she had some gifts so we would remember Gjirokastër. She gave me a pen in a presentation box, a newspaper article about Ismail Kadare and three black and white photographs of Tirana in 2012, from a collection of photographs by Robert Aliaj Dragot.

Donna had given considerable thought to the gifts. When she handed them over, she said that the photographs represented "freedom". I thought a lot about that. The photos were hard-hitting pieces of photo-journalism. One image was of a street market where lines of second-hand shoes and boots were on sale. In another, a young child peered out through a barred window. The third showed a pair of motorised cycle-trolleys used by Roma to collect rubbish. The "freedom" represented in the photographs seemed to be the freedom to be poor.

When the old regime was overthrown, people hoped that "freedom" would lead to better living standards. What kind of "freedom" was it that left large sections of the population struggling to survive? Was Donna using the photos to make a point about the economic cost of "freedom"? Or was she implying a more personal definition of "freedom" in the sense that that photographer was "free" to take the images? And what was it about Gjirokastër and photographs? Here more than in any other city, photographs seemed to be a kind of currency. They could be swapped or exchanged. They could be sold or given as gifts. Having photos in my hand as we walked around gave me access to this world of images. And now Donna was using them to try to communicate a deeper truth.

After we'd finished packing, I went to look for Donna so I could understand what she wanted to say. But I couldn't find her. A colleague said her shift had ended and she had gone home. I went out into the street, but there was no sign of her. So it was all left hanging, unresolved, and maybe that was her point. Maybe she just wanted to make me think. Ismail Kadare, Gjirokastër's own master of ambivalence, would have approved.

8: Tepelenë to Ballsh
The Old Industrial Heartland

Tepelenë: a very surprising sitting room
1988

From Gjirokastër, we headed north up the Drinos valley, past greenhouses and orchards, towards Tepelenë, where, said Pepi, an Albanian warlord called Ali Pasha had carved out a private fiefdom. Although the river was low at this time of year, there was enough water to support clusters of aspens that had turned a fiery autumnal orange.

The castle at Tepelenë was on a bluff above the river. The road bypassed the town centre, squeezed between river and castle. A smooth wall of stone towered skywards. Across the river, a mountain reared up from the riverbed and thin silvery streams cascaded down its flanks. Looking back towards Tepelenë, a line of apartment blocks along the escarpment faced up the valley.

A convoy of coal trucks was heading south; we had to pull in to let them by. Pepi said that the coal had come from Memaliaj, one of Albania's new towns; its coalfields were some of the richest in Albania. From the road, we saw lines of apartments that looked Spartan in the extreme.

We crossed the river and the road traced the foothills on the eastern side of the valley. We passed a dry reservoir and as the road began to climb, we saw goats accompanied by women spinning and knitting as they walked. The images through the window kept crowding one on top of another, sharp for an instant and then obliterated by the next in a never-ending stream. Tobacco racks, oxen pulling a wooden plough, cattle munching corn stalks, cloud-capped mountains, a bullock cart loaded with wood, cooperative farm buildings, more cows, hillsides traced with terraces.

Then a sweet smell started drifting through the coach. It was faint at first, no more than a whiff, then it got stronger and stronger. Pepi told us we were approaching Ballsh. Ballsh was an industrial city with an oil refinery, which was one of Albania's most important enterprises. The refinery nestled among the mountains. Lines of storage tanks ran up the hillside like enormous stepping stones. Wisps of vapour clung to the cooling tower. A chimney belched smoke. Over fields to the west, we could see a diesel train pulling oil wagons. Pepi told us that the railway linking Ballsh to Fier had been built by youth brigades in the 1960s.

2019

The new road followed the path of the old one along the Drinos valley. Every so often where corners had been straightened you could see a thin strip of asphalt that had been the old road. Just before Tepelenë, water gushes from the hillside at Uji i Ftohtë. Our Albturist group had stopped here for coffee on our way down to Sarandë. Back then, it had been little more than a truck stop. I remembered (or thought I remembered) a café below the road, but that can't have been right unless there had been a separate place reserved for visitors. Since then, Uji i Ftohtë has expanded. As well as restaurants, a series of terraced platforms have been built up the hillside next to the cascades. Roadside stalls sell herbs, olive oil, honey and fresh fish.

At Tepelenë, the road, as it did then, bypasses the town. As we'd driven through in 1988, Dag had snapped the castle walls and I'd taken a photo of the mountain on the other side of the river. It was Mali i Golikut where, in spring 1941,

Italian forces had tried to stabilise their lines after their botched invasion of Greece. Thousands of Greek and Italian soldiers died on the mountain. I also had a photo of the castle and the apartment blocks along the ridge. There was now a petrol station-cum-hotel on the outskirts, and once-cultivated fields by the river were fallow. But in essence, the scene was the same.

There was fierce fighting around Tepelenë during the National Liberation War. The town was liberated in September 1943 by the "Baba Abaz" battalion, more than a year before the liberation of Tirana. After the war, two of the battalion's leaders, Adil Çarçani and Hysni Kapo, rose to high office. Post-communist Tepelenë has remained a socialist stronghold. In March 1997, during the pyramid crisis, the town rebelled against what it saw as Sali Berisha's corrupt administration. In an echo of the old communist language, government officials were declared *armiqtë e popullit*, enemies of the people, and were dismissed from their jobs. Armouries were looted and roadblocks set up. Public buildings were torched and prisoners freed. In 2018, when Tepelenë was celebrating the 75th anniversary of its liberation, the Mayor, Tërmet Peçi, joined in a communist-era anthem praising Enver Hoxha.

Tepelenë's political affiliations are on show in the town. Martyrs' busts have been painted gold. A plaster design (is it a flame or a flower?) on the Bashkia is socialist pink. The town's museum has a pickaxe and rifle on its façade, two of the symbols most closely associated with the communist regime. Over the years, we had driven past the museum many times and it had always been closed. This morning it was open, and we ran up the steps, fearful that someone might lock us out. The woman in charge took 100 leks from each of us and gave us tickets. Her name was Kleda. She spoke good English and as we were the only visitors, she offered to show us around.

The first part of the museum was given over to pre-history, which meant lots of maps of Illyria and a few Roman remains - all the best stuff, said Kleda, had gone to

Tirana. Pictures of Ali Pasha took up a whole wall. Then we came to the section about Tepelenë's modern history. At the entrance to the galleries, an enormous board listed the names of 468 people who had been martyred during the National Liberation War, almost 9 per cent of the town's population. The board was installed in 2015 and paid for by the Bashkia.

The galleries outlined Tepelenë's struggle for independence. They described a series of uprisings against the Ottomans, the Greek incursion in 1912 and the struggle to evict Italians from Vlorë in 1920 in the aftermath of the First World War. The panels were the original communist ones. They even included a quotation from Enver Hoxha. Displays about Tepelenë during the National Liberation War used the old material, but they had been remounted on new pink boards. It was as if the Bashkia was deliberately associating itself with LANÇ, the communist-led National Liberation Front.

As well as songs, maps, photographs and memorabilia, the museum also had a large collection of Socialist Realist paintings. We asked Kleda why there were so many. She said that when the museum opened in the 1970s, the paintings had been specially commissioned, that was what happened.

At the rear of the museum, a door opened onto a small room. I assumed it was a storeroom and was expecting to see piles of stuff littered around. It was nothing of the kind. It was a mock-up of a communist-era sitting room with a settee and armchairs arranged around a doily-covered table. But it was the painting on the wall that grabbed attention. It showed Enver Hoxha on a visit to Tepelenë. Hoxha is standing with a group of villagers on a highpoint overlooking the river; Mali i Golikut is in the background. Hoxha is pointing towards cultivated fields along the riverbank while the villagers - a mix of young and old, male and female, military and civilian - listen respectfully. The painting was by a local artist, Aliosha Bilbili, and was dated 1985, the year Hoxha died. The shelf below the painting was filled with his books.

It was routine propaganda, but the point was it was Enver Hoxha on the wall. It seemed almost brazen, as if a taboo had been breached. When I asked Kleda about the picture she explained that she wanted the museum to have a communist-era room because "this is what tourists want to see". Kleda didn't think there was anything odd about displaying the painting; many houses from that time would have had one. She thought it had been inspired by a visit Hoxha had made in the 1960s, but wasn't sure of the exact date.

Tepelenë's politics came to the fore again in August 2017, at a time when Albania was under pressure from the European Union. If the country wanted to improve its chances of being granted full EU membership, it would have to "address the crimes committed during the communist dictatorship period".

There had been an internment camp at Tepelenë and the Albanian authority with responsibility for investigating communist-era crimes, AIDSSH (Authority for Information on Former State Security Documents), decided that the camp should be opened to the public. When I said to Kleda that we planned to go and see it, she became very defensive. We should understand that this was not a concentration camp, people had misunderstood, the prisoners had their families with them, they had access to doctors...

Kleda's response echoed comments made in March 2018 by Pëllumb Xhufi. Xhufi is a historian and former Vice Chairman of one of Albania's smaller political parties, the Socialist Movement for Integration (Lëvizja Socialiste për Integrim). Referring to a declassified CIA report, Xhufi said that conditions in the camp were "not bad" and that it was a "banality" to liken it to a Nazi concentration camp. Xhufi's comments outraged camp survivors and their relatives, but they went down well with defenders of the old regime.

Kampi 6 had originally been built by the Italians as a barracks following their occupation of Albania in 1939. When the communists came to power, they converted it into an internment camp primarily for dissidents from the north.

The camp operated from April 1949 until March 1954. The CIA report estimated that more than a thousand people were held there, mainly women and children. Prisoners lived in a single building divided into four rooms. Around three hundred slept in tiers of bunks in each room. Sanitary conditions were primitive and there were many deaths, especially among children and the elderly. Food was in short supply, as it was over the whole country. Able-bodied prisoners were used as forced labour laying railway lines, building factories and felling trees.

The camp was officially opened to the public on 23 August 2017. On the same day the following year, the Bashkia and AIDSSH organised a concert that would be "a celebration of life over pain and death imposed by the former Albanian communist regime". The date was significant. In 2008, the European Parliament passed a resolution declaring that from now on, 23 August would be the European Day of Remembrance for Victims of Stalinism and Nazism, also known as Black Ribbon Day.

The camp was in a run-down part of town, overlooked by apartment blocks and close to the old *zona industriale*. Cars had been dumped by the entrance. The gate was locked, but inside you could see the old barracks and a "Children's Forest" (*Pylli i Fëmijëve*), a grove of cypress trees planted in memory of the 300 children who died there. For a site that carried so much symbolic weight - a place where the wrongs of communism were to be publicly acknowledged - it seemed a very half-hearted tribute.

Memaliaj: coal and milk
2019

Nestling in an oxbow meander, in other circumstances Memaliaj might have been a delightful riverside town. But it was not built to be pretty. It was always a functional place - a grid of streets leading to a large square known as Sheshi Minatori, the Miners' Square.

When coal mining began at Memaliaj, the miners were originally housed in huts. Hoxha admitted that the Party had not shown "the necessary concern over the improvement of the conditions and treatment of the workers", particularly regarding their housing. Memaliaj's two-storey blocks were built in the 1950s and are some of the earliest examples of state housing in Albania. Some of them even have little architectural flourishes, like pediments over the doorways and patterned brickwork below the roofs. With each Five Year Plan, the mine expanded and the town grew to accommodate more miners. In 1954, a technical school was opened to train electricians and mechanics. The rows of four- and five-storey apartment blocks Dag and I had seen from the coach were built in the 1960s and 1970s, by which time Memaliaj had grown to a sizable community of around 5,000 people. Its mines were producing more than half a million tonnes of coal a year, about 25 per cent of Albania's total coal production. Much of it went by truck to the Metallurgical Combine at Elbasan. But like so many Albanian industries, the mine was unable to adapt to the new economic order and it closed in 1999.

The impact of the closure was devastating. Before 1990, miners were, relatively speaking, well paid and living standards in the town were above average. When the mine closed, incomes nosedived. Memaliaj now has the highest level of unemployment in southern Albania.

We stopped for a coffee in Sheshi Minator. A statue of a miner stood at one end of the square, a reminder of what had once been. Facing it, another *lapidar* commemorated the struggle against the "Nazi-Fascist invaders" in May 1943. The square was deserted. Then a man appeared with some cows. He led them across the square and into a derelict warehouse. He told us he had ten cows; every day, a tanker came to collect his milk and take it to a creamery in Gjirokastër. During communism, he'd worked in the mines. He'd worked there for twelve and a half years. At their height, the mines had employed around 3,000 people - everyone in Memaliaj had worked with coal. And now there was nothing; everything had closed, even the brick factory. He thought he was one of the lucky ones; he had work and could make a living from his cows. Most of the young folk had gone to Italy and Greece. He gave us both a hearty handshake when we left.

Ballsh: a refinery in the mountains
2019

For the next thirty kilometres, the new road continued to follow the route of the old. At Fratar, the roads diverged. The new one went straight to Fier; the old one to Ballsh and Patos. Almost at once, the surface began to deteriorate. On corners and inclines, the asphalt had washed away; other sections had slipped, sunk or crumbled. We had to go slowly, but it was quieter than the main highway and much more scenic, so long as you could put up with its twists and turns.

During the old regime, this road was a key industrial route, enabling crude oil to be transported from the oilfields at Ballsh-Hekal, Visokë and Patos-Marinëz to the refineries at Ballsh and Fier. The gradient must have been quite a challenge for the trucks shuttling back and forth. As we got nearer to Ballsh, we began to smell oil; soon enough you could see oil rigs and derricks scattered across the hillsides. But it was the smell that packed the punch. Thirty years on, it was still extraordinarily evocative, like reinhabiting a lost memory. For a few seconds, I felt just a frisson of how it must have been when Dag and I came along this road for the first time. And it wasn't just the smell: it was the location, the collision of oil and agriculture. Tarry sheep grazing among oil wells became one of the defining images of communist Albania. Even now, seeing leaky oil tanks amid such fertile land was both exciting and appalling.

After slow progress through the countryside, it was a shock arriving in Ballsh. It was busy and bustling, its main street choked with cars and oil tankers. Ballsh is another of

Albania's "new" towns, built in the 1970s when the planners decided that this mountainous location would be ideal for Albania's largest and most sophisticated oil refinery. The refinery was to be built on the east side of the Gjanicë river which flows on to Fier; the town was on the opposite hillside. Although there had been a lot of new building since 1990, the original estates, austere banks of five-storey apartment blocks, still dominated the upper reaches of the town.

The Deep Oil Processing Plant (Uzina e përpunimit të thellë të naftës) was commissioned during the Fifth Five Year Plan (1971-5) when Albania was still receiving technical and financial support from China. The refinery was one of a raft of major industrial projects that would confirm Albania's transition from an agricultural economy to an industrial one. Other projects in the same Five Year Plan included the metallurgical combine in Elbasan, the hydroelectric scheme at Fierzë and extensions to the Enver Hoxha Tractor Factory in Tirana.

Once the project had been agreed, a work camp was set up at Panahor, close to the construction site. The camp was a large one, holding more than 600 Albanians and a few Greeks and Italians. It operated from 1971 until 1984.

Construction was fraught. The project overran by two years and Hoxha sought scapegoats, flinging around accusations of sabotage for the delays. When the plant came on stream in November 1978, Albania's Vice-Minister of Industry and Mining, Rexhep Shehu, declared that despite "all the sabotage acts by the Chinese revisionists, a qualitative leap has been made in the field of oil processing". Official publications praised its "modern cracking and catalysis equipment" and - just as important - the refinery became a propaganda tool. It was proof of the modernity of Albania's industrial project, and pictures of its mazy pipe runs, distillation units and cooling towers were featured in magazines.

As well as embodying the triumph of socialism, the refinery had another attribute. It was profitable, and when the regime collapsed in 1991, the Ballsh refinery was one of Albania's few industrial plants to make a success of the transition. For the next eight years it remained under the control of the Ministry of Economy, Trade and Energy (Ministria e Ekonomisë, Tregtisë dhe Energjetikës), better known by its acronym METE. In April 1999, the government set up ARMO, Albanian Refining and Marketing of Oil. ARMO took over much of Albania's oil industry, including the refinery at Ballsh. In 2008, after pressure from the International Monetary Fund and the European Union, Sali Berisha's Democratic government agreed to privatise ARMO. That decision marked the beginning of the end for the refinery.

The plant was bought, sold on, and then rented to a company registered in the British Virgin Islands. In August 2016, it declared itself bankrupt and shut down, only to reopen in November under new management. In December 2017, a dispute over the supply of crude oil forced the refinery to close again. Workers' salaries were suspended, leading to protests outside METE's offices in Tirana. The refinery officially closed in September 2019. At the beginning of 2022, contractors began dismantling it and taking its metal away for scrap. The latest idea is to turn the site into a solar plant.

The prison camp at Panahor remains one of the refinery's unresolved legacies. During its construction, 93 prisoners died, buried in unmarked graves in the prison cemetery. Along with Burrel and Spaç, Ballsh was one of Albania's harshest prisons. An Amnesty International Report published in 1984, *Albania, Political Imprisonment and the Law*, drew on testimony from former prisoners and their relatives to paint a picture of life in the camp. Prisoners were woken at 4.30 in the morning, had breakfast at 5.00, began work at 6.00 and returned to camp at 3.00 in the afternoon. The main meal of the day was at 3.30 with lights out at 10 o'clock. Inmates were organised into brigades according to their skills. There was a builders' brigade, a carpenters' brigade, a trench-digging brigade and a brigade making concrete moulds. Prisoners were housed in prefabricated huts that were so cold in winter that many slept fully-clothed. Official records show that at any one time, more than half the prisoners were sick due to the harshness of the regime.

In March 2019, members of AIDSSH, the body that had pressed for the camp at Tepelenë to be opened to the public, visited Ballsh. They went with representatives from the International Commission on Missing Persons (ICMP). The delegation met with local officials to discuss exhuming bodies from the cemetery at Panahor. The EU provided funds for the exhumations and DNA testing. Eighteen months later, no timetable had been agreed, prompting some to wonder whether the government had lost its appetite for investigating past abuses.

When we had driven through Ballsh in 1988, I had taken photographs of the refinery. So had most of our group; you could hear the camera shutters clicking down the aisle. It was awe-inspiring in its way, an almighty clash of industry and nature: a mountainous bowl enfolding a huge industrial complex spewing steam and smoke. In the foreground, between the road and refinery, there was a field ready for planting and then a line of greenhouses. We had just a few seconds to take our photos before the refinery disappeared behind trees.

I must have taken the photos on the north side of Ballsh, on the road to Patos. There were several garages along the road and we pulled into one with a view of the refinery. The earthy field had been taken over by the garage; an inspection pit and a row of tatty workshops had been built on it. But the metal frames of the greenhouses were still standing. From the look of them they had not been used for decades. I lined up the photo as best I could, but trees along the roadside interrupted the view. Even so, you could see the cooling tower and chimney and some of the storage tanks.

These old photos can take you to dark places. When you start to scrape the surface, you realise how complicated things are and how much the past continues to cast its shadow over the present.

1988: The oil refinery at Ballsh, one of Albania's most successful enterprises, …

2019: …has closed with the loss of hundreds of jobs.

From Ballsh, road and railway followed the river. The railway had been abandoned. The river was disgusting.

This was, still is, oil country. Substantial reserves were found around Visokë in the early 1960s; there were plenty of oil derricks and the air was tainted with the smell of oil. Through the trees, you could see sections of the derelict railway supported on concrete struts.

A few kilometres north of Visokë, the road bent to the left. On the corner was a single-storey building which I recognised instantly. I'd taken a photo of it in 1988. The place even had a name, Ofiçine.

In itself, the building was nothing special: a line of offices with a tiled roof and large doorways that looked as if it had originally been an SMT, Stacioni i Makinave dhe Traktorëve, where farm equipment had been stored. When Dag and I saw it, it was the local headquarters for the Visokë oilfield. But what made it so memorable were the slogans. It was plastered in them, and I had spent hours at home studying the photo and trying to decipher them.

As well as the standard *Lavdi PPSH*, Glory to the Party of Labour of Albania, a board by the entrance featured three words in capital letters: *PUNOJMË, MBROJMË, MËSOJMË*. LET'S WORK, LET'S DEFEND, LET'S LEARN. Another slogan urged workers to work harder: Absence without action, Late to work, Minutes lost (*Munges pa aksion, Vonës në punë, Minutë kohë humbur*). To reinforce the message, next to the words were a clock face and a pickaxe and rifle. Another slogan read: Socialism requires people with culture and scientific knowledge (*Socializmi kërkon njerëz me kulturë dhe dije shkencore*). That had come from a speech by Enver Hoxha. There was more: a red flag with the heads of Marx, Engels, Lenin and Stalin on it and a painting of the house in Tirana where the Albanian Communist Party had been formed on 8 November 1941.

In the old photo, you can also see storage tanks and derricks. All were streaked with rust; one had lost most of its cladding. In front of the tanks was an oil pool where seepage

1988: From the crest of the hill, you can see how....

2019: ...Fier and Patos have expanded since the end of communism.

collected. The restraining wall was glistening; it looked as if there had been a recent spill.

We stopped to take a photo. The building was in a decrepit state. Roof tiles had been replaced by corrugated sheeting and the slogans had been chiselled off the walls. But the oil tanks were still there, and the seepage pool. As I walked over, a man came out of the building. I had the photo in my hand, but before I could say anything, he told me it was a restricted zone and I wasn't allowed to take photographs. I asked why, and he said it was a gas storage facility and entry was forbidden. I went back to the car and snapped a couple of quick shots through the window.

I had one more photo from this section of the journey. Just before Fier the road climbs a ridge and there's a fine view of Patos and the plain. I'd taken a photo from the coach just as the road began to descend. On the skyline was a brick tower - they were often used by the communists to support electricity or phone lines. Next to the tower was a quarry with a blackened kiln and conveyor belt. In the foreground was a terraced vineyard. Kirstie and I pulled off the road to take in the view. Patos had grown, and so had Fier. New developments ran north along the highway, through Mbrostar and on to Ardenicë. The vineyard had gone and the quarry had been reduced to rubble. But the brick tower was still there, and it was still supporting phone wires.

9: Myzeqe

Collectivisation and Internment Camps

Fier: a tale of two mugs
1988

It was dark by the time we reached Fier. The storm that had been threatening all afternoon had broken. Lightning lit the underbellies of the clouds. Thunder growled. Rain poured. We collected our bags from the coach and dashed into the hotel. We were tired and wet and it didn't help when rumours started: there were no single rooms; none of the rooms had bathrooms; none had heaters. As we waited, tempers frayed. When our turn came, we were given a twin room overlooking the square. It was basic but clean. We even had extra blankets. On the table between the beds was an old radio that crackled when you turned it on, but it worked. Outside, the rain was still falling and glistened on the cobbles. The streetlamp by our window buzzed.

In the half-hour before supper, Dag and I decided to brave the rain. It was almost shutting-up time, but a kiosk in the square was still open selling cigarettes, reels of (mainly pink) cotton, Bulgarian toothpaste, Polish razor blades and, curiously considering the lack of cameras, photograph albums. The shutters were coming down on a food store, but an assistant let us in. Packets of rice and pasta, bottles of jam and fruit juice, tinned fish and brown blocks of tobacco were displayed on shelves behind the counter. We wanted to buy

1988: The slogans have gone…

2017: ... but this Fier apartment block is still easily recognisable.

a bottle of red wine, and there were plenty of bottles: vodka, cognac, *raki* and *fernet*. I tried asking in Greek, then French. Dag tried German. In the end we gave up.

The hotel had a tourist shop, and after we'd eaten we went to see what was there. I bought some woollen slippers, two squares of tasselled carpet and a cassette of Albanian folk music. Purchases made, we joined the rest of the group in the lounge where a four-piece band was running through a medley of songs by the Beatles and Stevie Wonder.

2017

It had been pouring in 1988. It was pouring again now. The hotel we had stayed at, Hotel Apolonia, had closed so I'd booked into Hotel Fieri which was also in the main square. During communism, Hotel Apolonia had been for tourists; Hotel Fieri was reserved for foreign delegations and engineers working in the oilfields. The hotel had been privatised in 1994.

I was on my own for a couple of days and I ate supper under chandeliers in the hotel's Francophile restaurant, with gold-framed mirrors on the walls and paintings of French courtiers dancing in front of mirrors under chandeliers. After I'd eaten, I went outside. Part of the square had been cordoned off for pedestrians, but most of it had been given over to cars. No lights in the old Hotel Apolonia, but a Conad supermarket underneath it was open and brightly lit. Blue-tinted streetlamps marked the main boulevards running into the square. It was a chilly evening and there weren't many people around, but a kiosk by the hotel - was it the same kiosk that had been selling Bulgarian toothpaste in 1988? - was still open and every so often a customer came to buy chewing gum or single cigarettes.

I said to the man that I had some old photos of the square and asked if he'd like to see them. His name was Nimet and he invited me into his kiosk where it was a bit warmer. One of the photos was of a five-storey apartment block with three words across its balconies: *ORGANIZIM, DISIPLINE, EMULACION*. The block was next to the hotel. It had been painted orange and green, but structurally it was unchanged. I asked about the statue of Stalin. That, said Nimet, had been in a little park next to the apartment block where there was now a statue of "Heroi-Poet" Dino Kalenja. Nimet flicked through the other photos and then muttered, *"sistemi komunist"*. It was said so neutrally it was impossible to know what he really thought about the old regime.

1988

After breakfast, Pepi gave us the day's itinerary. We would be spending the next hour in Fier, so there was time for a walk. Then our coach would take us to Apollonia, one of Albania's most famous archaeological sites.

In the bright sunshine we could get a better sense of the square. In front of our hotel a garden was planted with flowers. There were also trees, lots of them. They filled the corner by the river. There were more people around than there had been last night, but it wasn't busy. Because there were no cars, you could walk down the middle of the road without danger. Only the foreigners used the zebra crossing by the hotel.

A fine old mansion stood by the crossing. The paint was peeling and the plasterwork cracked, but even in its dilapidated state it gave you just a hint of what pre-communist Fier must have looked like. The doors were open; a glass-fronted cabinet the length of the corridor was full of books by Enver Hoxha. At the end of the corridor we pushed open a door and realised we'd walked into Fier's library. A librarian came to see what we wanted, and we asked if there was a bookshop in Fier. She kept repeating, "not at all, not at all" and we weren't sure if this was an answer to our question or a response to our thanks.

Further down the street were two grey housing blocks with shops on the ground floor. One of them was the grocery store we'd been to last night. We hadn't seen it in the darkness, but on the wall was a mural of a red PPSH flag and railway tracks wrapped round a gun. The slogan said: Our Youth, Youth Action (*Rinia jonë rini e aksioneve*). At the other end of the building, another mural showed a female worker holding a pickaxe in one hand and a book in the other. The slogan said: Long Live Our Working Class (*Rroftë Klasa Jonë Punëtore*).

At the end of the street we came to another park with mature trees - pines, cedars and palms - and we wondered if this too had belonged to an earlier, more elegant Fier. A snack bar was open for pastries and luridly coloured soft drinks. A boulevard ran south from the park. There were flower beds and trees along the pavement, and its apartment blocks had balconies with wooden railings and flower troughs by their entrances. Another mural showed a dark-haired woman draped in an Albanian flag and a slogan: Socialist Albania Marches with Pride along Enver's Road (*Shqipëria Socialiste Marshon Krenare në Rrugën e Enverit*).

In a country where so much was mystifying, we latched onto the murals as something tangible. They were evidence of socialism in practice. But for all the fervour of the slogans, Fier felt lethargic and you wondered if the messaging had more to do with shoring up an ailing system than promoting revolutionary zeal. It seemed like the country had run out of energy. Everyone was waiting for something to happen.

2017

There were still some trees, but not many. From my sixth-floor window, I could see a dozen dark poplars around the Orthodox church. But of the cedars that had stood by the river, only six remained along with a bedraggled palm tree. Present-day Fier was defined not by its greenery but by concrete.

Fier had been one of communist Albania's more cosmopolitan cities. It was not large; in the 1980s, it had a population of around 36,000, but the plain around it was fertile and produced wheat and cotton. Fier also had a sizable industrial estate with a nitrate fertiliser plant and an oil refinery. Maybe that's why Enver Hoxha had taken such a close interest in its development. He was in Fier in February 1962 for a Party Conference, and he wrote approvingly in his Diary about the city's new squares, its asphalt roads and cheerful citizens. He returned the following spring with Spiro Koleka, who had recently been Chairman of the State Planning Commission. The two met with local planners and discussed the location for a new square which, Hoxha added, "will without doubt turn out to be beautiful".

The square in question, originally called Sheshi Stalin, is where the two hotels were built - both opened in 1966. A new road, Rruga Enver Hoxha, linked Sheshi Stalin and Sheshi Flamujve, Flag Square, where there was a fountain. This was the street Dag and I had walked along in 1988. Today I took the same route, from what was now Sheshi Fitorja along a congested Rruga Jakov Xoxa to Sheshi Pavarësia, Independence Square. In 2012, the fountain had been replaced by a huge globe of the world. Unfortunately, the globe soon developed structural problems; and in 2019, the Bashkia decided it was unsafe and removed it.

Apart from the obvious differences - in 1988 there had been no cars, people walked in the street, there were murals everywhere - the street was recognisably the same. The neoclassical mansion that had been the library was still there; so were the two apartment blocks, now painted green. There was something weird about the mansion, and it took a few moments to realise what had happened. At some point, two extra storeys had been added in the same style, transforming what had been a well-proportioned structure into an inflated piece of kitsch.

At least there was still a mansion, even it had been architecturally abused. It was of the very few reminders of

1988: The old buildings and murals have disappeared....

2017: ...under a café on stilts.

220

the original nineteenth-century town founded by a branch of the Vrioni family. In 1864, Kahraman Pasha Vrioni and his son Omer Pasha Vrioni commissioned French urban planners to design a town that would be a vision of Europe in what was still an Ottoman province. When the British writer and Albanophile, Edith Durham passed through Fier in 1904, she noted that "a very enterprising bey" had "rebuilt all the market-place with large solid-looking houses of stone, which have a surprisingly up-to-date appearance". The mansion was part of that development and is still referred to as Shtëpia e Vrionëve, the House of the Vrioni. It must have been completed by 1912, because a wall plaque states that Ismail Qemali stopped here on 25 November 1912, on his way to Vlorë to declare Albanian independence.

When the communists took power in 1944, the Vrionis were deemed class enemies and were harshly dealt with. The head of the family, Qemal Bej Vrioni, was found guilty of collaboration and was sent to the prison at Burrel where he was executed in 1947. Omer Pasha Vrioni's son, Sami, also died in prison in the same year. The Vrioni estates were confiscated and became a state farm. Other family properties were seized, including shops, warehouses and a flour mill called Myzeqeja built in 1936 and which, some say, was Fier's first industrial enterprise.

I was standing in front of blank wall on Rruga Jakov Xoxa, trying to decide if this was where the mural of a female worker with pickaxe and book had been. A man came out of a shop to see what I was up to. He introduced himself. His name was Ylvi. He owned the white goods shop in the adjoining block and spoke very good English. I showed him the photo. Yes, said Ylvi, there had been a mural on that wall. The *kafe* in the photo was now a clothes boutique. The arcade along the front had been turned into a jewellery shop.

I explained to Ylvi what I was trying to do and showed him the other photos. It was a Thursday morning, business was slow. "Come on," he said, "I'll show you where they all are."

So we set off on a tour of Fier. As we walked, Ylvi told me about himself and his city. His parents had been Chams from Mazarek, a village not far from Margariti in what had been Greek Chameria. They were forced to leave Greece in 1944 and came to Fier. Many Chams, Ylvi said, settled in Fier. Ylvi's father set up a small business, but two years later the communists nationalised it. His father died when Ylvi was only eleven; one of his older brothers had been a surrogate *babai*.

Ylvi seemed to know everyone. As we walked, we were constantly being stopped by friends and acquaintances and Ylvi had to explain what he was doing and show them the photographs. Walking with him was quite a revelation, an insight into the way the city operated. Personal connections were everything and Ylvi was very well connected. He said later that he probably knew around 2,000 people in Fier.

We walked down the street to Sheshi Pavarësia where old men were gathering under the trees, preparing for the day's cards and dominoes. Ylvi stopped in front of a café supported on concrete pillars overlooking the park. He was holding the photo of a squat, two-storey corner building that called itself a *gjellëtore vetshërbimi*, a self-service restaurant. On each side, running off at right angles, were single-storey shop units. On the building's façade - and this must have been why I took the photo - was a mural of young people with pickaxes and spades laying railway tracks. This, said Ylvi, was where I'd taken the photo.

It took a moment to see it. Behind the café on stilts, hidden from view, was the building that had been the self-service restaurant - or maybe it had been demolished, it was impossible to tell. But further along the street you could see the indented roofline of the original single-storey shops which matched the old photo. This was what remained of the old market area designed by Kahraman Pasha Vrioni's French architects.

Ylvi led me down a narrow road past the café and into a housing estate. He was now holding the photo of brick-built apartment blocks around a courtyard. "Courtyard" was flattering. The space was unpaved, puddled and strewn with rubble. Where we were standing seemed to have no connection with the photo. There was no courtyard and no apartments. Ylvi was enjoying this enormously. He told me to look more closely. And then I could see what had happened. The old blocks were still there; you could glimpse bits of them and their speckled roof tiles behind ad hoc extensions that had eaten up the courtyard. Some of the extensions were rendered and whitewashed; others were breezeblock with balconies protected by wire mesh.

As I stared and marvelled at the adaptations, Ylvi explained why people were so desperate to increase their living space. During communism, living conditions were cramped with a family of four allocated around sixty square metres. Sometimes there was more than one family in an apartment and everyone had to share a single toilet. At one time, there had been eleven people in Ylvi's extended family, so you could imagine how crowded they were. When housing stock was privatised, rather than moving into new accommodation, many families had taken the cheaper option of staying put and doing what they could to augment their living space.

While Ylvi had been talking, I was trying to think of an analogy for this redevelopment, and the best I could come up with was barnacles on a rock. Every household had added to their apartment. Everyone was competing for limited amounts of space. What had happened seemed to symbolise the transition from communism to a freewheeling version of Albanian-style capitalism: individualism grafted onto socialism.

We walked on past the Bashkia, which was being renovated and swathed in plastic. Next to it was Fier's theatre, Teatri Bylis. On the other side of the road was a handsome 1930s villa with a pillared entrance and balcony. It was Fier's Prefecture, *Prefekti i Qarkut Fier*, broadly equivalent to an English county council. To the right of the entrance were

1988: This has to be one of the most extraordinary transformations in Albania, ...

2017: .... an ingenious solution to cramped living conditions.

three plaques. I had a photo of them. The plaques in the photo had been splashed with paint and were so streaked with dirt it was hard to read them. Now they had been cleaned and their red stars restored. Paradoxically, they seemed to be treated with far greater respect now than they had been in 1988.

There was one more photo. It showed a snack bar, an *ëmbëltore*, surrounded by trees in a park. For the first time, Ylvi faltered. He explained that when he was growing up in Fier, there were parks all over the city and most of them had snack bars. He thought at first that I had taken the photo in the main square, among the trees by Hotel Fieri. Then he looked at it again. There were people around the *ëmbëltore*: soldiers in peaked caps and green uniforms; two well-dressed men, positively elegant by communist standards; a Roma woman in blue pantaloons and a red jacket. Suddenly, it came to him. Most of the trees had been cleared, but the *ëmbëltore* had been right here, by the Prefecture. Those two men were definitely actors - you could tell from their clothes and poses. Ylvi had worked in the theatre for a few months, and he knew that during breaks in rehearsals the actors went to the *ëmbëltore* for a snack. The soldiers were almost certainly based at the military offices on the main road. And the Roma woman - there had been, still was, a large Roma settlement set back from the road by the river. Of course Ylvi knew many of them, especially the ones like him who had become entrepreneurs.

We walked back along a *pedonalja* lined with trees and benches. It was part of a new park that had opened earlier in the year. The path went past Fier's new mosque and led to a children's play area and an ornamental fountain. A new arts centre was nearing completion. It was to be housed in the old Vrioni flour mill, Myzeqeja. The apartment blocks overlooking the park had also been given a make-over. They were painted bright colours - green, orange, red - and decorated with motifs drawn from nature: plants, plant fronds and leaves. Some of the leaves were painted, others were sculpted and hung on the exteriors.

Ylvi was broadly in favour of regeneration, but he didn't agree with all the changes. When the ground was cleared for the park, a 1930s villa was demolished. Ylvi had petitioned for it to be saved, arguing that it could have been turned into a characterful venue for public events. Ylvi had a strong sense of the history of his town. He understood the importance of holding onto some remnants of the past, especially when the pace of change was so dizzying. One villa had been saved. It was at the northern end of the *pedonalja*. A plaque on the wall said it had been built in 1935 and belonged to Nane and Dhimo Panajoti.

We were now back in Sheshi Fitorja, outside what had been Hotel Apolonia. The hotel shut in the early 2000s, and in 2005 it was taken over by one of Albania's new private universities, Kristal. Kristal's accreditation was withdrawn in 2014 when it emerged that students had been buying degrees. Since then, the main building had been empty, but the ground floor had been converted into shops. As well as Conad, there was a travel agency, an exchange office and a casino.

Ylvi asked again when we had stayed at Hotel Apolonia. I said November 1988. Ylvi said he started working there in June that year. He was twenty-two years old, it was his first proper job. He'd done his training at the Waiters' School in Durrës and learned what he called "food English", so he could answer questions about the menu but nothing more controversial. It was entirely possible that when Dag and I stayed at the hotel, Ylvi was serving our meals.

Casino Aladdin was next to Conad; it had Aladdin's lamps on the doors. This, said Ylvi, had been the tourist dining room. It was separate from the rest of the hotel to prevent mingling. "Let's go inside, he is my friend." As eyes adjusted to the gloom, a huge man, his neck bulging over his shirt collar, came over to greet us. Ylvi explained (yet again) what he was doing and then set about remembering what the dining room had been like. He tried the door that used to link to the other dining area. It was locked, but if it had been open it would have taken us into the Conad supermarket where the

Albanian dining room had been. The casino was one of the more bizarre transformations, a space deliberately insulated from its surroundings. In that sense, it wasn't dissimilar to the foreigners' dining room.

Would I like something to drink? Ylvi suggested we go to his flat. It was in an apartment block he owned on the ring road, only a few minutes away by taxi. We took the lift to the top floor and he opened the door onto a hyper-luxurious flat, no expense spared, the best TV, the best speakers, the best kitchen equipment. I perched on a leather settee that really looked too expensive to sit on while Ylvi went to the fridge. He offered me whisky; I said water was fine and then worried about spilling it on the settee.

Ylvi told me what had happened to him when the old regime collapsed, and how he'd built himself a new life. After his stint at Hotel Apolonia, he was appointed Head Waiter at the Kuscama restaurant near the Martyrs' Cemetery. He remembered a Romanian delegation coming to the restaurant at the end of 1989. They came in a convoy from Tirana. It was the first time Ylvi had seen so many cars gathered together in one place.

As the system began to unravel, Ylvi left the restaurant and set up a roadside stall selling coffee to the increasing numbers of people who now owned cars and were driving through Fier on their way to Greece. He made enough money to buy his own car and used it to take mountain tea, *çaj mali*, from Albania into Greece. The border was dangerous, especially in 1997 when the pyramid schemes crashed. There were masked men on the road, no police and Ylvi was carrying a lot of cash. It was, he said, a very scary time. Ylvi's siblings emigrated. One brother went to Boston, the other to Calgary; his sister went to Philadelphia. Ylvi said that so many Fieriots went to Philadelphia that people from Fier jokingly referred to it as Philadelfier.

Ylvi stayed in Albania. By 2007, he'd raised enough money to buy an old warehouse. He demolished it and built a new block with a showroom on the ground floor and executive flats above. He started importing white goods made by the Slovenian company, Gorenje, and now ran a very profitable business.

Ylvi opened the doors onto a rooftop terrace, and there it was spread out beneath us, his city reinventing itself with Ylvi playing a leading part. It was a fine view. From here you could see Fier expanding, pushing into agricultural land to the north and east. A new apartment block was being constructed next to Ylvi's on a site where there had been a flour mill. More land had been cleared to the south. But amid all the redevelopment there were plenty of reminders of the old world: warehouses with curved roofs, derelict factory units and on the hillside by the Martyrs' Cemetery, storage tanks for oil from the Patos-Marinëz oilfields.

It was midday; Ylvi had to go back to the shop. We swapped phone numbers and I went up to my room to write up my notes, but was distracted by the buzz of a chainsaw. Workmen were felling trees. I watched as one of the remaining cedars began to quiver as chunks were cut from its trunk. Workmen were pulling on a rope attached to its upper branches, ready to guide the tree down. The tree trembled, the men began to pull, there was a sharp crack and almost in slow motion, the tree crashed to the ground.

People had gathered in the square to watch and I went down to join them. It was like the scene of a massacre. Huge trunks and severed limbs were scattered across the road; the pavement was thick with sawdust. When the felling finally stopped, a single palm tree remained. When I asked why they were being chopped down, I was told that this was the first stage of a wider redevelopment plan for Sheshi Fitorja. It seemed crazy for the Bashkia to be cutting down mature trees to improve the environment. But it wasn't entirely negative. Some Albanians had seen commercial advantage in the felling and were using bits of tree trunk to display their wares. Another was using a log as a chair so he could sit behind his table on which he had laid out a few combs, some lighter fuel and some nail clippers. The man was in late middle age with a craggy face, deep-set eyes and a goatee beard. His name was Enver, and as he also had a weighing machine, I thought I'd get myself weighed. It cost twenty leks. He read off my weight and I asked if he thought that was about right for a person of my size. He thought it was. He asked if I wanted a comb, but I pointed to my head (and lack of hair) and he laughed. I gave him fifty leks, about thirty pence, and he touched his heart in thanks. Enver and Ylvi at different ends of the economic spectrum, both adapting to capitalism; one well rewarded, the other scraping a living that was measured in single leks.

I went back to my room and almost immediately the phone buzzed. It was Ylvi saying he was in the shop for five minutes. I didn't know quite what to make of that, so I asked if I should come to the shop. He said yes, he was shutting for the day, he had some free time, what did I want to do? Did I want to go for a walk, did I want something to eat? I was hungry, I'd only had *byrek* for lunch, so said food would be good. Would I like to eat in town or in a village? I said village.

We drove south along Rruga Ramiz Aranitasi. During communism, this area was another *zona industrial*. Ylvi pointed out some of the old factories: a meat processing plant, an oil press now privately run, and just before the road crossed the railway, a cotton mill from the early 1950s. On our left was the huge Gogo Nush fertiliser plant which had had its own power station. When the plant came on stream in 1967, Hoxha declared that its construction was "a multi-faceted victory for the people and the Party". The factory closed in the mid-1990s; the power station was decommissioned in 2007. But even in decay, it was an impressive sight with numerous factory units, chimneys and cooling towers still standing.

The restaurant Ylvi had chosen was called Rustika Kala; Ylvi had phoned ahead and requested a table by the fire. From the outside, as its name suggested, the restaurant looked like a fantasy castle. Inside, there were flagstones on the floor, an inlaid wooden ceiling and a large fireplace. On the walls were photographs of famous communist-era actors and actresses from Fier. It was the sort of place the town's well-to-do would flock to on a summer's weekend to enjoy the food, the views and the cooler air. Tonight, as well as us, a group of men were eating, and, of course, they were all Ylvi's friends. While we were waiting for our food, Ylvi called them over. They gathered around him and then he started showing them the old photos. He made it into a game; they had to guess where each place was. Ylvi was in his element, at the centre of the action. The more the men struggled, the funnier it became.

Back in Fier, Ylvi thought it would be good to round off the evening with a drink. But he was uncharacteristically on edge. Something was niggling. Then he said he wanted to give me something so I would remember Fier, a picture maybe or a book. I said he'd already done so much for me that I'd have no trouble remembering him or Fier. But Ylvi wanted to formalise the memory. He wanted to give me something I could take away.

A photography shop next to the café was open. The woman who ran it was a friend of Ylvi's. One of her best-selling lines was personalised mobile phone covers with pictures of babies, girlfriends or cars. It gave Ylvi an idea; why didn't we have some pictures put on a pair of mugs, one new, one old. But which pictures? We eventually decided the new one would be his shop and the old one the communist mural outside his shop. He was pleased, I was pleased. The mugs would be ready at ten o'clock the next morning.

When I went back the next day, Ylvi was waiting outside the café. He was holding two white boxes which he presented to me. I was very touched. I'd known this man for less than twenty-four hours, but his kindness and generosity had made my visit to Fier special.

Apollonia: a sanctuary in a changing world 1988

The ancient city of Apollonia was a few kilometres west of Fier. The road was narrow, straight and potholed. We bumped across a single-track railway line which, Pepi told us, had recently been extended south to Vlorë. But there could not have been many trains because people were using the track as a footpath.

The railway seemed to be a kind of informal boundary marking where Fier town ended and the countryside began. Beyond the railway, a few single-storey houses sheltered behind bamboo fences; then the landscape opened up and once again the plain stretched away into the distance. The rain had turned everything to mud. Muddy sheep grazed at the roadside. Ducks splashed in the potholes. An old woman who had just collected water from a standpipe picked her way gingerly through the puddles. In the fields, men were digging trenches and women with axes were breaking up tree stumps. Their children stood on the lip of a drainage channel and waved as we trundled past.

Apollonia was a large site, and on a warmer day it might have been more enjoyable. But in the cold it was a desolate place. Its grandest monument was the Bouleuterion, Apollonia's administrative centre where its town council had met. The façade was almost complete: six Corinthian pillars supporting a decorated architrave and tympanum. Roman bricks had been added later as a buttress. From there, we walked along what remained of the Stoa and climbed up to what remained of the theatre - in both cases, not very much. As we climbed higher, we realised that the best thing about Apollonia was its location. The city was only a few metres above the plain, but that was enough. Laid out before us was a huge, collectivised landscape running all the way to the coast. The fields were a mixture of muted greens and browns; stands of trees sheltered small settlements from the wind. And there were bunkers - a line of them immediately below the old city and more on the hillside. Just for the fun of it, Dag and I went into one and looked out through the gun slit. On the ridge above the city, field guns pointed west towards the sea.

When Apollonia was founded, it was close to the Vjosa river which gave it access to the sea. In 234 AD, a powerful earthquake shifted the riverbed and Apollonia's harbour began to silt up. The city declined and by the fifth century AD, it had been abandoned. Five hundred years later, Apollonia came under Byzantine control. They built a church and monastery outside the walls of the old settlement. Most of the stone for it was taken from the theatre. Given Albania's intolerance of religion, it would have been interesting to go inside, but the church was closed for restoration. Wooden props were supporting the south wall, as if the archaeologists feared the whole building might collapse.

In the museum, we were shown displays of terracotta pots and vases, household utensils and ancient weapons. Outside on the balcony, there was a collection of Greek and Roman statues, most of them headless. As well as restoration, archaeologists were also continuing to excavate the site. They were digging at the rear of the museum, where they had already exposed pillars and paving stones. The spoil was being sifted on the bank. Dag is a doctor, but you didn't need special anatomical knowledge to recognise what they were excavating. Fragments of body parts were mixed up in the soil: a finger, part of a leg bone, teeth and skulls. In one grave, a complete skeleton lay open to the elements. In another, a skull lay half buried in the mud, part of it stove in by a heavy blow. Some of our party collected fragments of bone to take home.

2019

The road had been improved since 1988 and Fier had spread westwards, over the railway and onto the plain. When the collective farms were broken up, many people used their plots to build new houses. They stood side by side with decrepit apartment blocks, a warehouse with *MARKSIZEM-LENINIZMIT* on the wall and lots of bunkers. One by the turning to Apollonia was large enough for someone to have put a chimney on it.

There had been some small changes in thirty years. Signage had been updated with information in Albanian, French and English. The paths by the entrance were marked out with brick edges and there were wicker baskets for litter. But the main difference was the trees. New ones had taken root and old ones had put on thirty years of growth. When I tried to line up a comparison shot of the Bouleuterion, the view was blocked by foliage. In the same way, it was hard to match general shots of the plain because of all the new growth. The plain itself had been broken into a myriad of small plots. The other striking difference was the new highway linking Fier with Vlorë. It swept past Apollonia to the west, cutting a straight line across the plain. The rapid rate of change all around made Apollonia seem like a sanctuary.

The monastery could easily have been mistaken for a fortified compound with the church at its centre. Thirty years on, the props had been removed and although a tree was partially blocking the view, the restored Byzantine brickwork glowed in the sunshine. New lights had been inserted in the dome and roof tiles had been re-laid. Even better, I could go inside. The air was scented with the sweet smell of wax from votive candles. The iconostasis was beautiful but not old; a plaque said that it had been destroyed in 1917 during the First World War and restored ten years later.

The museum was still on the first floor of the monastery, but it had been through a hard time. It had closed in 1991 but that hadn't preventing looting in the early 1990s. It had had been looted again in 1997. Many of its treasures had been moved to Tirana for safekeeping. It reopened in 2011.

The vast majority of its items were Greek or Roman. There were galleries full of statues, votive figures and stelae along with domestic items: clay pots and amphorae, keys,

1988: The Orthodox church at Apollonia…..

2019:….is now fully restored and open to the public.

ladles and buckets. There was also an Illyrian shield dated to the fourth century BCE. Its surface was decorated with circles; at its centre was a grotesque sticking out its tongue. The shield was important for the Albanian historical narrative. As at other sites, the role of the Illyrians in Apollonia's early history had to be made explicit. In its description of Apollonia, the Albturist guidebook says that there had been "a little Illyrian settlement at the place where the Hellenes settled". Within the Greek city, it continued, Illyrians had occupied "some of the highest posts in its administration and economic and cultural life".

It is quite possible that there was an Illyrian settlement at Apollonia that pre-dated Greek colonisation. It's known that a powerful Illyrian tribe, the Taulantii, occupied territory north of the Seman river. But even the arch-ideologue Enver Hoxha was cautious about asserting Illyrian influence without sufficient archaeological evidence. During a discussion of Albanological Sciences in 1969, Hoxha had told his audience that their research should have "anti-chauvinist, anti-idealist, Marxist-Leninist foundations". That was the only way to refute "foreign scholars who have anti-scientific views, otherwise we will not be able to do so, irrespective that it is our country about which these studies are being done".

In the same session, Hoxha spoke about the "foreign archaeologists and historians" who had excavated at Apollonia and Butrint: "we know that in their excavations they proceeded not from our interests but from their own". He was right about that. Butrint had been exploited by Italy. Apollonia had been plundered by French and Austrian archaeologists in the nineteenth and early twentieth centuries. The French archaeologist Leon Rey was more sympathetic to Albania. But it wasn't until after the war that Albania could take control of its archaeological sites.

The museum curator was on the balcony having a cigarette. His name was Adi. I said I had some photos from way back and asked if he'd like to see them. We went inside and I spread the photos on his desk. He was interested in all of them, but the one that really caught his attention was a photo Dag had taken of the excavations behind the museum. He said he hadn't seen that view before and asked if he could take a photo of the photo. I said how green the site had become with all the new trees. Adi said that the tree in front of the bell tower was planted in 1992 when the church reopened. It was a symbol of rebirth.

Adi had worked at the museum since it reopened in 2011. He told a story about one of the carvings in the portico. It was a fragment of a stela showing a woman holding a mirror. A chip was missing from the left-hand corner. The official version was that robbers who were trying to remove the stela had been disturbed by a vigilant policeman who had fired at them. His bullet had caught the edge of the stela. Adi had a different explanation. He thought that the policeman was working with the robbers, and when someone saw them trying to remove the stela, he fired the bullet to provide a cover story. At least the carving was saved, and only slightly damaged.

Myzeqe: old animosities linger
1988

A single-track, metal-girdered bridge took us across the river and back onto the plain. Soldiers were working in the fields. On a ridge above them was a graveyard. Cows grazed in the olive groves. After all the rain, the earth was heavy and glistening. A work party was digging drainage channels, the neat lines of the ditches marked by untidy piles of newly turned earth. Keeping these fields productive must be a never-ending task.

The plain stretched as far as we could see. This area, said Pepi, was one of Albania's most important agricultural regions, especially for wheat, cotton and sunflowers. Before liberation, much of it had been marsh; now it contained some of the country's largest cooperative and state farms.

The cotton harvest was in full swing. Bullock carts piled high with sacks were converging on a field by the road so the sacks could be loaded onto trucks. It took three or four men to control the bullocks and to help push the carts when they got stuck in the mud. Children sat on an earth embankment along the field's edge, watching the drama.

At Lushnjë, we had to wait while an old gun emplacement was blasted out of the ground. The thud of the explosion rolled across the plain.

We passed Lushnjë's Martyrs' Cemetery, bright with marigolds. Then it was more of the same monotonous, hypnotic plain. It seemed to go on for ever. At Dushk, the road was blocked by a bullock cart. The cart was loaded with winter feed and the animals were refusing to make the steep drop down from the road into the field. More sacks of cotton were stacked by the roadside. It must have had an early start; some men were asleep on the sacks. Images of Ramiz Alia had been painted on an apartment block wall.

A green and white diesel pulling half a dozen empty wagons rumbled past. Then a bridge over the Shkumbin river brought us into Rrogozhinë.

2019

We didn't stop on our way north, so the only photos I have of this part of the journey were taken from the coach. As we drove through Lushnjë, both Dag and I snapped photos of the town's industrial estate. As well as processing foodstuffs, Lushnjë also had a paper factory and a plastics factory. The paper factory had been built in the mid-1960s, the plastics factory a few years later. I managed to snap a couple of photos of the paper factory: its gates manned by soldiers, military and agricultural vehicles parked outside, a chimney dribbling smoke. Dag's picture showed a newer building with a garden and ornamental fountain which we assumed was the plastics factory.

The industrial estate was still there. Some units had tenants, but for the most part it was derelict. Kirstie and I walked past windowless warehouses, a listing chimney and rusting metal gates with a communist star. We tried to identify details from the old photos. We found a line of hoppers that we thought had been part of the plastics factory. But even when you managed to identify a feature, the context had changed. New fences and new houses blocked the view. Some things had disappeared. The garden and ornamental fountain had become a petrol station. A hotel with lots of blue-tinted glass had been built next to the paper factory.

The old road would have taken us through the centre of Lushnjë, where we would have had a brief glimpse of a *lapidar* in the central square. Next to the Martyrs' Cemetery was the Agricultural Research Centre (Instituti i Kërkimeve Bujqësore). It opened in 1956 and was still there, rebranded as the Centre for Agricultural Technology Transfer (Qendra e Transferimit të Teknologjive Bujqësore). Then it was back onto the plain.

For obvious reasons, these plains - Fusha e Thumanës, Bregu i Matit, Fusha e Vrinës, Fusha e Dropullit - were crucial to communist Albania. In a country where more than 70 per cent of the landmass is mountain, Albania would have struggled to feed itself without them. The plain we were now crossing was Fusha e Myzeqesë, Albania's largest plain. It stretches north for more than forty kilometres, from Fier in the south to the Shkumbin river, the traditional dividing line between northern and southern Albania. Fusha e Myzeqesë is not just Albania's largest plain; for the communists it also had profound political significance, because it was where collectivisation had begun.

The first Law on Land Reform came into force in August 1945, and so much importance was attached to it that Enver Hoxha himself went to Gorrë, a small village near Lushnjë, to present the land deeds to the peasant farmers. A second Land Reform law was passed in May the following year, to "correct the mistakes" of the first which was now judged to have been too soft on landowners and rich peasants (kulaks) who had been allowed to keep up to forty hectares of land for private use. This second law reduced the maximum holding to five hectares and banned the buying and selling of land. Peasants were encouraged to pool their private holdings, and on 11 November 1946 Albania's first agricultural cooperative was set up at Krutjë, barely a kilometre from Gorrë.

Collectivisation took time, but by March 1967 the authorities were able to say that all Albania's villages had been collectivised. And because of its leading role in collectivisation, the farms on the Plain of Myzeqe featured in official propaganda. An article in *New Albania* eulogised the plain as "an endless carpet of marvellous colours, combined so tastefully by the hand of man... Located in the heart of Myzeqe, it has rightly been called the granary of Albania."

The article also mentioned the *lapidar* in Lushnjë's central square. It was called Our Land (*Toka Jonë*) and, according to the article, symbolised "the victory of the broad masses of the peasantry, the final victory in their struggle for the land". Unveiled in 1987, late in the history of communist Albania, it was the work of one of Albania's finest sculptors, Perikli Çuli. At its centre a woman holds a sheaf of corn above her head. She is flanked by two men: one with a scythe, the other with a rifle. Around the monument's base, a stone ribbon illustrates farming's contribution to the Albanian economy.

From its inception, the *lapidar* was controversial. Some objected to the fact that a cypress tree had been felled to make space for it. But the real criticism lay in what it stood for. One commentator[1] has called it "shameful" because "it seeks to perpetuate those most bloody and tragic reforms in Myzeqe". The same commentator has reimagined the *lapidar*. Rather than holding a sheaf of corn above her head, the woman now holds a notice reading: *Arbeit Macht Frei*, a not-too-subtle message that recast Myzeqe not as "an endless carpet of marvellous colours" but as a vast internment camp.

---

1 Radi and Radi, http://www.radiandradi.com/kur-statujat-dhunojne-te-perditshmen-e-qytetit-jozef-radi

As we've seen, forced labour was an indispensable part of industry and agriculture, but it was taken to extremes in Myzeqe. In 1952, a work camp for 1,500 prisoners was set up at Vlashuk to dig a canal to bring water onto the plain. Three years later, the Council of Ministers issued an order "On the draining of the Tërbufi swamp and the reclamation of the Myzeqe plain", so another work camp was set up to drain 8,000 hectares of swamp at Tërbuf, north of Lushnjë. Other camps followed. Around Lushnjë, there were camps at Grabian, Savër, Gjazë, Gradishtë, Gjonc, Kafaraj, Hoxharë, Varibob and Bubullimë. There were another eleven around Fier: at Remas, Roskovec, Radostinë, Pojan, Hoxharë, Seman, Shtyllas, Ndërmenas, Libofshë, Kreshpan and Levan. Fusha e Myzeqesë had the largest concentration of internment camps in the whole of Albania.

There was a further twist to this story that was specific to Lushnjë and Fier. During the National Liberation War, a rival resistance group, Balli Kombëtar (BK), had been strong in Myzeqe. Hoxha dismissed its leadership as "feudal lords, big landowners and merchants, bajraktars, bourgeois intellectuals, senior clergy and other sworn enemies of the communists". When the war ended, many of BK's leaders and supporters were sent to the Myzeqe internment camps to dig ditches and canals.

But even communist-appointed officials in Lushnjë and Fier dragged their feet on collectivisation, much to Hoxha's irritation. He urged the Party to be vigilant and "to step up the class struggle in the countryside". Lushnjë's recalcitrance resurfaced in 1987, two years after Hoxha's death. In the same year that *Toka Jonë* was unveiled, Lushnjë's Bashkia did an astonishing thing. It commissioned two young artists, Edi Rama and Lad Myrtezai, to paint a mural about Myzeqe. The Bashkia offered them a wall in the town museum that was 15 metres long and 3½ metres high. Rama and Myrtezai called their painting "The Legend of the Land" (*Legjenda e tokës*).

Legjenda e tokës is a ferocious attack on starvation and exploitation. At the centre of the painting, a gaunt male figure is ploughing with an even more emaciated ox. To his left, a barefoot young mother suckles a baby. Another female figure is stretched over a coffin, mourning. On the right of the image, an army of skeletal peasants brandish sticks and scythes.

Two visions of Myzeqe in the same central square: one triumphalist, the other damning. When *Legjenda e tokës* was unveiled, some citizens were so appalled that they went to the Party offices to denounce the artists. Others were energised and found in the painting a style and sensibility that challenged Albanian artistic orthodoxy. Even now, it is a breathtaking piece of work, and even more so when you remember the context.

Post-1990, Lushnjë's uneasy relationship with the central authorities has continued. One of the most contentious issues harks back to that earlier struggle between the communists and Balli Kombëtar. In October 1943, the communists received intelligence that a large BK force had gathered at Lushnjë. In the battle that followed, twelve BK fighters were killed and their commander ordered the rest to surrender. However, a large number escaped to a hamlet called Matjan in the hills north-east of Lushnjë. The communists pursued them. The BK fighters were asked to join the communists. One did, 67 refused. Those 67 were shot.

Throughout the communist years, those associated with Balli Kombëtar and other non-communist liberation groups were persecuted. Since the fall of the old regime, the historical narrative has been revised to acknowledge the contribution of non-communist forces to Albania's liberation. But memorialising those fighters has remained problematic. Martyrs' Cemeteries were for communist martyrs, and post-communist administrations have been unwilling to change the convention.

In October 2016, the state did finally honour those 67 BK fighters shot by the communists. A monument was unveiled in Divjakë, a couple of metres from a *lapidar* commemorating communist martyrs. The two factions remain separated even in death. It is episodes like this that make you realise how fractured a country Albania still is. The weight of history is enormous. The past is not going away quietly.

Lushnjë to Rrogozhinë on the modern highway takes about twenty minutes. Most of the old road that meandered through collectivised villages has disappeared under the new. The only parts that still existed were the slip roads to the villages. We took the slip road into Dushk where Dag and I had seen images of Ramiz Alia on an apartment block. There were several four-storey blocks in the village, and that's probably where the banners had been hung. In the old economy, Dushk cultivated silkworms; it was still a farming community with polytunnels and orchards on the plain and olives on the hillsides.

A couple of kilometres before Rrogozhinë there was a turning to Tërbuf, where one of the first internment camps on Myzeqe had been set up. The village was namechecked in the Albturist guidebook. Thanks to drainage, Tërbuf was "no longer a hotbed of malaria nor the home of feudalism". It had become "the main region for the production of industrial plants and cereals". The road to Tërbuf ran in a straight line across the plain past smallholdings and new villas until we came to Çermë, a straggling village that would have been unexceptional were it not for a sign to Çerm Sektor and then another to Ç Kamp. Ç Kamp was a tiny collection of houses down a dirt track which had been an internment camp. At Çerm Sektor there was a modern pumping station, the only indication that this had once been marshland.

The work camp at Tërbuf was set up in January 1956. Testimony from survivors gives an insight into life inside the camp. Known as Reparti 309, the camp could hold up to 700 prisoners. Most were *armiqtë e popullit*, enemies of the people. They were mostly Albanian, but there were also some Greeks, some Yugoslavs and 24 women. Prisoners were tasked with digging a canal to take water from the plain to the sea. They were split into five brigades and were under pressure to do the work quickly. Conditions were extremely challenging, and the regime, as was its wont, started throwing around accusations of sabotage, trying to blame the engineers for the slow progress. The camp closed in March 1958 when the canal was completed. It became known as the Canal of the Prisoners (*Kanali i të burgosurve*).

Tërbuf was larger than I had expected. It was only ten kilometres from Rrogozhinë but it felt very remote. It had a new mosque, but most of the village consisted of communist-era housing blocks. We walked along dusty backstreets, past warehouses from the same period, but we couldn't see any sign of the camp. Maybe that wasn't so surprising. It had closed more than sixty years ago, and according to testimony even officials had found it hard to locate. Surrounded by reeds and water, the chances were that it had been reabsorbed into the landscape.

We stopped for a drink at a café overlooking the plain. Like so many, the couple who owned it had worked in Greece to make money so they could open a business in Albania. I said what a good view it was across the plain, and the man told me that in communist times Myzeqe had produced enough wheat to feed the whole of Albania; there was even enough to export to Greece. He described how the plain had been drained and fertiliser had helped increase the yields. There was pride in the way he described it. And then, maybe in case I misunderstood his nostalgia, he told me that back then, if he'd started a conversation with a foreigner like me, he could have been jailed. The trouble now, he went on, was that people in Albania didn't have enough money: "Look at the plain now, it's broken into small fields, just enough for one family. Who can make money from such a small farm?"

The Albturist guidebook described Rrogozhinë as "an important road and railroad junction". Because of its strategic location, it had a cotton gin, a soap factory and a sunflower oil press. Since the 1990s, Rrogozhinë's industry had collapsed. Bypassed by the new highway, what once must have been a busy town has become a backwater.

I had some photos taken somewhere between Dushk and Rrogozhinë. One showed a country road with farm vehicles parked on the verge. Another was of a train on an embankment pulling empty wagons. Because the road system had changed so dramatically, finding the locations turned out to be tricky. In one of the photos, road and railway converged. Dag had also taken a photo of the railway crossing a river. I puzzled over that for ages. The only place I could see on the map where road, rail and river came together was south of Rrogozhinë, between the two highways.

A minor road off the bypass took us through fields towards the Shkumbin river. The railway line joined the road and then we came to a road and rail bridge. It all fell into place. The embankment on the other side of the bridge confirmed it - that was where I had taken the pictures of the train. The bridge was a long one, around 400 metres, spanning both the river and a shallow valley. But its surface was so pitted we didn't risk crossing. Below the bridge an animal market was in full swing. Farmers in horse-drawn carts were converging on it from all over the plain. They were coming along dirt tracks between the fields, as they must have done for generations. In the distance, cars and lorries sped past on the new highway.

The next town was Kavajë. From our coach window, we had seen factories and a railhead. The railhead and a rusting gantry were still there. So were some of the factories. Their chimneys had undergone an imaginative transformation. Three of them had been topped with metal finials and turned into minarets.

North of Kavajë, development on a huge scale has obliterated much of the old world. Farmland has become real estate and the closer you get to Durrës, the more intense the development. In the town, the highway becomes a canyon running between hotels on each side of the road. But the old road system was still there. It was difficult to access from the highway, but we managed to get off the motorway at

Golem and onto a single-track road running parallel to the motorway. I think this must have been the old road. Although it was only metres from the highway, it felt like we'd shifted back to an earlier version of Durrës. That's not to say there weren't new developments along the road; there were. But there were also smallholdings with vineyards, orchards, hay meadows and even a few cattle grazing on the verges. At Shkallnur, we passed the remains of a cooperative farm. An open-fronted barn with a high roof looked as if it had been an SMT where motorised farm equipment had been kept.

We emerged by Durrës' bus station and took the road to Pezë. This was the way we had come with Edi in 1987. Back then, all this land had been part of the Hider Koka cooperative farm, Albania's largest, covering 4,500 hectares. Since then, as Tirana and Durrës expanded, it had become a kind of hinterland, a buffer between the two cities, a rural enclave where city dwellers could come for a taste of the countryside. It was also a place to get married, and competition between wedding venues had produced some extraordinarily elaborate buildings. Iliria Palace was a Baroque concoction with statues of Illyrian guards at the entrance. Golden Kompleks had statues on the roof and an enormous coat of arms.

The road continued along the valley of the Erzen river, through a rolling landscape of neat strips and pasture. We were now only a few kilometres from Tirana. It was a gradual transition from rural to urban; it happened almost without noticing. Then a familiar building, the twin towers of the "Stalin" Textiles Combine (Kombinati Tekstileve "Stalin"). We were back in Tirana.

10: Tirana
Hero City

Scanderbeg Square: the disappearing statue 1988

We were staying again in Hotel Tirana on Scanderbeg Square. Last year, Dag and I had been given a room at the rear of the hotel with a view over picturesquely dilapidated villas. This time we were at the front overlooking the square. Despite the early hour, plenty of people were walking or cycling to work. Every few minutes an elderly bus pulled up outside the hotel to disgorge its passengers. When the sound of the engine had died away, you could hear feet shuffling on the paving slabs.

Beyond the square to the south, mountain crests wrapped in a smoggy haze scribbled an erratic line along the horizon. The rising sun caught the tip of the minaret and shafts of misty, autumnal sunlight spread across the square, illuminating rooftop slogans. Then it did something so spectacular that I called Dag over to come and watch. Since last year a statue of Enver Hoxha had been erected in the square. As the sun rose, its light travelled down the statue and turned the metal gold. It was as if the dictator was being re-energised.

After breakfast, we went out and stood in front of the statue. Hoxha looked suave in a tailored suit, the trousers baggy around his ankles. His three-quarter-length coat was partly open, giving the impression that he was striding forward. Ten metres tall, the statue skewed your sense of proportion and made the people walking past look shrunken.

It was a beautiful morning, not a cloud in the sky, and in the sunshine we could see his face in detail. It was stern and unsmiling. Lips pursed, hair swept back, brow furrowed as if deep in thought, he stared down into the square. Even after death he had you in his sights.

2019

The statue was inaugurated on 16 October 1988, the eightieth anniversary of Hoxha's birth and just in time for our second visit to Albania. At the ceremony, Ramiz Alia told the crowd that it had been the "ardent desire" of the Albanian people to erect such a "majestic monument" so everyone could say: "We have Enver Hoxha here, in the middle of the capital."

Tirana became the Albanian capital in February 1920. It was a small community of less than 10,000 people whose lives centred on a bazaar and two mosques, Et'hem Bey, which still stands on Scanderbeg Square, and the Old Mosque (Xhamia e Vjetër) which was damaged during the Liberation War and never rebuilt. British travellers, Jan and Cora Gordon[1], visited Tirana in the mid-1920s and described the bazaar as "rows upon rows of meagre houses hollowed out into shops". Bernard Newman[2] was in Tirana ten years later. He found the bazaar "primitive", a place where "peasants squatted in the dust or mud while selling their wares". But he was more positive about King Zog's efforts to modernise the city. Newman noted that "a wide and pleasant boulevard, lined with exotic trees, leads to a large square, which houses all the government departments…The square is unfinished and at present unpaved, but one day at least it will be dignified."

When the communists took control in 1944, they inherited a city whose architecture was a mixture of Ottoman, Zogist and Italian Fascist. With Soviet help, the communists built industrial zones and housing estates that transformed Tirana.

1 Jan and Cora Gordon, *Two Vagabonds in Albania*, 1927, pp.3-4.
2 Bernard Newman, *Albanian Back-Door*, 1936, pp.219-20.

On 17 November 1969, the twenty-fifth anniversary of the city's iberation, Tirana was declared "Qytet Hero", a Hero City. By the 1980s, its population had grown to more than 200,000 and its factories produced almost a fifth of the country's industrial output. The "Stalin" Textiles Combine on the city's western outskirts was only one of a number of factories in a *zona industriale* that included a power station, a glass factory, a brick factory, a food processing plant called Kombinati Ushqimor "Ali Kelmendi" and a furniture factory, Kombinati "Misto Mame".

Scanderbeg Square at the centre of the city seemed to be the beating heart of communist Albania. In it were some of the country's most important institutions: the Bank of Albania, the National Library, the National Historical Museum. Along the eastern flank was the Palace of Culture. These buildings impressed with their mass; their bulk gave the square a sense of permanence. The Et'hem Bey mosque and the Clock Tower acknowledged Albania's Ottoman legacy. (The mosque was closed for worship but both it and the Clock Tower had Category 1 protection.) The statue of Scanderbeg, Albania's national hero, injected a semi-mythological element into the ensemble. With the addition of Hoxha's golden statue in 1988, the amalgam of Ottoman, Zogist and communist buildings had been welded together around a single figure. This was the Scanderbeg Square in my photos.

But in reality, the square was malleable. Ever since it had been conceived by King Zog, it had been shaped and reshaped by politics. In December 1950, the communists began putting their stamp on the square. A statue of Stalin was erected and it remained in the square until 1968 when Stalin was replaced by Scanderbeg. In the late 1950s, the old bazaar was demolished to make space for the Palace of Culture. In the 1970s, the Orthodox cathedral was demolished to make space for Hotel Tirana. Around the same time, Tirana's original Bashkia was demolished to make space for the National Historical Museum.

The Scanderbeg Square that Dag and I saw in 1988 marked the culmination of a political era, communist Albania's apogee. On a longer timescale it was just one version of many. But because it had been our first sighting, it made a deep impression and became the version by which everything that followed was judged.

1988

After a late lunch - macaroni, kebab, very sweet ice cream - we had some free time. Dag and I followed a street into the neighbourhood behind the hotel. A row of shops along the street were hardly shops at all, no more than doorways. The family squatted on the floor or sat on low stools behind loose cigarettes, razor blades and corked bottles of *shampo*. I bought a bottle; it cost four and a half leks. On the corner was the Flora bookshop, famous in Albania because it was where the young Enver Hoxha had worked and which became a communist cell during the Italian occupation. I bought a magazine, an edition of *New Albania*. On the front was a photo of Ramiz Alia celebrating May Day with Young Pioneers. Then we returned to the main square.

Scanderbeg Square was primarily a formal space for marches and rallies. But this afternoon there were plenty of people strolling. They were mainly civilians, but there were also some soldiers in high-collared khaki uniforms and peaked caps with red stars. A mobile kiosk by the Palace of Culture was selling snacks and brightly coloured drinks. At the far end of the square, gardeners were tending flower beds full of unruly red blooms. From there, we had an uninterrupted view down a broad boulevard, all the way to the Enver Hoxha University. On its roof were four letters, PPSH, which I now knew stood for Partia e Punës e Shqipërisë, the Party of Labour of Albania.

As the light faded, the fountains in the square turned red. People drifted away. The darkness seemed to exaggerate the size of the square. It made us feel vulnerable, by which I don't mean that we thought we were going to be attacked. It was subtler than that. It made you feel small, in the same way that standing in front of Enver Hoxha's statue made you feel small. The square was real enough and the wind was biting. But at the same time, there was something dreamlike about it. It was hard to put into words.

When we got back to our room, I jotted down some phrases in my notebook. The square was "a victory for belief", "a construct of rhetoric", "imagination made real". I was trying to capture the fusion, as I saw it, of reality and otherworldliness because there was something slightly dissociated about the space. You had to keep remembering where you were. This square was Albania's equivalent to Trafalgar Square. From our window, Hoxha's statue glittered under the spotlights.

2019

That version turned out to be short-lived. On 20 February 1991, Hoxha's statue was pulled down and everything changed. Unsurprisingly, the upheaval impacted on the square. Scanderbeg Square had never officially been pedestrianised - it was just that with so few vehicles it had seemed that way. When restrictions on car ownership were lifted, the square became a giant roundabout. That was how it had been in 2005. When I next visited in 2012, road lanes had been marked out and there were pedestrian crossings. The crossings only worked when enough people wanted to cross and the weight of numbers forced drivers to give way.

The square arrived at its present form in 2017 and is now officially pedestrianised. Hoxha's plinth has disappeared beneath the paving stones, but all the buildings in the square continue to be used. What has changed is the visual context. Enormous skyscrapers looming over the square have recalibrated the sense of scale. The fifteen-storey Tirana International Hotel, for many years Albania's tallest building, now looks Lilliputian.

To make space for the skyscrapers, there was another wave of demolition. In the early hours of Monday 18 May 2020, the same day that the National Theatre was demolished, diggers flattened the remains of the Ottoman neighbourhood where the Flora bookshop had been. In August 2022, work began on the Scanderbeg Building, also known as Tirana's Rock. Shaped to resemble a bust of Scanderbeg, when completed it will be 85 metres high, small compared to its neighbour, Mount Tirana, which will be more than 200 metres high. Behind the Tirana International Hotel, a 34-storey hotel is being built. When completed, it will be 125 metres high.

Many have criticised the decision to allow so many skyscrapers in what historically has been a low-rise city centre. But high-rise infiltration is not new. When the fifteen-storey Hotel Tirana opened in 1979, it changed the visual dynamics of the square. I'm not a fan of the skyscrapers, but communism was overthrown more than thirty years ago and Tirana has no obligation to preserve its central square as a memorial to a discredited regime. Scanderbeg Square is just doing what it has always done: it is reflecting political power.

Usually when we're in Tirana, we stay in a small hotel on Rruga Mine Peza. For the sake of research, Kirstie and I had booked into the Tirana International Hotel for a couple of nights. The sweeping staircase, one of the hotel's grandest features, had preserved its communist-era tiles etched with a geometric pattern.

When I stayed here with Dag, I took photos from the front and rear of the hotel. One of the photos from the rear was a view over a jumble of Ottoman villas and communist housing blocks. The neighbourhood had been demolished; in its place were new apartments and offices. If it wasn't for the mountains along the horizon, you could be forgiven for thinking that these were two unrelated locations.

Another photo showed Hotel Peza on the corner of what had been Bulevardi Stalin. Further along the boulevard, two tall buildings faced each other across the road. Both were built in the 1970s. The one on the left was designed by Petraq Kolevica, one of communist Albania's leading architects, and was the headquarters of China's Civil Aviation Administration (Agjencia Ajrore Kineze). Facing it was an innovative building designed by another influential architect, Maks Velo. Velo's tower was headquarters for ATSH, the Albanian Telegraphic Agency (Agjencia Telegrafike Shqiptare). ATSH was an immensely powerful organisation, responsible for filtering foreign news and disseminating information about Albania.

Hotel Peza had become the headquarters of an insurance company. Kolovica's block had been turned into apartments. But Velo's tower had gone. Although it was a Category II Cultural Monument, it was weakened by an earthquake in 2019 and a decision was taken to demolish it.

I also had photos of Scanderbeg Square. One shows the Palace of Culture, the Bank of Albania and government buildings with slogans on their roofs: *RROFTË KOMITETI QENDROR I PPSH* (Long Live the Central Committee of the Party of Labour of Albania) and *LAVDI VEPRËS SË SHOKUT ENVER HOXHA* (Glory to the Work of Enver Hoxha). Hoxha's statue stands between the Bank of Albania and the National Historical Museum. In the modern equivalent, the statue has gone. Next to the bank you can see the dome of Tirana's new Orthodox Cathedral. Behind the bank, a 25-storey skyscraper, Alban Tower, is being erected.

Since its redesign, Scanderbeg Square has become one of the city's most used public spaces. All the major buildings had survived transition, but there were several small changes. The communist stars on the National Historical Museum's mosaic had been removed, and for some reason the aproned worker had relinquished his book and now had a sack slung over his shoulder. But otherwise it was as bright and gaudy as it had been before 1990. Hotel Tirana had also been modified. Its communist-era window blinds gave the hotel a chequered façade. Since privatisation, the blinds had been replaced with smoked glass, so that in the sunshine the hotel now appeared to be striped.

1988: The Palace of Culture and government offices in Scanderbeg Square....

2019: ...are overshadowed by new apartment blocks and skyscrapers.

Of themselves, these changes barely register, but cumulatively they have an impact. I had a photo taken from the south side of the square. It shows Hotel Tirana, the sloping roof of the Et'hem Bey mosque, a government ministry and part of the Palace of Culture. When I tried to take a modern equivalent, the elements were all there, but something wasn't right. It was like trying to force jigsaw puzzle pieces together. Then I realised what had happened. Since I had taken the original photo, the ministry had been extended and the plaza had been raised to accommodate the entrance to a museum, Bunk'Art 2. Spatial relationships had been disrupted and it was no longer possible to see the buildings in the same way.

The revamping of Scanderbeg Square has also had an interesting visual consequence. When the square was relaid, the engineers built it with a 2.5 per cent slope. That translates into a two-metre difference in height between the centre of the square and its edges. The slope invited interpretation. Was it supposed to mimic the curvature of the Earth? Or was it more specific to Albania? An Albanian friend told me that Edi Rama had said that the slope symbolised "the power of the individual": a person standing at the centre of the square, at its peak, can take control of the space and see everything. In a country where for decades public space had been seen as the "enemy", places where individuals were vulnerable to state surveillance, you could argue that this slope was an attempt to *personalise* public space, to give individuals (rather than the state) control over it. Trees and bushes around its edges reinforced the notion of "safe space" by providing citizens with private spaces within the boundaries of the square.

The slope had another effect, which only became apparent when I tried to match the old photos. Because the surface was curved, it was impossible to make exact comparisons. The visual context had been altered. For example, because of the curvature of the square, the flights of steps up to the Palace of Culture have had to be adjusted. There are now six steps up to the terrace; in 1988 there were nine. During

1988: Enver Hoxha's golden statue in Scanderbeg Square....

2019: ...has become a distant memory.

communism, there had been ten steps down from the square to the sunken gardens behind Scanderbeg's statue. After the space had been renovated, there were only four. The result is that, in a literal sense, the curved surface of the square has made it impossible to *see* the square and gardens in the way that Dag and I had *seen* them in 1988.

The National Historical Museum: a narrative revised
1988

Our group gathered on the steps of the National Historical Museum. In the entrance hall we were greeted with a larger-than-life statue of Enver Hoxha.

The exhibits on the ground floor dealt with Albania's early history: fragments of Neolithic pottery, Bronze Age weaponry and Iron Age ceramics. But the main focus was on Illyria. As we went around, Ilir spoke about the importance of the Illyrians and how modern-day Albanians regard themselves as their descendants. We were shown fragments of Illyrian armour and weaponry, Illyrian farming implements and a map of Illyrian settlements.

Scanderbeg's resistance to the Ottomans in the fifteenth century was described on the first floor where there were displays of weapons - swords, pikes and crossbows – and an enormous mural of Scanderbeg marshalling his mountain warriors.

Rifles and pistols arranged in the shape of a double-headed eagle represented the League of Prizren. A tableau of the Declaration of Independence in Vlorë included a statue of a portly Ismail Qemali, Albania's first Prime Minister. Then came the First World War and out of the chaos that followed, a politician called Fan Noli led what Ilir called "a bourgeois-democratic revolution". Ilir was interrupted by one of our group who asked, "what's bourgeois?" Ilir was taken aback and I wasn't sure if the question was genuine or a wind-up. After a moment, the questioner asked, "is it the enemy?" "Yes", said Ilir, "it is the enemy", and he continued with his potted history. After Fan Noli came Ahmed Zogu, first as President and then King. Someone asked why there were no pictures of him in the museum. Ilir replied, "we don't have pictures of traitors on display in our country."

The final part of the exhibition dealt with the Liberation War. Explanatory panels in Albanian described the formation and development of the partisan movement under the guidance of Enver Hoxha. Around the walls were pictures of partisan leaders; Hoxha's was the most prevalent. There were more pictures of Hoxha above the cabinets: Hoxha by turns stern or avuncular, suited or in military uniform, Hoxha relaxing with peasants or surrounded by children. The display climaxed in a hall with a huge Socialist Realist mural showing partisans engaged in hand-to-hand fighting with German troops. One partisan was lunging forward with a rifle in one hand and an Albanian flag in the other. Smoke from a burning German tank darkened the sky.

Every museum is an exercise in ideology, but here it had been pushed to the limit. This was an account of an independence struggle that had begun with the Illyrians more than two thousand years ago and was finally achieved in 1944. That was the moment Albania had been waiting for, and its mastermind was Enver Hoxha.

2019

When it opened in 1981, the purpose of the National Historical Museum was to lay down an account of Albanian history that culminated in the victory of communism. It was selective in its material, choosing - as Ilir had told us - to ignore King Zog altogether. With the old regime's collapse, its stranglehold on the historical narrative went too. In 1992, the year when Albania's first non-communist government was elected, the museum closed. When it reopened four years later, it had been stripped of Enver Hoxha and had a new Pavilion. It was called The Genocide of Communist Terror in Albania, 1944-1992 (Gjenocidi dhe Terrori Komunist në Shqipëri, 1944-1992).

The images and displays were stomach-turning. Around the walls were grainy images of labour camps, gibbets, firing squads and corpses. There was a gruesome mock-up of a cell with a tiny window and a blanket to sleep on. A chain and handcuffs hung from the wall. This wasn't anonymous suffering. Boards listed the names of people who had been killed by the regime. Some families had fared particularly badly: 13 members of the Vata family had been killed between 1946 and 1951; 28 members of the Marku family were killed between 1945 and 1953. Most of the deaths occurred in the 1940s-50s, but there were later ones too. Another board listed the names of those killed trying to cross the border in 1990. After a while it became difficult to process all the names.

Across Albania, there had been 82 prisons, of which 48 were internment camps. Altogether, there had been 17,900 political prisoners, of whom 5,157 were killed, 9,052 died in prison, 30,383 were sent into internal exile.

This Pavilion was also where members of other resistance groups were remembered - Balli Kombëtar and Legaliteti - as victims of the communists, along with intellectuals and clerics: Muslim, Bektashi, Catholic and Orthodox. Politicians who had been members of the Communist Party and who were later executed were also remembered.

Displays chronicled the final moments of the old regime. There were images of Hoxha's statue being pulled down. Young "Martyrs of Democracy" were commemorated. Then, in March 1992, the election that brought the Democratic Party to power. Photographs showed Scanderbeg Square filled to bursting and Sali Berisha giving a two-fingered victory salute to the crowd. What the communists had done was an affront to human decency, but was it "genocide"? Was the Pavilion really suggesting that Enver Hoxha had set out to annihilate a nation? And why was Sali Berisha taking the credit for the overthrow of the old regime? The pendulum had swung from one extreme to another. Albania's continuing political struggle was being played out in the museum.

The Genocide of Communist Terror in Albania closed in 2008. The Pavilion reopened in 2009, closed again and then reopened on 20 February 2012, the 21st anniversary of the toppling of Hoxha's statue. The Pavilion had a new name, the Pavilion of Communist Terror (Pavioni i Terrorit Komunist). Sali Berisha attended the opening.

The displays in the Pavilion of Communist Terror were much the same as they had been in the Genocide gallery, except that information about the two non-communist resistance movements - Balli Kombëtar and Legaliteti - had been moved to the Pavilion of the Antifascist National Liberation War. There were also two new Pavilions: an Icon Pavilion with a fine collection of more than sixty icons, and a King Zog Pavilion. The Zog displays were not particularly informative - some photos and a family tree that traced Zog's descendants back to a warlord called Zogu Le Grand. But the fact that he was there at all showed how far his rehabilitation had come.

Enver Hoxha had not been entirely removed. There was a picture of him at the Conference of Pezë in 1942 and another as one of the leaders of the General Council of the National Liberation Front. And in truth, it would be even more damaging to the credibility of the revisions if he had not been mentioned. Like it or not, it would be hard to tell the story of the National Liberation War without him.

Even with the help of the old photos, it was hard to rekindle the strangeness of communist Albania. Over the years I often thought about Edi, our guide on that first trip in 1987. His was the first authentic Albanian voice we'd heard when we got into the coach at Hani i Hotit. He was our conduit, the person with the knowledge and authority to explain (or not) what we were seeing.

When I started going through the photos in a more systematic way, I found some pictures of Edi. There was one of him in the coach and others at Hoteli i Gjuetisë and Shkodër. I wondered what had happened to him. I contacted an Albanian journalist friend and asked if he knew Edi. Of course he knew him, everyone knows everyone in Tirana. A few minutes later I got a text with Edi's number and a note saying that he was expecting my call. So here we were in the foyer of the Tirana International Hotel about to meet up again after more than thirty years.

I knew it was him when he walked in through the doors, a little more stooped and a little greyer, but still with a full head of hair. We shook hands and then ordered coffee. We found seats in a quiet alcove and Edi filled us in on what had happened to him since 1991.

During communism, Edi had been an English teacher. He'd also worked at Kinostudio which back then had been a dynamic production centre, making feature films, documentaries and animations. When everything collapsed, many of Edi's friends went abroad; but he decided to stay and use his language skills. Proficient English speakers were in short supply; as Edi put it, "English was a job, it was a profession."

For a few years, he worked for a Norwegian shipping company that started a catamaran service between Bari and Durrës. Then he worked as a fixer and translator for foreign TV companies who were now able to travel freely around Albania. He worked on a *Disappearing World* documentary called *The Albanians of Rrogam* which I had seen when it had been broadcast in July 1991. For Edi, that meant visits to Manchester when the film was being edited and subtitled. He'd also worked with German and Canadian film companies. His last assignment had been with *Top Gear* who wanted to film a road trip through Albania. They called the programme *The Mafia Road Test*. Edi thought the idea was terrible and he hated the presenters. He described a day on location at Ksamil where the team had wanted to use the cable ferry across the Vivari Channel. First they wanted to go in one direction, then the other, ignoring an ambulance that was waiting to cross. That was it as far as Edi was concerned, that was when he decided to retire in 2011, the same year as me.

I said how impressed we had been in 1987 with his ability to toe the ideological line without seeming to endorse it. Edi said his family had a "bad biography" because his father had worked abroad. On one occasion, Edi himself was suspended from his teaching job and sent to work in the country. But because he was such an accomplished linguist, he had a bit of leverage, and when Albturist started putting on more tours, he was allowed to become a guide. Most of the tours were at the weekend; if it was a weekday tour, the authorities would provide cover for him at school.

There were several important things about being a guide, but the most important was to have a trustworthy driver. You didn't want to be working with someone who reported what Edi called "indiscretions". Albturist ran seminars where academics instructed guides what to say about the economy, geography and so on, but it was always a fine line. You didn't want to be so doctrinaire that you lost credibility, but you obviously couldn't criticise the regime. So you had to be subtle. He told a story about an academic from the London School of Economics who had been on several Albturist tours and prided himself on asking difficult questions. As they were driving through Dropull, he asked why the government had felt it necessary to put barbed wire around the Greek minority villages. So Edi asked his driver to do a detour and take them into Derviçan. In the village square, people were sitting under a plane tree drinking coffee. Edi said to the academic that as far as he could see, there was no barbed wire.

On another occasion, they were driving from Sarandë to Gjirokastër. All the guides knew there was a labour camp on the outskirts of Sarandë; they didn't usually come this way at night because people would ask about the spotlights. On one occasion, they got their timings wrong and Edi was horrified to see prisoners jumping down from the back of a lorry. There was no way he could disguise what they had seen; sometimes you just had to admit it. On balance, Edi preferred British or German visitors, because they were better informed. One time, he had a group from Austria; at the end of the tour, one of the group took his microphone and said what a good job Tito had done in Albania...

I asked Edi if visitors like us had been followed as we walked around. Definitely not! You had to apply for a visa months in advance, so any vetting would have been done at that stage. Itineraries were planned in advance; hotels were pre-booked; luggage was inspected on arrival. In other words, by the time you got into Albania, you had already been so well investigated that there was no need for tailing.

The only time he'd heard of people being followed was in Korçe, where foreigners were suspected of leaving religious material in the Martyrs' Cemetery and that was against the law.

Not everything about what Edi called "state socialism" had been bad. Albania had had a free health service; folk music and traditional culture had flourished; there had been respect for education. Education was a particular concern for Edi. When communism ended, private universities had sprung up all over the country. Some were so bad they had been forced to close. He thought that more would follow.

Edi admitted to feeling some personal responsibility for the decades of "state socialism". People like him who didn't support the regime had kept their heads down and didn't make a fuss. Looking back, he wondered if he should have done more. But for all Albania's current problems, he remained optimistic. He trusted in the younger generation to make a difference. Then he got up to go. His leg was hurting; he had a problem with a sciatic nerve that was making it difficult to walk. I said I would be coming back to Albania soon and that I would very much like to continue our conversation.

The Martyrs' Cemetery: exhuming the past
1988

Our last full day and it's one for umbrellas. Cloud hangs low. Tirana is swathed in a fine mist and the air smells of coal. Beyond the statue of Scanderbeg, the University buildings look ghostly and insubstantial. The mathematical symmetry of those tiered arches and windows is unsettling, as if a painting by de Chirico had been made real.

After breakfast, we were taken to the Martyrs' Cemetery. A narrow road twisted and climbed through forests. We were dropped at the foot of a broad flight of steps that took us up onto a terrace with a huge statue. It was Mother Albania. She stood like a ship's figurehead, her clothes blown back against her body by an invisible wind. Her right arm was raised, and in her hand she held a laurel wreath and communist star. Next to Mother Albania, in a plot bordered with red flowers, was Enver Hoxha's tomb. It was a simple memorial, just a marble slab with his name and lifespan, 1908-1985, picked out in gold letters. Above his name was a single laurel leaf. Two soldiers stood guard. The graves of other martyrs spread in a crescent around the hillside. As well as name and dates, each grave had a single laurel leaf and a five-pointed gold star. A pale sun broke through the mist and we had a fine view over fields and forests to the city.

2019

Visiting the cemetery had been like going into the country. A cordon of fields and trees had separated it from Tirana on the plain below. When the communists were overthrown, that cordon became valuable real estate. Trees were felled and embassies were built there, for Kuwait, Saudi Arabia, Austria, Libya, Hungary and Croatia. The road has been re-engineered and was now a dual carriageway. The Cemetery has lost its remoteness, but superficially at least it looked much as it had done in the autumn of 1988. Mother Albania (Nëna Shqipëri) is still a dominating, even intimidating presence, and the slogan on the plinth, Everlasting Glory to the Martyrs of the Fatherland (*Lavdi e Përjetshme Dëshmorëve të Atdheut*) works as well in post-communist Albania as it did during the dictatorship. But there have been significant changes.

In May 1992, only a month after Sali Berisha was elected President, Enver Hoxha's body was exhumed and moved to the public cemetery at Sharrë on Tirana's south-western fringes. Family members were forbidden from witnessing the exhumation. Some years later, Hoxha's son Ilir[3] wrote an account of what had happened:

> We spent the night at the gates of the cemetery. Then, under searchlights, the grim work began. We heard the sound of pneumatic drills. They were working in haste to finish the task before sunrise. This kind of work needed to be done secretly, at night, away from the eyes of people. At last they had finished, and we were allowed to approach the exhumed coffin. There were doctors there to certify that Enver Hoxha was really dead. It was eleven o'clock. They bore the coffin away and we were allowed to follow. They reburied it, directly in the earth, in the People's Cemetery.

Traumatic as it must have been for the family, it's hard to see how Hoxha could have remained in the Martyrs' Cemetery. Along with Hoxha, at least twelve other leading communists were exhumed. For Sali Berisha's incoming Democratic administration, these exhumations demonstrated his party's rejection of Albania's communist past. Only two of the communists buried next to Nëna Shqipëri were undisturbed: Qemal Stafa and Vasil Shanto. Maybe their survival was serendipity. Or maybe it was because they were both

---

3 Ilir Hoxha's account of the exhumation is in an online memoir, *My Father, Enver Hoxha*, at: http://www.oneparty.co.uk/compass/compass/com13605.html

northerners, as was Sali Berisha. Both died before the regime was formally established and so, to a degree, were exonerated from its excesses.

In 1998, Berisha's outgoing Democratic administration took another controversial step and sanctioned the interment of "Heroi i Demokracisë" Azem Hajdari, in the same spot that Hoxha had occupied. Hajdari was a student leader in the winter of 1990 when students persuaded Ramiz Alia to abandon the one-party state. Hajdari was also active in setting up the Democratic Party and sat as a Democratic MP. He was assassinated in September 1998. Although by then Hajdari had fallen out with Berisha, the symbolism was clear. From now on, non-communist martyrs could also be buried in a Martyrs' Cemetery.

There was one other post-communist addition to the upper terrace. A memorial commemorated 22 Albanians who were executed by firing squad in February 1951 after being found guilty of plotting to blow up the Soviet Embassy. It was one of the most notorious mass killings carried out in the early years of the communist regime. The generalised inscription on the memorial - Victims of the Communist Terror (*Viktimat e Terrorit Komunist*) - could equally apply to all those thousands of other people who died during the dictatorship.

Three gardeners were planting roses by Azem Hajdari's grave. I explained what I was trying to do and showed them the old photos. In 1988, red floral borders were a dominant motif. A red border framed the plots on each side of Nëna Shqipëri. A red hedge ran along the whole of the eastern side of the cemetery. Those borders had gone. So too had the palm trees which had been such a feature on the upper tier. One of the women said that a few years ago, the palm trees had become diseased and they'd had to remove them. They'd planted new ones along the wall by Nëna Shqipëri. Another photo showed the whole of the cemetery with the graves arranged in steps. The women said that the graves furthest away were *jo politik*; they were where soldiers and

1988: Enver Hoxha's tomb was removed from Tirana's Martyrs' Cemetery in 1992.

2019: His place was taken by student activist Azem Hajdari.

policemen who had been killed on active service were buried. One had died in Afghanistan. When they came to the view over the city which had been all fields and trees, the women chorused "*halal, halal*" and laughed at their joke about the Kuwaiti Embassy. Then I showed them the pictures of Enver Hoxha's grave. One of the women ran a finger along the red hedge behind Hoxha's plot. They all liked the red flowers but they made no comment about the rights or wrongs of removing him.

Then it was their turn to ask questions. How old was I, where did I live, how big was my pension? They patted me on the back, and I asked if I could take a photo of them. Yes, they said, but only if it included the roses. They took off their floppy hats and linked arms while I took the photo. Then it was time for them to get back to work. One of the women walked over to a topiarised bush, wrenched it apart and, like a party trick, pulled out her besom which she'd hidden inside.

1988

After a visit to the Ethnography Museum and a tour round the diplomatic quarter, we were taken back to the hotel. There was still some time before our flight, so Dag and I set off for another walk. A number of boulevards ran into Scanderbeg Square; we chose a dead-straight, over-sized one with hedges between the carriageways. Traffic consisted of horse-drawn carts and bikes. It was hard to believe we were walking along a major thoroughfare in the heart of a European capital.

Apartment blocks lined the boulevard. Washing hung from the balconies; roofs were forested with aerials. Between the blocks were older villas, once-handsome buildings with tiled roofs and bow windows, but now in a poor state of repair. We passed a derelict mosque. Peasant women squatted on the pavement selling leeks. (We had been told that it was technically illegal to sell private produce, but so long as it hadn't been stolen or cooperative equipment misused, no-one was going to make a fuss.) A church had been converted into a cinema. The façade was covered in concrete and the windows bricked up.

We left the main boulevard and cut through more housing estates along narrower roads. During the Liberation War there must have been a lot of fighting in this part of the city because there were a number of commemorative plaques. Each one had a red star, and even without a word (or hardly a word) of Albanian, their meaning was clear enough: *demonstrata, Italia fashiste, revolucionare antifashiste.*

An Enver Hoxha slogan had been written in fancy script on a wall:

LAVDI veprës se ndritur e të pavdekëshme të shokut ENVER HOXHA
GLORY to the shining and immortal works of Comrade ENVER HOXHA

We stopped to try and read it and a bunch of schoolchildren appeared from nowhere. One was wearing a very smart uniform, a smock with a white collar and necktie. They seemed to find us very amusing. And then on the corner, a sign painter was at work putting the finishing touches to a slogan in capital letters:

RROFTE KOMITETI QENDROR I P.P.SH.
LONG LIVE THE CENTRAL COMMITTEE OF THE PARTY OF LABOUR OF ALBANIA

Paintbrush in one hand, ruler in the other and a small pot of red paint at his feet, he was taking great care over the lettering. There are slogans all over Albania, but you never think of someone actually painting them.

We came out on another boulevard that ran along the side of a large park. Women were sweeping the paths. Soldiers across the street kept pace with us, throwing glances in our direction. We crossed the park and turned onto the main university boulevard, past government buildings guarded by soldiers and then back to the hotel.

Edi was waiting on the steps. He'd not been with us to the cemetery and apologised for his absence. He explained that he'd been called back to school to invigilate an exam. Some of the students, he said, were having trouble with the conditional.

2019

I knew for sure that Dag and I had walked along Rruga e Kavajës because I had a photo of a plaque commemorating a student uprising on 20 January 1944. I found it on the wall of a youth centre next to Tirana's Chamber of Commerce. Someone had scrawled *Partizani* in yellow spray paint beneath it.

I also had photos of the mosque and church; both were on Rruga e Kavajës and it was easy enough to match them. Xhamia Dine Hoxha had been built in the 1920s. It had closed in 1967 and its minaret pulled down. It reopened in 1996 with a new minaret and a new zinc dome. By the doorway, men sat under umbrellas selling bottles of scented oil and religious trinkets. Zemra e Krishtit, Sacred Heart, was further along the street. It was a Catholic church in a severe, neo-Romanesque style built in 1939 at the beginning of the Italian occupation. During atheism, it had been converted into Kinoteater Rinia. It reopened for worship in 1991. A crowd of well-dressed people were mingling on the steps about to celebrate a baptism, so I went back later when it was quiet. The interior was plain, just whitewashed walls and brick arches. Because its original murals had been destroyed, a local artist, Shpend Bengu, had been commissioned to paint new ones. There were also two commemorative plaques. One named three Catholic martyrs, Shtjefen Kurti, Mark Dushi and Zef Bici, all from Tirana who had died during communism. The other, dated December 2017, thanked

Mrs Valentina Berberaj for her contribution to the cost of renovating the roof and façade.

There was another church on Rruga e Kavajës that Dag and I hadn't seen in 1988. It was a pretty building, set back from the road at the end of an alley. A plaque described it as Kisha Katedrale Engjillëzimit, the Cathedral Church of the Annunciation. But if it was a cathedral, why was it so small? And why was it in such a secluded spot? The story of the church is closely connected to Fan Noli, the driving force behind what Ilir had called Albania's "bourgeois-democratic revolution".

Bishop Theofan Stilian Noli, better known as Fan Noli or the Red Bishop, had been part of the same émigré community in Egypt as Nasho's grandfather, Jani Vruho. Unlike Jani, Fan Noli returned to Albania after the First World War. He became an MP and in July 1924 formed a government committed to political and agrarian reform. It was a turbulent time in Albania, with conservatives pitted against radicals. Fan Noli's administration lasted five months, until December 1924 when it was overthrown by Ahmed Zogu. Thereafter Fan Noli lived in exile, first in Italy and then America.

In the early 1960s, when Fan Noli was in his eighties, he made it known that he wanted to visit Albania before he died. Around this time, plans for the redevelopment of Scanderbeg Square were being finalised, part of which involved the demolition of Tirana's Orthodox cathedral. Hoxha was uncomfortable about allowing Fan Noli to visit, but reluctant to ban him. Hoxha also seemed unwilling to alienate the Albanian diaspora in America. So the authorities agreed to pay for a new Orthodox cathedral. They also agreed that the old cathedral's sacred objects, including the Bishop's Throne, could be reinstalled in the new church. Given the regime's hostility towards religion, it was an astonishing decision.

The new cathedral was consecrated on 21 March 1965. But it was too late for Fan Noli, who had died eight days earlier in Florida. Hoxha commented on Fan Noli's death in his Diary. He praised him for being "anti-feudal" and "anti-Zogist". Fan Noli, he wrote, was one of Albania's "outstanding political-literary figures". Even so, Hoxha must have been relieved that his visit never took place.

Unlike many Orthodox churches, the interior was light and airy. At the centre of a new iconostasis was a painting of the Last Supper. And there, to the right of the altar, was the high-backed Bishop's Throne brought from the old cathedral. It had a golden icon on the backrest.

The janitor was sweeping the steps. In a mixture of Greek, Albanian and English, he told me that during communism, the church had been converted into a sports centre with a gymnasium and swimming pool. It had reopened in 1996, after a three-year restoration. He explained that his family were Orthodox Christians from Smyrna. But because he had a Turkish grandfather, during the 1923 population exchanges they had been sent to Istanbul. Later his family had gone to Greece, but during the Second World War, when everything was confused, they somehow ended up in Albania. He wanted me to admire the church. Everything was new - the only thing missing was a Pantocrator for the dome, but unfortunately the money had run out.

I still had a number of photos to match. One was of a plaque commemorating a school revolt in January 1944. I also had a picture of the sign painter and the Enver Hoxha slogan in fancy script. I was reasonably sure that after the mosque and church, Dag and I had left Rruga e Kavajës and taken one of the side streets into Tregu Çam. But as there were at least four streets, and with the photos as my only guide, it was impossible to know which one it had been. Tregu Çam is a densely populated market area. In the mornings, its narrow streets are made even narrower by stalls selling everything from shoes and clothes to household items and toys. Shirts are hung on racks on the walls, so even if there had been a plaque, it would almost certainly have been hidden from view. And just to make the task even more challenging, several Ottoman houses were being demolished. I walked past one that had been reduced to a pile of splintered laths and masonry. If a plaque had been on the wall, it would have been pulverised along with the building.

I stopped for a moment, unsure what to do. A small, wiry man with a weather-beaten face was putting his bike away in a garage. He was wearing a Germany 2006 Fifa World Cup top. He asked if I was lost and I told him what I was trying to do. His name was Syrja. I showed him the photos and he called over a friend. As they looked through them, they commented on the vehicles: that jeep was an ARO from Romania; that car was a Polski Fiat; the pick-up truck outside the mosque was a Polish Żuk.

Syrja had been an engineer during the dictatorship and now lived on a small pension. He spent most of his time cycling. He cycled around Tirana and thought nothing of cycling to Kavajë for a swim, a round trip of over a hundred kilometres. He offered to take me on a tour of his neighbourhood to see what he could find.

Syrja had lived in Tregu Çam all his life. He knew the shopkeepers; he knew about the history of the buildings; he knew which families lived in which apartments; he knew their children. It was a struggle to keep up with the volume of information. As we walked, we kept meeting people Syrja knew. We stopped for a few words with the white-coated assistant in Bulmet Jugu that specialised in cheeses from southern Albania. Then we met the artist who had repainted the interior of Xhamia Dine Hoxha. Syrja said that when the mosque had been closed it had been used as a *magazinë per festa*, a warehouse where they'd stored flags and floats for festivals. In the old photo, you could see part of a 1920s villa next to the mosque. Two families had lived there, said Syrja. At the end of communism, the villa had been sold. The ground floor was now a *birrari*; upstairs was a coffee bar called Estja. Syrja wanted me to understand the significance of a *birrari* so close to the mosque. It demonstrated, as he put it, *tolerancë dhe respekt*. Everyone in Albania - *Ortodokse, Katolike, Mysliman* - they all got on.

We continued up the main road towards the Catholic church. Then Syrja stopped at a road junction close to the villa where Radio Tirana was based in the 1960s. This, he said, was where I'd taken the photos of the sign painter and the children under the fancy slogan. The corner had been redeveloped. Grill bars faced each other across the road, but houses further up the street were shielded behind rough brick walls exactly like the one in the photo.

I also had a picture of a bread shop. Men by the door were gesticulating towards a jumble of metal frames on the pavement. Those frames, said Syrja, fitted onto the back of the truck that brought the bread from the bakery. To the right of the shop, three women in headscarves were chatting by an alley. Syrja stopped outside a fashion boutique called Style Ador with an ATM in the wall. Next to it was a pizza restaurant. This was the bread shop, Syrja announced. I looked but couldn't see it. Syrja started pointing out the features: the balcony, the downpipe... I still couldn't see it. "And the alley? where's the alley?" He took me by the arm so we were standing in front of the pizza parlour. It was a glitzy place; the walls had been painted black and featured a large picture of Albert Einstein. A corridor ran along the wall. "That's the alley," said Syrja. It was a miraculous transformation, one repeated a thousand times across Albania as old shop units have been remodelled and reinvented for the new world.

I said how grateful I was for his time, and as we walked back towards Scanderbeg Square, Syrja started talking about the bad reputation Albanians had abroad. He said that visitors to Albania would see how friendly Albanians really were. Anyone could come now, from Germany, from England, from France, even from Serbia. Syrja's sister lived in Germany; he'd been to see her many times but she missed Albania. Syrja was very pro-German, in fact he was very pro-Europe, very pro-West. Albania, he said, is a European country that belongs with the Western nations. We shook hands and I complimented him on his memory. "It's all in here," he said, pointing to his head.

1988: A bread shop on Rruga e Kavajës....

2019: ....has become a clothes boutique - another astonishing transformation.

I was on my own again, staying at Hotel Kruja on Rruga Mine Peza. The TV was on in the garden for a football friendly between Turkey and Albania. You could hear the cheers, groans and whistles from the bars along the street where fans had gathered to watch. Sprawled on one of the garden settees were three people I'd not seen before, two men and a woman. They were grungier than your average Albanian. One was a heavily built man with a goatee beard, earring and dark glasses resting on his forehead. At the end of the match - Albania won 3-2 - he caught my eye and asked where I was from. He introduced himself. He was Vaga, a rap artist. Albanians knew him as Vagabondi - *Vagabond* had been a term of abuse during the dictatorship.

Vaga spoke English with a strong Detroit accent. He reckoned the transition from totalitarianism to democracy was taking far too long: "I'm scared, man, how long does a transition take, nothing's changed, there's no light at the end of the tunnel." Vaga thought the whole of Albania was in the grip of depression, it was endemic, it spared no-one. The young people were so depressed that every month thousands of them left the country: "It makes me sad, we've lost 300,000 people, 10 per cent of our population, they're so depressed they'll spend €20,000 to go to England and wash dishes, that's a hell of a lot of money to wash someone else's dishes, why don't they wash dishes here and put the money into the Albanian economy. If they'll spend €20,000 to wash dishes in England, think what they might do for a few thousand euros here."

What made everything so much more sinister was that Vagabondi didn't understand what was going on: "The system is so opaque, so corrupt. I watch the news, I have more chance of understanding the situation in Syria or Iraq than understanding the situation here. Most times in life, you smell what you smell, but not here. If you see a dog, it's a dog, but in Albania it's not a dog, it's something else…"

Vagabondi's anger was directed at Albania's political elite. He thought they were all philistines. He went through them, counting them off on his fingers. "I like Rama, but he's the best of a bad bunch, know what I'm saying?" Rama's father, he went on, was a communist who signed the death warrant on a young poet. The President, Ilir Meta, had been caught with thousands of euros in his car and the court said the evidence wasn't strong enough. The leader of the opposition, Sali Berisha, had been Hoxha's private doctor, his *private fuckin' doctor*. "During the war you had Churchill, then after the war, you got rid of him and when you needed him again, you got him back. I understand that, that's democracy. But here, here, who do you go to?"

He gave me a brief critique of Albania's neighbours: "They all hate us!" Greece, he said, gave us democracy and I love them for that, but they are racist. Montenegrins hate us. Macedonians hate us. Serbs are ethnic cleansers. "You know who's the worst? The Albanians. They hate gypsies most of all; man, if your daughter married a gypsy she'd better get the hell out of it and go to America, otherwise they kill you."

"I love my country, I got tattoos all over, but you know what (lowering his voice only a little), we were supporting Turkey, and when Albania played England in the World Cup, we supported England, we wanted England to win the World Cup, like they did in 1966."

The words spilled out, thoughts stitched together with repeated motifs, moving seamlessly from Albania to Iraq and 9/11 to wartime Britain and back to Albania. He kept repeating, "there's no light at the end of the tunnel". But despite the seriousness of what he was saying, he could still laugh. Vagabondi loved his country. He had chosen to stay, and like others had put his faith in the young. But the pressure was so remorseless, he feared that soon there would be no young people left.

The next morning, Nazmi was on the reception desk doing paperwork and updating his Facebook page. When he wasn't running the hotel, Nazmi was an artist; he was a fine landscape and portrait painter. In 1988, he had been a student studying

Fine Art at Tirana's Liceu Artistik, "Jordan Misja". When he saw the photo of the sign painter, he immediately said *klasa e dyte*, second class. This man, he said, was not a fine artist; he was employed on the day-to-day stuff, painting slogans and promoting *njeriu i ri* and *gruaja e re*, Socialism's New Man and New Woman. After he'd done his military service, Nazmi was employed by the state, painting pictures not slogans. He was once told to paint a portrait of Enver Hoxha. He did it in three days, a record! Nazmi said that Enver Hoxha's face was so well-known, he could have painted it with his eyes closed.

In Nazmi's view, the old regime had been fascistic: everything had been propaganda, especially its art. Its biggest mistake had been collectivisation - people, he said, want to work for themselves, they want their own animals and their own land. Collectivisation led to food shortages, sometimes even starvation. In the factories, if the work took three minutes to complete, that was it - he brushed his hands together to emphasise the point - the work was done. But despite its errors, Nazmi judged the regime as 50-50, which surprised me; I thought he might have been more condemning. Some things were good: food was cheap, the currency was stable, and where people were still able to work for themselves, the quality of individual craftsmanship remained high.

I still had one photo that, so far, no-one had been able to identify. It was of a building site where workers were adding another storey to an apartment block. People who had looked at it thought the apartments must have been on a main thoroughfare because the road surface was good quality asphalt, most likely Rruga e Durrësit or Bulevardi Zogu i Parë. I asked Nazmi if he recognised the block. He didn't. So I decided to walk up Rruga e Durrësit and come back down Bulevardi Zogu i Parë to see if I could find it.

Both streets had plenty of apartment blocks. They dominated Rruga e Durrësit, but unlike the block in my photo, these apartments faced the road rather than being at right angles to it. I stopped at a kiosk to buy a bottle of water and asked the man if he recognised the block. Like the

1998: Transferable skills? Street art during…..

2019: …and after communism.

others, he homed in on the road surface: only *rruga kryesore*, the major roads had such good quality asphalt. He thought the block was on Unaza, the ring road. If I turned right at the roundabout, he thought I'd find it near the Harry Fultz Institute.

Unaza was a chaotic mix of cafés, street traders, government offices and new developments. But I could see why people had suggested I look here because there were also ranks of communist-era apartment blocks set at right angles to the road. I walked slowly, picture in hand, comparing each block as I passed. This kind of scrutiny makes you realise that although superficially all the blocks look the same, there are subtle differences. On some, the balconies were at the corners; on others, they were in the centre. Sometimes, a single window separated the balconies; other times, they were separated by two or even three windows. To make identification even more difficult, many of the blocks had sprouted extensions and had been painted bright colours.

I thought I had found a match near the junction with Bulevardi Zog i Parë, but when I asked at a hardware shop, the men said the blocks were new; before they'd been built, there had been a *lulishte*, a flower garden, on the corner. They too pored over the photo, but they couldn't place it. They said there had been so many changes since 1990 that sometimes it was difficult even for residents to recognise their own neighbourhoods.

Sunk into the pavement on Zogu i Parë were cast-iron manhole covers from communist foundries in Dibër, Korçë, Vlorë, Kukës and Tirana's Uzina Partizani. The cover from Kukës even had a date: 1973. Above ground were new offices and apartments and a statue of King Zog, that "treacherous bandit chief" as Hoxha called him. Not far from the University, there was a line of apartment blocks, some of them set at right angles to the road. One was on the corner where Rruga Dervish Hatixhe meets Zogu i Parë: the number of storeys - five; the arrangement of the balconies - at the corners and in the middle; the windows - two on each side of the balconies. Everything fitted. The building had been painted orange and red. As I took photos, a man in a cherry-picker was touching up the paintwork.

And then I spotted an inconsistency. In my photo, the central balconies were separated by a window. In this block, the balconies were next to each other. I am not an architect, but I suppose it would be possible to increase the size of the balconies so that they absorbed the window space. But let's be honest, it's unlikely. Much as I wanted to say that I'd found the block, I couldn't. But it was a very near thing.

House of Leaves: a final twist

Opposite the new Orthodox cathedral and shielded by trees is a red brick villa with grilles over the ground-floor windows. The villa was built in 1931 for Jani Basho, a pioneering physician and obstetrician. Like many of his generation, Basho was trained in Austria. He spent fourteen years in Vienna studying medicine, and when he returned to Albania in 1927, he set about modernising its health services. He became Director of the Military Hospital and introduced Albania's first gynaecology service. King Zog made Basho his personal physician. Basho became wealthy. He built two villas in the centre of Tirana: one to live in, the other as his obstetrics clinic. The clinic had been the villa with grilles over the windows.

After 1944, Basho continued to work as an obstetrician, but his villas were confiscated. The clinic was taken over by the Sigurimi, Albania's all-powerful state intelligence service. It became their nerve centre where people were taken for interrogation and where information was collected and stored. The Sigurimi was disbanded in 1991. In May 2015, the villa was opened to the public as a museum called The House of Leaves (Shtëpia me gjethe) on account of the ivy clinging to its walls.

When the museum opened, Prime Minister Edi Rama spoke about "this dark part of our heritage" in which no-one, with the exception of Enver Hoxha, had been immune from fear. Rama hoped that the museum would make public "the entire edifice of surveillance and persecution" so that Albania could confront its past directly and fearlessly.

Graphics show how the Sigurimi's tentacles reached into towns and villages across Albania. It permeated the armed forces, the economy and political intelligence. It scrutinised biographies and monitored foreigners and diplomats. Homes were bugged and phone calls intercepted. It was said that public toilets were the only safe space to express "dangerous thoughts".

Like East Germany's Stasi, the Sigurimi went to great lengths to disguise their bugs. They secreted them in clothes, shoes, handbags, radios, pipes and ashtrays, picture frames, saws, drills and lathes. They used high-end equipment to record conversations: reel-to-reel tape recorders, mini cassette players and Uher portable tape recorders. It all looked very familiar. I had been using the same equipment in the 1980s to make radio programmes for the BBC. Communist Albania must have been profitable for Uher.

Upstairs, there were diagrams of torture and a list of the crimes that warranted arrest: spying, being an enemy of the Party, attempting to escape, subversion, terrorism, sabotage. Another section dealt with propaganda. There were film posters, photographs of Enver Hoxha and a picture of partisans posing outside Radio Tirana. There were publicity shots of Scanderbeg Square and photographs of hotel rooms and a restaurant where a band was playing and foreigners were enjoying a drink. I understood that when I had received copies of *New Albania* and *Albania Today*, they had been propaganda. But looking at the photos of the hotel, I don't think I had quite realised how enveloping that propaganda had been.

Albturist was part of the system. It reported to Sigurimi's Fifth Branch which oversaw the surveillance of foreigners. Albturist was also there to ensure that visitors went away with a good impression. The places we visited, the hotels we stayed in, the food we ate, the buses we travelled in - it was all part of an effort to give us a positive image of Albania. The propaganda worked. When we went home and said to everyone, you really should go, we were doing the regime's bidding.

Visiting Albania back then had been an adventure and it had lived up to expectation - so much so that my interest in the country has lasted for more than thirty years. But the opacity continues to be troubling. Trying to make sense of what we saw on those first visits is one of the reasons why I keep going back.

The architect of that state, Enver Hoxha, died in April 1985. His statues have been pulled down and his books burned. His regime has been disowned by all but a very few. But he continues to cast a long shadow. The old photographs are a record of the world he created, but they remain enigmatic. There seems to be something uncomfortable lurking beneath their surface. Albania is still reluctant to give up all its secrets.

Afterword

Out of the Shadow?

In the summer of 2023, the Albanian Tourist Union issued a warning: a labour shortage was threatening to derail the country's expanding tourist industry. Without greater efforts to recruit and retain Albanian staff, Albania would have to bring in workers from Sri Lanka and India to meet the shortfall.

Labour shortages are just the latest indication of a problem that has dogged Albania since it reopened its borders in July 1990: Albanians who want to improve their life chances leave. Albania's Ministry for Europe and Foreign Affairs has estimated that since 1990, around 1.4 million Albanians have left the country. That's the equivalent of about 35 per cent of its working population.

By far the largest numbers of those leaving, around 75 per cent, have gone to Greece or Italy. But there are also sizeable Albanian populations in Western Europe and North America. The Albanian Embassy in London estimates that around 140,000 Albanians currently live in the UK.

Migration from Albania to the UK became a national issue in 2022, when thousands of Albanians started crossing the Channel in small boats. Figures for the year ending in March 2023, recorded that 12,451 Albanians made the crossing, 28 per cent of the total number.

Hostile UK rhetoric about "Albanian criminals" stung the Albanian government. In November 2022, Edi Rama, the Albanian Prime Minister, appeared on British television to complain that the British government was "fuelling xenophobia". Rama spoke again to the BBC in March 2023 and accused British authorities of scapegoating Albanians: "Unfortunately, we have seen ourselves and our community being singled out in this country for purposes of politics. It has been a very, very disgraceful moment for British politics,, he told BBC Radio 4's *Today* programme. When called to Parliament to give evidence to the Home Affairs Committee, the Albanian Ambassador, Qirjako Qirko, complained about a "campaign of discrimination": "Everyone who is responsible for this activity should apologise, he said.

Emigration from Albania is nothing new. It has been a factor in Albanian life since the fifteenth century when thousands of Albanians migrated to southern Italy for religious reasons. In the sixteenth and seventeenth centuries, Albanians went to Istanbul in search of political and military preferment. In the nineteenth century, Albanian diasporas gathered in cities like Cairo, Alexandria and Istanbul where they kick-started the *Rilindja*, the independence movement that led to the creation of an Albanian nation state in 1912. During the dictatorship, Albania's borders were closed. But since the 1990s, mass emigration, driven primarily by poverty, has shrunk the workforce and decimated communities.

However challenging the circumstances, the decision to leave the country of your birth is not one to be taken lightly. After much soul searching, my friend Ylvi decided to stay in Albania. When we met up with him in October 2021, he was buzzing; coming to a final decision had been a huge relief. Earlier in the year, he had opened a new shop in Vlorë. To cement the family's long-term commitment to Albania, Ylvi's sons had now taken over the business in Fier. In Himarë, both Spiros and Oresti have decided that running successful businesses is sufficient reason to stay. Conversely, Donald, my friend in Krujë, took a different view and has gone to Canada. When Kirstie and I were in Sarandë in 2021, Almet's restaurant had closed. He had taken the plunge and joined his son in Greece.

AFTERWORD

Albanians started coming to the UK in the late 1990s. In 1999, during the Kosovan war, more than 3,000 Kosovan Albanians were airlifted to the UK. Small numbers of Albanians from Albania also started to come. Mirkena was part of that first wave. She came to England in 2002. She now teaches Albanian at University College London. When I began learning Albanian, she was my teacher.

She told me that one day, while she was studying Translation and Interpretation of English at the University of Tirana, she saw some brochures for Bristol University. She applied and was accepted on a Masters course in International Relations. She didn't have enough money for the fees, so she had to work as well as study. She had three jobs. One was in a sandwich bar where her teachers came to get their lunches. Mirkena was so embarrassed she used to hide until they went away.

It was, Mirkena remembers, a lonely life: "I didn't have friends; no-one knew anything about Albania." But she stayed because she wanted a better life. She was awarded her Masters in 2004, got married and started to put down roots in England. In 2009, after working as a translator and proofreader, she joined the staff at UCL's School of Slavonic and East European Studies (SSEES). Then she started teaching Albanian to diplomatic staff at the Foreign Office: "I remember queueing in front of the British Embassy in Tirana, being very worried if they would give me a visa, and then in 2012, one of my students was the British Ambassador. How can that be true!" Mirkena identifies that moment as the one when she finally started to feel that she belonged: "I felt good about myself. I'm settled here and I've got all my friends. My children go to school here. We human beings, we always want the best. It wasn't easy. I think that's why I'm not scared of life anymore. I had to do it all myself."

Another of my teachers, Mirela, came to England in 2016. She grew up in southern Albania, near Sarandë. Both her parents are from Albania's Greek minority; Mirela has Greek and Albanian as mother tongues. After completing a

PhD at the University of Tirana, she taught for several years in the University's Faculty of Foreign Languages. She started teaching at UCL in 2017.

For Mirela, getting work in the UK was relatively straightforward, but there was still a considerable emotional cost: "The most difficult part is when your parents get older and they need you more." She has had to adjust to different social norms and behaviours, but she also wants to celebrate her Greek and Albanian heritage. It's a delicate balancing act: "You try to adapt to the country and society where you live but of course there are always things that draw you back to the place where you were born and where your parents, family and friends are."

Luljeta came to the UK in 1999. I met her through a friend who knew I was interested in Albania; he invited me to come and meet her. Luljeta was one of ten siblings. She grew up in northern Albania; her family was poor: "Luxuries were unknown to us. For example, an extra egg would be a luxury or a glass of hot milk when we were making yogurt." But there was a strong family bond: "We shared beds, chairs, clothes and shoes. We ate from one plate and drank from one cup."

When she was nineteen, Luljeta was married against her will. Her husband was violent; she tried to commit suicide. In the chaos that followed the collapse of the pyramid schemes, family members started to emigrate. Luljeta's husband came to the UK. A few months later, Luljeta and their two small children followed him. They crossed from Vlorë to Italy in a small boat. After sleeping rough for several weeks, they were taken to a refugee camp in Rome where the Red Cross organised visas for them to travel on to France. In November, they were given papers allowing them entry to the UK.

It took another six years of legal wrangling before Luljeta was formally granted Indefinite Leave to Remain. By then she was working in a hotel and doing cleaning work in her spare time. One day, her husband packed the car and said he was going to Albania for a couple of weeks. He never came back. Luljeta was left on her own with three children to look after: "From that day on, I knew we were alone. We had no-one on our side and no-one to support us. It was going to be just me and my children."

Eventually Luljeta built up enough customers to start her own cleaning business. She bought a house and raised her children. Despite the obstacles, she never gave up: "Have a dream, have a plan in your life. Never be a doormat for anyone. No-one is better than you. Keep aiming higher and higher in your life. There is always a way to succeed."

Luljeta's story is extreme. But her desire to improve her life and give her children a better chance is shared by thousands. In the UK today, there are Albanian academics, musicians and artists; Albanian doctors, teachers, journalists and lawyers; Albanian restauranteurs, barbers, plumbers and roofers. Albania can ill afford to lose people who are so driven, so determined to succeed. Its loss is another country's gain. Until Albania manages to escape from the shadow of its past, it's hard to see how the pattern will ever be broken.

Acknowledgements

One of the greatest pleasures of writing this book has been the opportunity to talk to so many Albanians about their country's past, present and future. Thanks go to everyone who has given me their time and hospitality, and who have shown me places I would never have found without their help. Special thanks are due to Ylvi Sulejmani, Donald Meca, Nasho Vruho and the Maja family who run Hotel Kruja in Tirana. I was also delighted to meet up again with Edi Kurtëzi, our guide on that first visit to Albania, whose urbane good humour and insights are always one of the highlights of a trip to Tirana.

In the UK, thanks go to Gill Evans and Steven Williams who both advised on the initial pitch. Thanks also to James Ferguson and the team at Signal Books who had faith in the project and to James Pettifer for his encouraging response to the original manuscript - James' *Blue Guide* continues to be a prime source of information about Albania. Thanks to Miranda Vickers for her endorsement of the book's central premise and for writing the Foreword. Melanie Friend and Arta Dedaj-Salad have offered much needed encouragement while the book was being written.

More broadly, my language teachers at University College London, Mirkena Shqarri-Palluqi and Mirela Xhaferraj, have not only taught me Albanian but have also broadened my knowledge of Albanian history and culture. The Anglo-Albanian Association has also played a crucial role in providing a window on Albanian life. Thanks are due to the AAA's Chairman, Stephen Nash, and President, Sir Noel Malcolm, for their efforts to promote a positive image of Albania.

Most of all, thanks go to my family who have lived with this project as it has taken shape. It was my father-in-law, Dag Beardwood, who first suggested we go to Albania in 1987. He was an admirable travelling companion and is much missed. Since then, my partner Kirstie and our son Joe have accompanied me on visits to Albania. Kirstie's support throughout the project has been crucial to its completion. I dedicate this book to her.